GOVERNOR SMYLIE REMEMBERS

GOVERNOR SMYLIE REMEMBERS

by Robert E. Smylie

FOREWORD BY HOWARD BERGER

University of Idaho Press
MOSCOW, IDAHO
1998

Published by the University of Idaho Press, Moscow, Idaho 83844-1107
Printed in the United States of America

02, 01, 00, 99, 98   5, 4, 3, 2, 1

Library of Congress Cataloging-in-Publication Data

Smylie, Robert E. (Robert Eben), 1914–
Governor Smylie remembers / by Robert E. Smylie ; foreword by Howard Berger.
p. cm.
Includes index.
ISBN 0-89301-212-2
1. Smylie, Robert E. (Robert Eben), 1914– . 2. Governors-Idaho—Biography.
3. Idaho—Politics and government. I. Title.
F750.22.S69A3 1998
979.6'033'092—dc21
[B] 97-35116
CIP

Unless otherwise indicated all photographs in the text are from the personal files of Robert E. Smylie.

COVER PHOTO: Governor Robert E. Smylie at his typewriter composing one of his speeches. ISHS 77-163.46.

To Lucille

CONTENTS

List of Illustrations · IX

Foreword · XI

Acknowledgments · XV

1. The Idaho Connection · 1
2. The College of Idaho · 12
3. Becoming a Lawyer · 31
4. The Law, the War, and Lucille · 39
5. Eight Years in the Attorney General's Office · 48
6. The First Campaign for the Governorship—1954 · 63
7. The First Governorship—1955–59 · 79
8. The Second Campaign for the Governorship · 105
9. The Second Governorship—1959–63 · 115
10. International Travels—Russia, Argentina, Brazil, Japan, and Mexico · 127
11. A Museum, a Judge, and a Commission · 150

12. The 1962 Campaign · 158

13. The Third Governorship—1963–67 · 183

14. The Sales Tax of 1965 · 192

15. National Recognition, Defeat, and the "Descent from Glory" · 205

16. Thirty Years Unwinding in the Afterglow—1967–97 · 215

Index · 227

ILLUSTRATIONS

With my sisters · 5
The football player · 16
A page from *The Trail* · 28
Receiving the oath of office as attorney general · 50
The Board of Land Commissioners · 52
Dwight D. Eisenhower given Idaho potatoes · 55
The original campaign car · 66
Election night 1954 · 75
Being sworn in as governor · 80
Celebrating my inauguration · 81
At the inaugural ball · 82
Speaking to the legislature · 84
Republican officeholders, 1955 · 85
Members of the tax committee · 96
In Nixon's vice-presidential office · 98
At my desk · 99
At the Fiesta del Pacifica · 102
The family at the governor's home · 103
The Girl Scout tea, 1955 · 114
Joe Albertson and myself at a store opening · 116

Typing my own speeches · 118
Nelson Rockefeller at Boise airport · 123
Governors in Red Square · 129
Japanese representatives visit Boise · 145
Declaring "William E. Borah Day" · 153
Idaho candidates with Dwight Eisenhower · 159
Lucille · 164
Former president Eisenhower with the Smylie men · 180
With Senator Goldwater in Sun Valley · 181
At the Territorial Centennial Ball in 1963 · 186
The house at Norwood · 209
Receiving the Conservationist of the Year Award · 214
Visiting the White House in 1986 · 216
A family dinner at the Top of the Hoff · 219

FOREWORD

BORN ON HALLOWEEN 1914 in Marcus, Iowa, Robert Smylie grew to manhood in the American heartland. Leaving Iowa in 1934 he turned westward and spent the next four years at the Albertson College of Idaho in Caldwell. Graduating in 1938, Smylie enrolled at the Law School of George Washington University in the nation's capital. After practicing law in the District of Columbia, serving in the United States Coast Guard during the Second World War, and marrying Lucille Irwin, he returned to Idaho as assistant attorney general of the state in 1947. In 1954, Robert Smylie defeated Democrat Clark Hamilton to begin the first of his three terms as governor.

By 1958, Governor Smylie could catalogue a host of achievements. Among those successes was an increase of $.75 in the minimum wage, a five-day work week for state employees, $15 million in appropriations to state agencies, the creation of an Idaho Department of Commerce, an appropriation of more than $9 million for public assistance, $692,000 for the teacher retirement fund, and the reopening of Lewis-Clark State College in Lewiston. While securing significant appropriations for highway construction his first term, Governor Smylie claimed notable budget reductions by reducing the state employee payroll. Robert Smylie also proposed and succeeded in amending the state constitution so that a governor could run for a second term and thus be able to carry out policies over a longer span of time. Citing a multitude of legislative achievements and running as the only Republican opposed to the right-to-work law, Governor Smylie was reelected over Democrat A. M. Derr in November 1958.

In his second term, 1958-62, Governor Smylie oversaw massive appropriations of over $90 million for highway construction and improvements. He also became an active booster of the Gem State's marvelous investment opportunities promoting the interests of the state in matters of business, land, and water. This brought him attention as a national leader and he was appointed chair of the Western Governor's Association in 1959.

Winning easily over Democrat Vernon K. Smith in 1962, Smylie made his third term his most ambitious. Calling for increased funding for secondary and university education in Idaho, Governor Smylie became a vocal advocate for an Idaho sales tax. Smylie claimed that this bold, yet necessary, move would vastly improve the educational system in every county in the state. Governor Smylie also worked to create an Idaho Park System—an effort which would culminate with the creation, in 1966, of Harriman and Farragut State Parks.

The years 1964-66 were of enormous importance for Robert Smylie. Governor Smylie backed Governor Nelson Rockefeller in his unsuccessful showdown with Senator Barry Goldwater for the Republican nomination in 1964. Governor Smylie also participated in that year in a very public effort to oust Dean Burch as chair of the Republican national party and was vociferous in his efforts to return the GOP to a more centrist position. Arch-conservatives in Idaho were outraged, and in August 1966, Smylie lost the GOP primary to Goldwater-booster Don Samuelson of Sandpoint, becoming an early casualty of the political divisiveness that has caused tens of millions of Americans to simply turn their backs on politics entirely.

In his introduction to *Paradox Politics: People and Power in Idaho,* Randy Stapilus states that Idahoans "display a cheerful political perversity" and "cherish not just rugged, but aggressive independence." In the pages that follow, one will discover the singularly wonderful mix of cheerfulness and aggressiveness that embodies the political life of Robert E. Smylie. One is struck by the plain fact that this autobiography is a book about politics and is a record of how one man governed. The former governor records, without mawkish sentimentality and without rancor, his campaigns, his administrations, his legislative successes, his failures, and his errors. But above all, the work is a fascinating look into the art or craft of administering a small, demographically homogeneous state.

This memoir therefore is a work of instruction. It teaches how to run a winning campaign in a small, overwhelmingly rural state, without a great deal of money. It teaches how to lay out a legislative agenda, accepting the fact that while not every goal is attainable, one can still achieve much. Leonard Arrington wrote in his two-volume *History of Idaho* that Robert Smylie "was a man of action rather than a politician who enjoyed status." That is not entirely true. As this well-crafted memoir testifies, Robert Smylie was a doer, but he was also a politician who immensely enjoyed being governor. He saw the wonderful possibilities for Idaho at a point in time when he could bring his vision to fruition. In the last analysis, then, this volume also teaches how to be a good governor, a successful governor, a popular governor, without ever losing grace, wit, humor, and joy. This instructive book is a rare opportunity to explore the vision, the temper, and the method of Robert Smylie and the many contributions he made to Idaho.

DR. HOWARD BERGER
Professor of History
Albertson College of Idaho
May 15, 1997

ACKNOWLEDGMENTS

LET ME HERE and now acknowledge the encouragement of those who have helped with the completion of this memoir. Louise Shadduck, Betty Penson Ward, and Harold West deserve my thanks for their encouragement and for their insistence that I complete the text. I am indebted to Judy Austin, Editor of *Idaho Yesterdays* for help in checking some of my historical data. Dr. Howard Berger, Weyerhauser Professor of History at The Albertson College of Idaho, provided sound advice and technical assistance. David Bonine helped with the completion of the text, and I am undyingly grateful to my longtime secretary Bernice Callsen and to Connie Anderson for their assistance in getting this text on paper. Lee and Connie Farmer helped by reading transcribed dictation for me after my eyes grew too dim for use. Lastly, I am grateful to my lovely Lucille for bringing order to my thoughts when sometimes they got addled.

I shall always be grateful to the people of Idaho who gave me the opportunity to serve them and thus made this memoir possible.

ROBERT E. SMYLIE

July 4, 1997

GOVERNOR SMYLIE REMEMBERS

CHAPTER ONE

THE IDAHO CONNECTION

If you want to be governor of Idaho, the odds are dramatically improved if you happen to have been born in Iowa. There is an Iowa–Idaho connection, and it finds its most noteworthy instance in the governor's office. The connection has held true for five governors, including Frank Steunenberg, James H. Hawley, John M. Haines, Dr. C. A. Robins, and myself. The connection for me began on Halloween night, October 31, 1914, in a little town called Marcus in Cherokee County, Iowa. Marcus then had a population of about 150. My father was the school superintendent and also coached basketball. He was off with the basketball team at a game on the night I was born.

I do not remember a great deal about Marcus, and it is difficult to differentiate between what I have been told and what I actually remember. We moved early in my life, and my first solid memories occur in a town called Hartley, about thirty miles north.

Father had been elected superintendent of schools in Hartley, and we moved there when I was two. Most of the little Iowa towns were very similar. They all had a railroad and there were at least two passenger trains a day, which in those days provided much needed excitement. I think the largest town I ever lived in as a child was Missouri Valley, Iowa, population 4,200.

I still try to remember those very early years of my life. We lived in a large, square house in Hartley, and sometime along about then Father acquired a player piano with roller records that were very easy to play, which may explain why no one in my house ever seriously considered taking piano lessons.

I can remember the years of World War I when my uncle, Dr. F. M. Cole, had gone off to France with Pershing's expeditionary forces as a medical officer. My Aunt Leila traveled as far as New York with him and stayed there doing Red Cross work of one kind or another. They brought their English bulldog to Hartley and left him with us for almost two years. We enjoyed the dog, and for many years we referred to that bulldog as old Pug Dog. Pug was by then quite elderly and rather resented anything that got him out of a warm place on the carpet in the sunlight. He was a good companion for a very small boy, and I never had another dog that was quite the same as Pug.

One principal memory of life in Hartley was a trip my family took to Morningside College in Sioux City to see an invitational basketball tournament. Apparently my folks hoped my athletic prowess ran high because there was a little basketball suit that had been made especially for me. I wore it sort of as a mascot when we went to the Hartley High School basketball games.

Another memory of life in Hartley, Iowa, that had a lasting impression on me during my formative years was the Armistice celebration. In November 1918 when news had been received that the armistice had been signed, a spontaneous celebration was held which my whole family attended. My sister Dorothy had been born by that time, and, with my older sister Frances leading the way, I was permitted to push the baby carriage as we went downtown to listen to the band and hear the speeches. It is the first real political event of which I have a vivid memory.

In 1919, we moved to Missouri Valley, Iowa, where Father had become superintendent of schools. Missouri Valley was, as I have mentioned, much larger and was quite exciting. It was a railroad junction, and for the first time we lived in a town which had a library and two grade schools. My sister Dorothy and I went to First Ward School. The Carnegie Library permitted us to have a library card at the age of seven. I succeeded in teaching Dorothy to read after I had learned in order to prevent my having to read books to her. I remember we had a first grade teacher named Alice Brandriff who was very big on reading. She encouraged our journeys to the library and was extremely helpful in getting us interested in books that we might not have read had it not been for her enthusiasm. I first heard of Sir Walter Scott's Ivanhoe, Robin Hood, and many other legendary characters from Miss Brandriff's recitations about them in her first and second grade classes.

Missouri Valley was on the main line of the Chicago Northwestern Railroad between Chicago and Omaha, and it was the route chosen by the government for President Harding's funeral train in 1923. He had been in Alaska and had returned to San Francisco, where he died in a hotel. I remember going down to the station in Missouri Valley with my father to watch the train go through. It was draped in black, and it was a very impressive ceremony. Missouri Valley was one of the stops where they serviced passenger trains, and the train was in Missouri Valley long enough to be put in shape to go on to the next division point.

Though Father was superintendent of schools in most of the towns in which we lived, he also taught a class or two in history. History was his passion and an area in which he considered himself some sort of expert. Because he taught history, he used to receive textbook samples from the publishing companies, and he was permitted to keep them. They made up the bulk of his personal library. My sister and I became inveterate readers of history because he allowed us easy access to his small library.

My father also had a typewriter in his study at home, and he permitted us to use it. We were curious, as youngsters usually are, and I learned to type with two fingers, a trait that I still have. I never felt compelled to learn to type correctly, and, as a consequence, all through the years that I was in the statehouse, I did all of my composing on a typewriter with just two fingers. Even as governor of Idaho, I typed the same way I had learned in Father's study on that old Underwood upright so many years ago.

We did not have an automobile after the First World War. When we went to visit Grandmother in Hull, Iowa, where Mother had been born and raised, we always traveled by train. To get from Missouri Valley to Hull in 1923 and 1924 required three train changes over a distance of about 120 miles. Those annual summer treks to Hull were exciting because Father always put me in charge of the trip. At the age of six or seven, I felt very important. I had to be able to identify where we had to change trains and to what towns we would be taking them.

In 1924 we moved back to a very small town named Corwith where Father again taught school. It was in Corwith that I saw my first motion pictures. They were *A Tale of Two Cities* and *The Hunchback of Notre Dame*. They had been made available to the little country school districts by the Iowa state education office in Des Moines. That was the first time most of the children in Corwith had the privilege of seeing a motion picture since the town had no theater.

While we lived in Corwith Father purchased a Ford Model T touring car. It made many trips to the small towns located around Corwith, and we were now able to take trips to Hull when we pleased.

We lived in Corwith for two years and then moved on to Rock Valley, a town in northwest Iowa of about 1,500 people. In Rock Valley I acquired my first bicycle by selling magazines for the Curtis Publishing Company—the old *Saturday Evening Post*, *The Country Gentleman*, and *The Ladies Home Journal*. The first reward I was given was a pin, which was indicative of membership in The League of Curtis Salesmen. After that you began to accumulate points that would ultimately entitle you to get a prize from their catalog. After lugging magazines many miles throughout the Iowa countryside, I finally got the bicycle they featured and forthwith quit The League of Curtis Salesmen and terminated my brief association with the *Saturday Evening Post*. Instead I took to delivering the *Des Moines Register–Tribune*. The Sunday paper was the only paper that came to Rock Valley, and so it

With my sisters, Frances and Dorothy, and Pug Dog in the summer of 1918.

was a fairly easy task on a Sunday morning to go out and deliver the hundred newspapers that I managed to sell.

In Rock Valley, I finished grade school and began my first year in high school. There I wrestled with algebra, Latin, and the other courses that were characteristic of the high school curriculum during the 1920s. I played basketball at Rock Valley High School, but freshmen weren't permitted to play football, so my athletic skills in that area were neglected. The Rock Valley gymnasium was little more than a cracker box, and we didn't play very much basketball.

Later we moved to Jordan, Iowa, which was the smallest town I ever lived in. I do not remember it having more than twenty-five souls. It had a consolidated high school, and Father was both superintendent and history teacher. Jordan was not notable for much of anything except being halfway between Boone and Ames, Iowa, and on the main line of the Chicago Northwestern. There was much to dream about watching those great old trains, like the Mountain Bluebird and the City of Portland, go past the doorstep headed west. It probably had an effect on my life because I remember thinking that one day I would ride one of those westward-bound trains.

In 1931 we moved to Cresco, Iowa, where I graduated from high school, and my father decided on a new career and purchased a service station, which he owned until the beginning of World War II, when he returned to teaching. I was a senior in 1931, and it was the first time I had ever been in a school where my father was not the principal, the history teacher, or the superintendent of schools. It was the first time I felt as if I were accomplishing things due to my own efforts. If I received decent grades, it was because I earned them. Also, I played both football and basketball with some skill. But all in all, at Cresco, Iowa, I finally was free of family supervision and the liberation did feel good.

There were three teachers in the Cresco High School who made a noteworthy impression on my memory and in my education. Miss Myers, who taught English, was the first person to really get me interested in English composition. Mr. Boyd Thompson, who was the all-purpose coach, coached basketball, football, track, and baseball, and I suppose would have coached wrestling if there had been a team. And there was a Mr. E. Keith Popejoy who taught band and also taught economics. This was a strange combination, but in those early years of the Great Depression everything was a little strange. People worked at what they could and at anything for which they would be paid.

In addition to myself there were thirty-eight other boys in that senior class—one of whom was Norman Borlaug, who became a Doctor of Philosophy in Agronomy and was later a Nobel Peace Prize recipient for his work in creating the green revolution in the third world. Another was Ervin Upton, who became first a professor and then dean of the College of Agriculture at the University of Minnesota. It was a fairly remarkable class, and I had occasion to meet a good number of them again at the fiftieth anniversary of our graduation in 1982.

It was about this time that I decided that I wanted to be a lawyer because of the impression made upon me by a local attorney. His name was Frank McGill, and he practiced in the little town of Rock Valley, Iowa. He seemed to me even then to have found a way to enjoy life, to have a reasonable amount of both influence and affluence, and to have come to be looked up to as a pillar of the community. I greatly admired him and, in retrospect, he seems to have been one of the most respected men in the community. That was enough to make any young person seek to emulate him. There had been a brief period when I was quite furious with him for marrying the English teacher, on whom I had a crush, and it took quite a long period of time for me to forgive him for that transgression.

Looking back, other people who also seemed to have made a deep impression on me in those early years all were, in one way or another, involved in political affairs. I was quite impressed with the fact that my maternal grandfather, who loaned me his first name as my middle name, had been town clerk of Hull, Iowa, for many years and had declined on several occasions to run for the office of county supervisor. His reason was that he would have to give up his shoemaking business and move to the county seat, and he did not want to do that.

My grandfather on my father's side was a Methodist minister who served a score of churches in northwest Iowa and was presiding elder of two or three of the Methodist church districts. He was once unsuccessfully considered for Bishop of the Methodist church, and he used to put it rather slyly that there was more politics in the Northwest Iowa Conference of the Methodist church than there was religion. I remember hearing the tales of Lloyd Harding, who was a college classmate of my father at Morningside College and who later became governor of Iowa. He ended his career in a scandal that made him not very useful politically in Iowa, but he was a great speaker, and he used to make speeches in other states and was quite active on the commencement circuit throughout Iowa.

I also remember John Hammill, who was governor of Iowa when he came to our little school in Corwith and traveled up north of the town to dedicate a place called Eagle Lake State Park. Hammill was one of the early park builders in the Midwest and deserves a great deal of credit for the establishment of Iowa's splendid park system. I remember meeting Frank Mossman, who was the president of Morningside College, on several occasions as he traveled about the state. There was also Guy Gillette, who was a lawyer in Cherokee, Iowa, and who later became a United States senator, and, of course, there was also the truly flamboyant Lester Jesse Dickenson, who served Iowa for about fifteen years in the Congress and the Senate.

I was also extremely impressed with the old state capitol building on the campus of the University of Iowa in Iowa City. It was built and then abandoned when the capital was moved to Des Moines. I first saw it when I attended what was called in those days the Iowa Brain Derby. At the derby I contested with other high school students from around the state on our knowledge of American history, and I think, if my memory serves correctly, I finished eighth.

Whether the presence of all these political personalities and the general commitment in my family to public service predestined me to be interested in public affairs is, of course, hard to determine, but early on I became an avid follower of national political conventions. I was literally thrilled to listen to Franklin Delano Roosevelt accept the Democratic nomination for president in Chicago in 1932. He flew from Albany to the convention in Chicago to make that speech, and he was the first candidate for president ever to accept the nomination while the convention was still in session. It was a breakthrough as far as American history was concerned, and it was profoundly exciting to a seventeen year old who was listening to that sort of thing for the first time on the first radio that his parents ever owned.

The difficulty after graduation from high school in 1932 was that there wasn't really much of anything that anybody could do. The farm boys went back to the farm, but those of us who lived in town had great difficulty finding employment. Very few of us—in fact I can think of only two people in our class—went straight to college. I finally got a job driving a local bakery truck six days a week on a delivery route that served towns located within a radius of about forty miles of Cresco. I went to work at five in the morning and usually finished up about five at night. That added up to a lot of hours, but they didn't pay us by the hour—they paid us by the week. We got fifteen dollars for our troubles, but that was the Depression.

Because my grades were adequate, I had received a scholarship to Luther College at Decorah, Iowa, and another one to the State University of Iowa at Iowa City. Simply because there wasn't any money to match the scholarships, it was impossible to take advantage of either of them. I was not unique. Nearly everybody in the class was in the same situation. Very few of the young men had jobs, and I don't know that any of the ladies did either. If you did have a job, you usually weren't paid very well.

Even so, those were happy months and years. We went ice skating on the river. We went dancing at a little town called Spillville, which had a dance hall where the big bands out from Chicago used to stop and play one-night stands on weekends. I think it cost thirty-five cents for admission to the dance hall. We had some great times dancing to musicians like Jan Garber, Guy Lombardo, Red Nichols, and other bands of the early thirties. We played pool on Allen Shackelton's pool table, and gathered at the Cresco Carnegie Library, which became sort of a postgraduate club for Cresco High School.

The town, like the rest of the country, slid into the depths of the Depression in 1933. It seemed quite unlikely that any of us would ever be able to go to college, so a group of us became avid readers. I don't know exactly when it was that the Book of the Month Club was organized, but sometime in 1933 I managed to have enough money to be able to join and to occasionally buy some books that, as my memory serves, usually cost two or three dollars a copy in hardback. Two selections that I remember quite well were a series of essays by Christopher Morley entitled *Internal Revenue* and a book by Walter Hindus called *The Great Offensive*, which was a story of the economic revolution in

Russia driven by the Communist party under the leadership of Joseph Stalin. Hindus was sympathetic to the Russians and seemed hopeful that they would be able to pull themselves out of the economic morass that the czars and imperial government in Russia had created. It didn't work out the way Hindus anticipated.

At Christmas in 1933 my aunt, Mrs. F. M. Cole, from Caldwell, Idaho, came to visit us. She was there for five or six days, and after she left I received a letter inviting me to come and stay at her house in Caldwell and attend the College of Idaho. It was one of the great liberating moments of my life. I suspect that had it not been for that letter I might still be driving a bakery truck in Iowa. I decided immediately to accept Aunt Leila's invitation. I was sure that it was an opportunity that would never come again, and it presented me with a means of taking off on my own into what I was quite sure was a very exciting world.

My father supported me in this decision. However, the idea that the eldest son (my brother Bill was seven years younger than I) would now be leaving did not meet with complete family approval. My mother was especially disturbed that I was "going away." She wondered how I would get my shirts laundered, and she wondered how I would ever be able to take care of myself. But I had reached my decision and continued on my plan to leave for Caldwell and enroll at the College of Idaho.

From year's end in 1933 until September in 1934, I began a frantic bout of money saving so that I would have some cash to take with me when I began my great adventure. I had a job and I saved nearly every penny. When I finally left for Caldwell in September, I had $198 and a $50 World War I savings bond, which probably was worth exactly $50. I did spend money to buy a suit because Mother insisted, and I bought a dressing robe which I believe I still have but very seldom wear.

Winter, spring, and summer passed rapidly, and I became a sort of local hero with my friends because I was "going off to college." I did have some serious second thoughts about my plans. I would be leaving my father to run the family service station mainly by himself, and I anticipated he was going to have a very difficult time of it in the next few years. But it seemed to me, as it seemed to him, that either I would take off on my own then or I would never leave.

Very soon it was September. I went down to Cedar Rapids and caught a bus taking me west to Caldwell, Idaho. The bus ticket cost sixteen dollars. I had not planned on paying for transportation, and thus it was that my capital was seriously reduced by the time I arrived at college.

CHAPTER TWO

THE COLLEGE OF IDAHO

DURING THE DEPRESSION I learned that hitchhiking was a thoroughly respectable mode of travel. Very few young men going back and forth from college used any other mode of transportation. It was common then to get a college pennant, put it on your suitcase, and stand by the side of the road. In those years we must have been kinder, gentler, or simply less fearful. You usually managed to get picked up fairly easily. I think the longest ride I ever hitched was from Blair, Nebraska, on the Missouri River, to Salt Lake City. On that trip I beat the Portland Rose from Cedar Rapids, Iowa, to Caldwell.

I recall many interesting experiences hitching between Iowa and Idaho. I remember especially a haystack near Sutherland in the hay country of western Nebraska. We used to head for the haystack and use it for a dormitory overnight. In the morning you could always bathe and shave in the irrigation ditch nearby. The local people also used the ditch as a swimming pool, and much to our surprise we found that very often the swimming was coeducational and that on some warm September nights dress was optional. Another place along Highway 30 where I always tried to stop was Lava Hot Springs, east of Pocatello, Idaho. There you could get a warm bath in the mineral hot springs, and there were some pretty good sleeping accommodations that could be purloined around the edges of the state pools.

But that first bus ride west was a very thrilling experience. I had never been west of the Missouri River, and I had heard all my life about places like North Platte, Cheyenne, Salt Lake City, the Rocky Mountains, the Green River, the Bear River, and the Snake River.

I particularly remember the Hagerman Valley and Thousand Springs and then the long ride across the desert from Bliss to Boise. In Boise you stopped in those days at the Idanha Hotel, which was then the interstate bus stop. I tried to clean up a little bit because I would soon arrive in Caldwell.

Dr. and Mrs. Cole had left Caldwell on a short vacation and were not going to be at home when I arrived, so I was met by my uncle, Robert Smylie, who was superintendent of schools at Notus, Idaho. I stayed at his house for two or three days until it was time to start football practice at the college.

The first weekend Uncle Bob and his family and I traveled up the Payette Canyon to McCall and across to New Meadows and back down through Council and Weiser to Caldwell. It was my first experience with the Payette River, and it has been a life-long love affair. I remember the beautiful green water in September and the fact that the country was almost untouched. There were not many people in Long Valley in those days, and it was a very beautiful drive for a young fellow just arrived from the flatlands of Iowa. After the weekend, my uncle deposited me at 1704 Dearborn Street, the Coles' residence. It was the beginning of a splendid experience and, in retrospect, a splendid life.

Caldwell was a quiet, unassuming town in 1934, but to me it seemed terribly exciting. It was the largest place I had ever lived in and I thought it was quite a bit more sophisticated and intellectual than any town I had ever experienced. Most of the community was clustered around the corners of Main and Kimball Streets, and Cleveland Boulevard ran east and south out of town toward Nampa past the College of Idaho campus. The Coles lived one block off Cleveland

Boulevard and three blocks west of the campus at the corner of 17th and Dearborn Streets. Within the limits of the town we had a swimming pool, a golf course that was being constructed in the old alkali slough, and a Carnegie Library that was built to serve the high school. The streets of Caldwell were all paved and two very impressive railroad trains arrived regularly. One of them was the Portland Rose, which was the famous old train on the Union Pacific. Its arrival was always an occasion. Common to many small towns in Idaho, railroad tracks ran straight through the center of town and all of the crossings had to be watched carefully because freight trains used the tracks as well. Caldwell was primarily an agricultural and commercial town. It was the county seat, and the district court met there, although it was not a very busy court. Frequently, we had to wait four or five months to find a criminal trial that we could attend as part of an assignment in one of Dr. Hayman's classes at the College of Idaho. The fact that criminal trials were that far apart would be a state of affairs that I suspect the sheriffs and prosecuting attorneys of these modern times would envy.

My room in the Coles' house was in the basement, and it was about twelve by fourteen feet. It was the biggest room that I had ever lived in all by myself, and I was quite impressed with the accommodations. There was a shower bath and I could use the living room if I asked Dr. Cole in advance. When I arrived I found evidence that another boy had lived there. He was my erstwhile cousin Eugene Cole, and I say erstwhile cousin because we were not really related, but, as was the custom in the twenties and thirties, people like that were cousins just as your parents' friends were uncles. Eugene had developed several places to secret things away, and I, as he, made frequent use of these cubbyholes. Eugene and I thought that Aunt Leila didn't know anything about those hiding places—a fact which I learned was not the case some years later.

When I departed Caldwell for law school, I left a half pint of whiskey in one of those hiding places, even though it was not my custom in those days to leave whiskey unattended. When I returned four or five years later, it had been moved very surreptitiously, but noticeably, to a different location, and only one person could have done that.

Of course Aunt Leila was quite sure that neither Dr. Cole nor I would touch liquor because good men didn't touch liquor and we were, quite obviously, good men.

The Coles' residence at the corner of 17th and Dearborn Streets was on the same block as several other places where college students lived. Happily, this block also accommodated one of the sorority houses, which was a block up the street from the old Steunenberg residence where Governor Steunenberg had been assassinated in 1905. Frank Steunenberg was governor from 1897 to 1901. He called out federal troops in 1899 to put down unrest between mine owners and workers in the Coeur d'Alene district. In 1905 he was assassinated, and the resulting trial pitted William E. Borah against defense attorney Clarence Darrow. The individuals charged were associated with the Western Federation of Miners. Harry Orchard was convicted; three of the union leaders, including William D. "Big Bill" Haywood, were found innocent.

The morning after I moved to the Coles', I walked the three blocks to the campus, crossed 20th Street, and began what amounted to an entirely new life. There was a building called the Stadium, and that was where Coach Basler was going to meet the football players. I had played one year in high school, and I thought I knew something about the game. I went to that first meeting of the team as what would now be called a walk-on player. I am not sure I would have done this if I had not been Uncle Bob's nephew. He was a great football enthusiast who had played brilliantly for Morningside College, and he was sure that I could play football for the College of Idaho. As I remember, we got some sort of a physical examination and were issued practice uniforms and told to report back for practice the next morning at nine o'clock. We then began practices twice daily until school started ten days later.

Later that afternoon I took a look around the campus. The College of Idaho then consisted of Blatchley Hall, Finney Hall, Sterry Hall, Voorhees Hall, Strahorn Library, the Field House, the Stadium, and the Hat. For those who were not around in those early days, the Hat was the little square building down on Cleveland Boulevard at the entrance to the campus which had, once upon a time, been a station stop on the

The football player in his sweater, 1935. The sweater is still around.

interurban railroad between Caldwell and Boise. In 1934–35 the Hat served as a stop for the buses which ran every hour on the hour between Boise and Caldwell.

That first afternoon at the College of Idaho Mr. Hampson, the groundskeeper, was busy mowing the grass and getting the campus cleaned up for the onslaught of students. Sterry Hall was open, and I walked in and took a look around at some of the classrooms. The college seemed to me to be not much different from the little private colleges that stretched across the state of Iowa. Sterry Hall looked very much like Old Main at Luther College at Decorah and the Main Hall at Morningside College at Sioux City. All were founded as church-related schools, and one wonders if ministers were equipped with catalogues so architectural plans for the central building of a campus could be mail ordered. They have a striking similarity across the country.

A week later it was time to register for college classes, pay tuition, buy books and school supplies, and come fairly close to ending up broke. As I remember, I enrolled in the required fifteen hours of classes, five of which were a class in beginning German, which I was to take from a professor named Knute Overgaard. Unfortunately, I soon found that fifteen hours of credit classes was a bit too much when one also practiced football five hours a day. Having heard that if you persevered at football you could probably get a job that would pay part of your tuition, I was determined to make the team. If I had not made that decision, I'm not sure I would have been able to stay in college for the second year, but this had tragic effects on my scholarship as a German student. Very shortly Dr. Overgaard was telling me that it might be well for me to decide to resign from the class before I got thrown out. I walked home and told my aunt that I was going to drop German. She thought the decision was a bad one, but a forgivable one. I withdrew from the class just in time to prevent receiving a failing grade.

I had always planned to go on to law school if I could manage to finish college. Dr. Paul Murphy, who registered me for school in that first year in 1934, told me that I should take courses in history and economics and those should be my major and minor areas of study. Political science, which is now the accepted pre-law curriculum of choice, was not yet an independent discipline at the college or elsewhere. Thus, history and economics were the areas of study in which I concentrated. I also thought it would be wise to undertake what training I could in forensics, such as debate and oratorical endeavor. I did so with a view to preparing myself for what I anticipated would be needed later on in the courtroom. As it turned out, I didn't need these skills much in the courtroom, but I did put what I learned to fairly decent advantage in the political arena.

During the course of that first registration period I met a fellow named Bill Young from Parma and a boy from Caldwell named George Greenfield. Our lives would be entangled for the next fifty years. All three of us went to the George Washington University Law School. After our four years in Washington, D.C., I came home first and was already attorney general by the time the others arrived. When Bill Young came back from law school, he started farming, practiced law, went on to serve for many years in the Idaho House and Senate, and was later named clerk of the Idaho Supreme Court. Bill Young was Speaker of the House when I was sworn in as governor. George Greenfield was the Democratic state chairman the year that I was first elected governor of Idaho, and George would serve in several positions to which I was happy to appoint him during my years as governor.

I have a notion that I picked the right year to enroll in the College of Idaho. I still have the notion that *when* you go to school is as important in the formation of your intellect and character as who teaches the classes that you attend. In any event, the class of 1938 at the College of Idaho ended up being a fairly accomplished group of people and included Young, Greenfield, Robert Sloan, Jim Toole, Cyril Slansky, and a host of young women, many of whom became school teachers of consequence and note.

With registration completed, classes commenced and we began to get to know the old professors who had been staffing the college almost from the beginning. Indeed, they were the real purveyors of our collegiate experience. Majoring in history with a minor in economics steered me in the direction of Professors Herbert H. Hayman, E. C. Preston, Francis C. Springer, as well as the obligatory courses in mathematics under Professor Joseph Rankin and chemistry under Professors Joseph Roblyer and Henry House. We were required to enroll in a course of religious education, but it was permissible to take a sort of quasi-history course in lieu of that requirement. I remember taking a course from Dr. James Millar in my freshman year in comparative religion.

The first year in college was relatively uneventful. I got to play a little on the football team, at least enough to make a letter, as I remember it, and to learn a little bit about how the game was played at the college level. I was a B student and ended the year with about fifteen dollars left and no prospects of any further financial assistance unless something unexpected showed up. I had joined the local fraternity, called the Orions, and had participated pretty generally in almost all of the college activities. I had permitted somebody to talk me into running for editor of the student newspaper and was solemnly defeated and thereafter had the good sense not to run for elective office on campus again, but I did undertake to have my say in campus affairs by participating in the proceedings that elected other people to office.

When school was out in the spring of 1935, I did not have a job and so hitchhiked my way back to Iowa. I hoped I could get a job in Kentucky, where my sister was an army nurse at Fort Knox. The job was supposed to be carrying chain on a surveying crew that was laying out the original boundaries of the gold vault at Fort Knox. Unfortunately the job never materialized, and so I returned to Cresco without anything on the horizon.

I had worked at various jobs around Fort Knox and had a little money, but not very much. I think I remember that when I returned to Cresco and the folks' house, I had something in the neighborhood of thirty-six dollars.

Then I received a letter from Coaches Loren Basler and George Stovel at the college suggesting that perhaps if I came back to school and played football there might be a job. There was no promise of work, only a hint, really, but it was enough to perk me up a little and to get my legs in motion. I decided that the choice was between having thirty-six dollars and nothing to do in Cresco, and having thirty-six dollars, a long hitchhike, and maybe having something to do in Caldwell at the college. The choice was pretty easy to make, and I got the folks to take me down to the big highway at Cedar Rapids, and I mounted my thumb.

Hitchhiking was easy in the fall of 1935, and the first ride I picked up took me as far as Grand Island, Nebraska. That was almost a third of the way to Caldwell, and my spirits rose in consequence of that happy circumstance. That night I slept in the usual haystack in Sutherland, Nebraska, and bathed in the "international memorial irrigation ditch," but waited to shave until I got to Lava Hot Springs in Idaho where the water was warm and the weather was a trifle more salubrious.

From Lava Hot Springs I hitched a ride that took me all the way to Boise. I arrived in Caldwell in time to report for football practice just as though I were going to go to the college. I had a promise that I could live in the basement again at my aunt's house and help around the house for meals, but tuition and money for books was going to be scarce. They used to say at the time that being broke and having to work hard built character. If that were the case, there was a lot of character being built in Caldwell in those days. Hardly any of us had any money. We enjoyed life tremendously, and we got quite a bit accomplished, but there was not a good deal of money for foolishness or for anything but penny-ante poker.

That first football practice in 1935 became crucial to completing my college education. It was necessary to put my case to Coach Basler and Coach Stovel. I was no shrinking violet, and I told them that if I was going to remain in school and be able to play football, I was going to have to have some financial help.

Both Basler and Stovel must have remembered me as not much of a lineman. My freshman year, although tolerable, was certainly not of star quality. However, someplace along the line I must have learned a thing or two about how to play. I also suspect that someone on the team did not return, because the coaches apparently had aid that they could distribute to people they thought worthy and well qualified. When practice was over that afternoon, Basler and Stovel called me into their little office and told me that I could have what they called an NYA scholarship. The NYA was a New Deal agency called the National Youth Administration. You received a grant and in return performed a service on campus. Each one of the grants was enough to pay your tuition and nothing more. My grant required me to be secretary to the head of the Department of Philosophy and Religion, under Dr. James Millar. I had no aptitude as a secretary, very little knowledge of religion and none at all of philosophy, but I received the job, I suspect, because I was an improving guard on the football team. So even in those Depression days it can be said that one of the primary ways you built a football team was to have to play for pay.

The papers you signed when you accepted an NYA grant involved an assignment of your salary to the college. Of course you would draw a salary if you had already paid your tuition, but in my case I didn't have the money to do that, and the NYA grant assignment took care of paying the tuition for the first semester, as well as the second, if I continued to hold the job.

Now I had my tuition arranged and a place to eat and a place to sleep, but I didn't have any books or college supplies and I had only sixteen dollars left. I told George Stovel about my plight to see if he had any ideas. He said he would think about it. He must have thought quite well because the next day he came back and said that he thought maybe I might fit into a job slot that they wanted to fill at the Butler-Miller Hardware Company in downtown Caldwell. I asked to get away from practice early that evening to interview for the position.

After about a thirty-minute conversation, Mr. Butler and Mr. Miller both said that they thought it would be a good idea if I came to work for them. They wanted to know if I could make sign cards for their window displays, and, although I knew nothing about it, I promptly said that I could. I hurried back to the college the next morning and got Colin Matthews to teach me how to make them. Colin was the head of the Art Department and a new man on campus. He taught me enough that I was able to carry off the task quite well and thus hold on to my job at the hardware store. The pay was thirty dollars a month. I regularly swept the place out and designed their signs and window displays. I can't remember how many hours were involved, but they were substantial. The thirty dollars I earned was just enough to be able to buy some corduroy jeans, some college supplies, and some books. I was off and running in my second year in college.

The football season that year was neither a disaster nor an unqualified success. We had had a conference championship in my freshman year, and this had taught the fans in Caldwell to expect wonder at all times and all places. We started out in 1935 with fairly good success. We played six games in a row without dropping one and then lost the last four consecutively. The last four, of course, were the important ones. They were the conference games, and thus the championship that we had won the year before went down the drain. We lost to Willamette, Linfield, Whitman, and, worst of all, Eastern Oregon College of Education. The first three were almost forgivable, but that last one made us a second-rate team in the eyes of the Caldwell fans. I was, however, able to make my own way as left guard on that team and on the succeeding teams the next two years.

Thirty dollars a month at the hardware store doesn't sound like a great deal to pay for clothes and books and college supplies, but there wasn't anything left over for spending money. As a consequence, I began to consider other sources of income. Happily I had learned somewhere along the line how to play poker with sufficient care to never lose much money, and I would occasionally win a little. There were always some students who had adequate allowances who could participate in furnishing a little spending money for impecunious types like myself. I also engaged in a clandestine term paper writing project for hire that was modestly lucrative at times. The going rate was about ten dollars a thousand words. I could write English prose with sufficient skill to produce a pretty good paper in a fairly short time. I don't know what the college would do now if they knew that I had indulged in those peccadilloes, but it provided me the means of having an occasional night out with some of the co-eds.

None of us had very much money and some of us had none at all, but we had an awfully good time in those years. The college proms, the dances at Middleton and Nampa, the talk sessions at the local hangouts like Gaines-Bowes and McCluskey's—all of those were fun times. There were no automobiles on the campus so everybody walked everywhere. You even took a girl to the formal and semi-formal dances on foot. That involved walking down Cleveland Boulevard to the Odd Fellow Temple at the corner of Kimball and Cleveland where all of the dances were held. It was great fun to dance to the big band music of the local "pep" bands.

Some of the upperclassmen were a major influence in those first years at college. There were Bill Scott from Twin Falls and Raymond

White from New Plymouth. Both were pre-medical students. There were Russel Cook and Howard Campbell from Nampa and Middleton, respectively, who were studying the usual arts and sciences curricula. Three of them were seniors and one was a junior and somehow or other I became fairly close friends with all of them. I think it may have been because I was two years older than most of my classmates, having stayed out of school for two years after high school graduation. These upperclassmen were very good to an unworldly young fellow from Iowa. They taught me how to study, how to make dates with the girls in the sororities, how to smoke surreptitiously, and how to drink Scotch whiskey and gin. They even taught me how to organize a run to Ontario to buy liquor in Oregon before it was legal in Idaho. White and Scott were forerunners of that long line of pre-med students who found that a degree from the College of Idaho was a great asset when they were trying to gain admission to medical school. Dr. Arthur Curtis Jones and Dr. James Coughlin, who were in my class as freshmen, would travel the same route. Scott transferred back from Stanford to finish his science degree at the College of Idaho for that reason. The science department, under Dean Orma J. Smith, with the assistance of Professors Roblyer and House, was just then getting up to speed, and it would produce a list of first-rate scientists and physicians.

Dr. William Judson Boone, who had founded the college and was its president, was present on the campus in the school years of 1934, 1935, and 1936. We saw some of him, but these were the last two years of his life, and he was more observed than really known. He was an imposing presence, and his character very obviously dominated the entire school. He was the reason we didn't smoke on the campus and also the reason why the intersection of 20th Street and Dearborn Avenue, just outside of Voorhees Hall, was a sort of environmental disaster. It was the largest cigarette stub receptacle west of Chicago. But strangely, everybody obeyed the unwritten rule that you didn't smoke, and it is interesting to note that it was almost thirty years before that rule was abrogated in any substantial way.

Dr. Cole, my uncle, was Dr. Boone's personal physician, and he was in attendance when Dr. Boone was found dead in his little laboratory in the basement of his house on Ash Street. I remember him coming home to dinner that evening and relating the fact that Dr. Boone had passed away. I suspect that we, like everybody else in Caldwell, wondered what would happen to the college now that its founder, mentor, and guiding spirit had died.

As might be expected of the faculty that Dr. Boone had gathered together, the people who ran the classrooms at the college rallied around and took on the task of running the school through the 1936–37 school year. They were a notable group. There was Dean Smith, of course, and Dr. Joseph Roblyer, Henry House, Dr. Joseph Rankin and his wife, Sarah, Dr. E. C. Preston, who taught history, and Paul Murphy, who was a professor of romance languages. It would be unfair to say that these people were underpaid. They were scarcely paid at all, but they taught school and they taught it with great skill. I do not know exactly what was going on at that particular time in the history of the college. The faculty may not have measured up to the standards now imposed on faculty in terms of academic degrees or formal training, but they did have something going for them in the way of teaching people how to be of service to their community, how to be reasonably accomplished scholars, and how to lead productive, useful lives.

During those years it seems, in retrospect, that current events continued to develop my interest in political affairs and to intensify my desire to participate somehow or other in great public events. I remember one occasion, in 1936, when George Greenfield and I borrowed his father's old Chevrolet and drove up to Boise to attend a political rally where John Daniel Miller Hamilton, then the Republican national chairman, made a speech in Public School Field on behalf of Alfred M. Landon, the Republican candidate for president. Mr. Hamilton was an impressive character and made an excellent speech, but he and Landon only carried Vermont and Maine against FDR in that year. Both Landon and Hamilton faded into history after that.

I recall being in the newsroom of the *Caldwell News Tribune* on the evening of the general election in 1936. A great number of people were gathered there to watch the returns coming in over the Associated Press wire. Late in the evening, it became apparent that Barzilla W. Clark, the mayor of Idaho Falls, had been elected governor. He was thought by the Republicans present to be untrained and perhaps not quite up to speed for the job. I recall one of the gentlemen saying that we were "not to worry," that he had been living here for thirty years and that he didn't know anybody in the state who was capable of ruining it in two years.

The year of Landon's landslide defeat, 1936, was also the first time that I voted. I went down to the little church at the corner of 16th and Everett Streets and cast what must have been one of the least effective ballots in Caldwell's history since everyone I voted for lost. I voted at that precinct in that little church from that time until I moved my legal residence to Boise in 1967.

In the fall of 1937, President Franklin Delano Roosevelt came touring down through Boise Valley to take a look at Hubert Peckham's onion farm near Wilder, Idaho. The president had come into Boise on a special railroad car called the Magellan and then came down the valley by automobile. As I remember there were three automobiles. One had the president and Mrs. Roosevelt and Governor Barzilla W. Clark in the backseat. They were preceded by one car, apparently the Secret Service, and they were followed by a third car, which had Mr. Peckham and some dignitaries in the backseat. They stopped very briefly in front of Sterry Hall at the College of Idaho, and we were all very excited that a president had come to call. Mrs. Roosevelt was presented with a bouquet of roses, and after about five minutes the presidential cavalcade was on its way again.

Things are much different these days. I suspect that if the president tried to come to visit the College of Idaho campus now, there would hardly be room in Caldwell for the required entourage. By contrast, on FDR's visit there was no visible security. Nobody policed the crowds gathered in front of Sterry Hall, and, to my knowledge, nobody policed the roads out to Wilder and to Parma, where he got back on the railroad car and traveled on to Portland to dedicate a phase of the Bonneville Power Administration's new dam on the Columbia.

This was certainly enough to excite almost anyone's appetite for political affairs, and the Orion fraternity decided that the time had come when we should select a president of the student body. We put together a little campaign that elected Bill Young and we were successful in other elections and took control of the Board of Directors of the Associated Students. I already had my eye on the job of being business manager of the 1938 *Trail*, the yearbook, because I apprehended that unlike the other elected positions, there was some money to be made in that one. Winning the election in 1937 was premonitory to being in charge of the Board of Directors of the Associated Students when the time came to elect the business manager and editor of the yearbook. That decision was pretty certain to lead to my election in the spring and to the post that I desired to hold.

It is a tribute to the skill with which we put the political machinery together that it elected the director of the Associated Students again in 1938 and 1939. By 1940 I was in law school at George Washington University and I lost interest in such local events at the College of Idaho.

After football season ended most of my extracurricular activities were centered on the debate team. We had an intramural contest in those years that we called the Walters Debate. This was named after T. A. Walters, who had been assistant secretary of the Interior and who had lived on Dearborn Street in Caldwell. Some time back in the twenties he had put up a small sum of money to provide a prize of twenty-five dollars for the winners of the intramural contest, who then went forth to do battle on behalf of the college. In all of the last three years that I was in school, I was a member of the debate team, and in my junior and senior years I was a partner with George Greenfield. He said I didn't debate very well, but I talked quite loudly, and we usually went to Linfield College in McMinville, Oregon, to attend the invitational debate tournament. George often won a prize. He was a very skillful debater and became a very skillful trial lawyer in later years. In our senior year, we went to the National Convention of the Debate Fraternity in Topeka, Kansas, at Washburn College. We had a good two-and-a-half-week trip, at college expense, that was well worth our hard work. George Greenfield and I wanted to go to see Alf Landon, who lived in Topeka, and we wrote to get an appointment. We were told that if we were to stop by the house we could see him. We did do that and had a visit with the old gentleman. I thought he appeared much older than he in fact was. He lived many, many years after that, and his daughter has just retired after a distinguished career in the United States Senate.

By now I was thought to be worthwhile enough as an employee to be able to work full time during the summer at the hardware store. I think I got the magnificent sum of thirty dollars a week for my trouble. It was enough to provide a small store of spending money when I returned in my junior year. I also worked the next two summers in the hardware store before going east to law school. It was interesting work. I got to know almost all the people in the business community in Caldwell and became familiar enough with the banker that he lent me twenty-five dollars on my own name.

It was in those years that the Caldwell Night Rodeo was organized, and either the first or second year I had some fairly extensive responsibilities with respect to the operation of it. By now the golf course had been completed, and we played golf almost every evening. I also operated a softball team in the city league for the hardware store. All in all it was a bucolic summer experience in a small town in western Idaho, but it provided enough pleasure to keep me in Caldwell rather than to hitch back and forth to Iowa.

I suppose the senior year is always the most important year or the best year for almost everybody who goes to college. It was for me. There was a football trip to play San Jose State in San Jose, California. We went down on the train, through Salt Lake City, west across the long dike that divides the Great Salt Lake, through Reno, and over Donner Pass. We arrived in San Francisco and had a chance to see that great city just as the bridges were being finished. I think maybe I was one of the last passengers on the ferry boat from Oakland to San Francisco. That was a notable experience.

Unfortunately, we were not very good football players that year. We lost the game sixty to six. It was a sensational beating, but the trip was worth it. We had a new coach, O. Page. He had been one of Alonzo Stagg's football players at the University of Chicago.

The trip to San Francisco and the spring trip to Topeka, Kansas, which occupied a good deal of time, were the principal extracurricular events of that year, but the item that dominated almost all of my time was the 1938 edition of *The Trail*.

The fellow who had run for editor of the yearbook did not seem to have much interest in it, and after I was appointed to be business manager of the publication, I undertook to do most of the editing myself. In those years that involved putting the book together, seeing that all of the pictures were organized, and writing most of the copy.

We decided to try to put out a modern, first-class book that would bring the publication of an annual at the college into the twentieth century. In a sense we succeeded. The book was, I think, the best one that had been done up to that time and set a standard by which later books would be measured. In the spring and summer of 1937 we took most of the pictures and planned most of the layouts. George Greenfield and I took a trip to Seattle to see a man named Walter Ervine who was head of Western Color Type and Engraving Company, which would do the engraving for the book. We stayed at the Washington Athletic Club and had a marvelous time in what was one of the biggest cities either of us had ever seen. We hitchhiked to and from Seattle and got hung up in

A page from the 1938 College of Idaho yearbook, The Trail, *for which I served as business manager.*

Walla Walla, Washington, without any money. I had to wire Dr. Cole for five dollars to get home.

Most of my spare time in the college year of 1937–38 was spent putting the finances of the yearbook together. This involved shaking down the business community for ads and contributions and pleading with Jim Gipson, Jr., of Caxton Printers to give us additional things for the book without charging us. It was a successful enterprise, and I think I showed a profit of about fifteen hundred dollars or so. In any event, it permitted me to send some money to my sister, Dorothy, who was in nurse's training at the Norwegian-American Hospital in Chicago, and to have a modest sum left with which I could get my credits squared away for transfer to George Washington University.

Almost before I knew it, four years had gone by and we were preparing to graduate. I had not been a great scholar, but I graduated in the upper quarter of my class. That was enough to insure me admission to the law school at George Washington.

Commencement that year was in the old First Methodist Church located on Kimball Street and Blaine Avenue. I am not sure how many people graduated that spring, but it must have been between eighty and a hundred. The next fall the college would have seemed a strange place to go back to, simply because of the fact that almost everybody I knew had graduated with me. The commencement address was made by a Mr. William Jeffers, who was then president of the Union Pacific Railroad. He had apparently been secured as commencement speaker by the new president of the college, Raymond Hotchkiss Leach, who served only one year.

I spent the summer of 1938 in Caldwell working at the hardware store and enjoying myself generally as a former college student who had no particular immediate responsibilities. I tried to prepare myself mentally for making the big break to go east to law school. In late summer Fred Miller and Carl Butler, who ran the hardware store, sat me down one afternoon and told me that if I didn't get out of town I would probably never do it and would end up working for them. It was sobering because it was that kind of thought that had led me to leave Cresco and driving the bakery truck to come west to the College of

Idaho. But it was Dr. F. M. Cole, my uncle, who finally said what my father had said once before—that if I didn't have the courage to do it now, I would never have the courage to leave. And so as the summer drew on toward fall, I told Butler and Miller that I was leaving their employment. My first sojourn in Caldwell had been a rewarding experience, and it was the commencement of the education of a young man who was now fairly certain to be on his way.

CHAPTER THREE

BECOMING A LAWYER

In mid-September of 1938, I learned that a cattle train was being made up to leave Caldwell on the sixth of October from the stockyards at 20th Street and the railroad and that it would be possible to get passage in the caboose as far as Grand Island, Nebraska. I quickly signed on for a free trip and announced in ringing tones to all who would listen that I was leaving on the sixth to go to Washington, D.C., to begin law school.

Having made that decision and having passed the point of no return, I had to figure out a way to attain some reality for my plans. As usual in those Depression years, the big problem was money. I had saved a fair sum from my work during the summer, and I decided to see if I could borrow some additional capital in order to get started in Washington after I got there. Mrs. Lila Stubblefield loaned me $200 and with that, and the proceeds of my summer's work, I cleared my debts at the college so that my transcript could be transferred to George Washington University and went down to see Mr. J. M. Carl at Alexander's Men's Store in Caldwell and bought a suit and three shirts. The suit cost $37.50 and the shirts, as I remember, cost $2.00 apiece. With that large a purchase, Mr. Carl threw in a necktie, and I was then fully equipped to take off on my trip east.

I have often been asked why I chose to go to law school at George Washington University. Aside from the fact that George Washington would accept someone who graduated from college in the top fourth of their class, there were other factors influencing my decision.

George Scatterday was a young lawyer in Caldwell who had just returned to join his father in practice, and he had been educated at George Washington University. He told us about how he had worked most of the time he was in the law school as an elevator operator on Capitol Hill on Senator Borah's patronage. He said that George Washington was the only law school he knew of where you could work full time and go to law school full time. For this reason, there was no other real choice. George Washington was not yet the glittering law school that it is now, but it was a good school and one which would furnish a serviceable legal education.

In the meantime, 1938 had been an election year in Idaho and D. Worth Clark, the congressman from Pocatello, was running against James P. Pope, the incumbent Senator, who was a Democrat. It was a hotly contested election and many of the Republicans organized a crossover vote to benefit Congressman Clark because Senator Pope was not very well liked. There was a regular cabal of Republicans from the old Gooding machine who participated in this effort (Frank Gooding, one of Idaho's early power brokers, served as governor between 1905–9 and U.S. Senator between 1921–28) largely, I think, at the insistence of Senator Borah. The Republican rebels contributed funds to Congressman Clark's campaign and actively organized a crossover vote so that Republicans were voting in the Democratic primary for the purpose of voting for Congressman Clark. My uncle, Dr. Cole, and my quasi-uncle, Ike Westcott, were a part of the group organizing this endeavor. I asked my uncle to inquire of Senator-elect Clark about the possibility of a patronage job on Capitol Hill as a way to earn a living while I went to law school. He did so and Congressman Clark said that he would "see what he could do."

Equipped with my new suit, my old suitcase, my rusty, trusty bathrobe, a pair of brogans, and what was left of my $260, I left Caldwell October 6, 1938. I had decided to use the cattle train as a way of getting east rather than hitchhiking because I thought the weather would be difficult. It turned out to be a wise decision. It was raining when we left Caldwell, and it was raining all the way to Grand Island, Nebraska. As a matter of fact, it rained all across Nebraska and into Iowa, and I didn't really see any sunshine until I got to Grinnell, Iowa, where I stopped to visit some old friends, one of whom was at Grinnell College. I also went on up to Cresco to visit my folks before I left for the east.

I had talked Bill Young into going east to law school with me, and I had to spend the next two weeks jarring him loose from Parma, where he had gone after graduation. I finally sent him a telegram saying that I was leaving from Iowa City, Iowa, on a certain day and hoped he would join me at the bus station. He did. Together we went on to Chicago, visited with my sister and her nursing friends at the hospital in the Windy City, and then went on to Washington, D.C., by bus. We arrived in Washington about eight o'clock in the evening the night before Thanksgiving.

Earl Burton, a Caldwell boy who was already attending graduate school, met us at the bus station and took us to the *Time* magazine news bureau in the old *Washington Post* building on Post Square where he was working. Later we walked up Connecticut Avenue to a fraternity house on R Street, where we spent the night, and then we celebrated Thanksgiving Day with Earl Burton and his friends, the Coes. Richard Coe, the son of the household, was a student at George Washington and also worked in the drama department at the *Washington Post*. He worked there all of his life and ultimately ended up being editor of the drama section and a character of very considerable note around the town. Earl Burton died early, but Richard Coe's path and my own crossed from time to time over the years that intervened. Most recently we encountered each other at a White House reception hosted by President Reagan in 1987.

Bill Young and I were the first of five people from the class of 1938 of the College of Idaho who ended up in Washington that year. Robert Sloan followed us and entered an accounting course and became a certified public accountant. George Greenfield and Don McClenahan came later, and they entered the law school. About a year later Mary Alice Stubblefield, who was employed by the Civil Service Department, came to Washington to take a job there. By odd coincidence, none of us stayed in Washington after the war was over and our education was completed.

After we arrived in Washington, Young and I spent diligent hours trudging up and down the avenues looking for work. We did this under the guiding hand of a lady named Mary Palmer, who was a clerk in Congressman Clark's office and who was very kind to us. The people in Senator Borah's office were especially helpful. They were Cora Rubin and Joe Bergey, both of whom later came back to live in Idaho. We finally picked up a couple of jobs in the post office during the holidays and worked until Christmas Eve, but unfortunately we didn't get paid until after the first of the year. Christmas Eve came and we were flat broke. We went down to a restaurant called the Deauville on Connecticut Avenue and spent our last five dollars on scotch whiskey. We had our room and board paid for until the tenth of January and we were guaranteed two meals a day and a place to sleep, but being fresh out of the coin of the realm was pretty disheartening.

I finally confessed to Mrs. Palmer in Clark's office that we were broke and she loaned me twenty-five dollars, which I was to repay out of my first pay check. At the same time she told me that as soon as Clark got sworn in on the twentieth of January, I would have a job as a capitol policeman on his patronage. This was a great reassurance to me. At the same time, Bill Young encountered some good fortune in getting a mail clerk's job at the Reconstruction Finance Corporation. We now had anticipated earnings, but we had no cash. Some time after the first of the year, we each got a check for twenty-five dollars from our parents and that tided us over until there was a pay check that could buy some more room and board.

The assurance of employment meant we could check out possibilities at the law school, and we did just that. Our transcripts had arrived, and so we applied for admission. After about a week we were told that we would be admitted to the class commencing in February, and we enrolled. I was working on the Capitol Police Force from four in the evening until midnight. I went to school in the daytime from eight until two. Bill Young had a daytime job so he went to the evening classes. Although we took pretty much the same courses, we didn't attend classes together.

In the fall of 1939, I listened to Senator Key Pittman of Nevada and Senator Borah open the debate on the revision of the Neutrality Act, which restricted the U.S. government and its citizens from becoming involved in activities with "belligerent" nations. Borah was opposed to any revision. Being loyal Borah Republicans, we were very much in favor of his position. The debate was the forerunner of the end of the neutrality farce and the beginning of the legislation that led to the creation of a peacetime draft and preparations in earnest for war. But mostly in those weeks and months in pre-war Washington, we enjoyed the last mellow light of its time as a country-town capital of the great democracy. When war came, things would never be the same.

Having listened to those debates and having listened to the conversations between some of the senators whom I met in Senator Clark's office, including Senator Harry Truman, I concluded that it was not a question of whether we were going to go to war, it was a question of when. I decided that the thing to do was to go to law school in the hope that perhaps it might be possible to finish the program before we actually entered the war. I never went home after that for vacation. Instead I attended law school classes twelve months a year, and was thus able to finish before I was drafted in 1942. That self-imposed rigorous schedule made life in law school even more difficult than it would have been without the self-imposed discipline.

They like to tell freshman law students that they should look sharply to the left and sharply to the right because a year hence two of the three of us would not be there. They also liked to tell you that the law was a jealous mistress and she left no time for frivolity. Both of these maxims turned out to be correct. The attrition rate at George Washington University Law School was about sixty-five percent for reasons which they rather kindly called a lack of scholarship. This was shorthand for saying that you were flunking out. A full load in law school and a full forty-hour work week kept you busy and kept you out of trouble, if you had any inclination for trouble, and you had no funds with which to finance trouble anyway.

That decision to go nonstop through the law school was to be the defining moment which affected everything that came after. It made me concentrate exclusively on my studies. It permitted me to graduate in June 1942. But most important of all, it permitted me to come back from the war years with my law degree tucked underneath my arm and my admission to the bar already accomplished. Had that not been the case, I wouldn't have been ready when Robert Ailshie asked me to become assistant attorney general in Idaho in 1947.

Commencing classwork in the law school brought me into contact almost immediately with a veritable flock of great professors and teachers. There was Hector Galloway Spaulding, who taught equity, Charles Collier, who taught constitutional law, William Friar, who introduced me to the vagaries of evidence law, William Cabell Vanbleck, who taught conflicts of laws, and Carville Benson, who taught domestic relations and criminal law. Somehow or other in these first fourteen hours of credit in the first semester in law school I learned how to study and how to address myself to the comprehensive examinations that concluded every course and on which your final grade depended. In that first semester, I managed to get five A's and two B's and thereafter I went straight through the entire eighty hours without breaking my chain of A's. This permitted me to finish second in the class, to be an associate editor of the *Law Review*, and to be introduced to the law firm of Covington, Burling, Rublee, Acheson and Shorb, where I began working in the fall of 1939.

Looking back, I don't seem to remember much about the law school that was outstanding. It was sort of a blur of study and case books and lectures and examinations and then more of the same. Everybody in the law school in those days had a job and was working at it as well as attending law school. I met several interesting students along the way, some of whom I found reason to remember in later life. There were two persons in the law school who served as governors of various states during my time as governor of Idaho. I remember district and circuit court judges by the handful who went to school there, went home, and later were appointed to the federal bench.

Most of our entertainment occurred in a place called Bassin's Coffee Shop, which was located close to Stockton Hall where the law school was housed. We spent hours there talking about classes, politics, and the looming war, and drinking endless gallons of coffee. It was in this old law school hangout that I learned the habit that has afflicted me all of my life. I found that in the law school there was hardly anything you couldn't do better if you had a coffee cup in your hand. I would continue that habit or indulge that addiction down to the very writing of these memories.

Bill Young and I did not have much money so we did a lot of things that were free. We went to Corcouran Gallery of Art, to the Phillips Gallery, and, of course, to the Smithsonian Institution. Dick Coe used to get us tickets for free in the pigeon loft at the National Theater. We saw the great Tallulah Bankhead play the lead in *The Little Foxes*. We saw Claire Boothe Luce open her own play as the lead in *The Women*. Occasionally we went to Constitution Hall, where free tickets were also available to students at the university, to listen to the National Symphony. But mostly those years were a round of library work, law lectures, study, and streetcars, which were the major means of getting back and forth.

We lived on Connecticut Avenue within walking distance of Dupont Circle. The old Mount Pleasant Line on the Capital Transit Company became our workhorse. It went to Capitol Hill, it came within five or six blocks of the university, and it generally served almost every transportation need you could imagine.

While I busied myself in law school, dark clouds were gathering and it became apparent that war was imminent. Earlier there had been no guards at the Pennsylvania Avenue gates of the White House. Now they appeared. Mrs. Roosevelt used to drive her own car to the beauty parlor. Now she was driven. Temporary buildings began to appear on the Mall between the Reflecting Basin and the Washington Monument. The drumbeat was distant, but its volume was increasing, and by

December 7, 1941, Washington had changed dramatically and began to look like the capital of a nation at war.

As did every man, I had registered for the draft in 1940. I was fortunate enough to end up with a fairly high number when they conducted the lottery. I had registered in Caldwell, Idaho, which was still my official residence, and the draft board in Canyon County was looking over my shoulder as I conducted my studies.

I had a friend who was an admiral in the Navy. We discussed whether or not there was any point in being in a hurry to accumulate a war experience. He told me that he didn't think I needed to hurry—that the war would be going on for some years and there would be plenty of time for everybody to participate. He advised me to wait until Uncle Sam sent for me and then go and do whatever was required of me. I thought it was sound advice and followed it.

CHAPTER FOUR

THE LAW, THE WAR, AND LUCILLE

IN THE FALL of 1939 while I was in law school, I was offered the opportunity to become a law clerk at Covington, Burling, Rublee, Acheson and Shorb. I made $135 a month as a Capitol Policeman and taking the job in the law firm only paid $100. I did some checking around, primarily with United States Senator D. Worth Clark, about whether or not it would be wise to take the job. His advice was that it would be, and I found out later that he had asked Lucille Irwin whether this was a good idea. She just happened to be Judge Covington's secretary. Lucille's advice was that I ought to pay the law firm for the opportunity. So, after due deliberation, I took the job and stayed on with the Capitol Police Force until they caught up with me and turned me loose. When Senator Borah passed away in January 1940, however, I was one of the policemen chosen to be an honor guard at his funeral services in the Senate Chambers.

Covington and Burling was, and I suspect still is, one of the most prestigious law firms in Washington, D.C. It had been founded by Mr. Covington and Mr. Burling in the years after World War I and had grown by the time I arrived on the scene in 1939 to be a firm of about forty lawyers. There was one other senior partner, named George

Rublee, who was a graduate of the State Department in the years during World War I. He specialized in international law and in banking law.

The firm's offices at 15th and H Streets, N.W., were about two blocks from the White House. They had about them a sort of hushed cathedral-like air that suggested that important things were being done and that law was incidentally being practiced. The office occupied the sixth and seventh floors of the Union Trust Building, and on the sixth floor there was a library that would have been the envy of many small law schools. Many of the junior partners and associate members of the firm had been clerks in the Supreme Court of the United States. Several of them had worked, at one time or another, for Justice Brandeis, Justice Cardozo, or Justice Holmes. Most of them were graduates of Harvard Law School and tended to look down on the peons who went to George Washington. Nevertheless, there was considerable collegiality and camaraderie in the firm that made being there a learning experience of the first order. It would be fair to say that the experience I gained at Covington and Burling was such that it would indeed have been more appropriate for me to have paid for the opportunity rather than being paid a salary.

The law clerks, who were permitted to sit at the feet of the learned and the mighty, were called junior law clerks, although we were not much more than what might be referred to as "gofers." In those days, we ran the errands and had charge of the duplicating machinery and kept our books and papers in a small room off the conference room, and the secretaries in the office named the three junior law clerks "the boys in the back room."

The three of us who began together—James Ellison, Charles Olson, and me—were joined some time later by another lad named George Elmore, and we spent two years in a setting and an environment which was conducive to the most rigorous and enduring legal training possible. We worked from nine in the morning until a quarter to five in the afternoon, and I went to law school in the evenings.

Every once in a while one of the lawyers would give one of us research to do, and we could have the "joy" of preparing a memorandum. As time wore on these assignments grew more regular and more excessive. In the fall of 1939, with lawyers leaving the firm for work associated with military preparations of one kind or another, we began receiving better professional assignments. Writing a memorandum for John Laylin that dealt with whether or not bar silver and the storerooms at West Point could be regarded as a defense item was a thrilling experience. The end result of our labor was a legal defense of the U.S. government's right to lend the silver to Great Britain, which then used it to "win" the support of Saudi Arabian sheiks during the Second World War.

The firm's clientele included a list of some of the corporate greats of America—General Motors, Dupont, DeSoto Bank, the American Canning Association. Very often there were assignments for agencies of the government, such as the Department of the Treasury and the Department of State.

One of the partners in the firm was Dean G. Acheson, who left the firm to become assistant secretary of state in 1939. He was later secretary of state under Mr. Truman and wrote the definitive history of the Marshall Plan in his book, *Present at the Creation*. I knew Mr. Acheson well and visited with him occasionally after I became governor of Idaho. He was one of the saints of the Democratic party and always regarded me as sort of an apostate because I was a Republican governor.

Over the course of 1939 and 1940 our assignments in the back room grew more and more important. I had the opportunity to help get the export licenses for the steel pipe that El Paso Natural Gas needed to build a pipeline to Monclova in Mexico. That, in turn, would provide fuel for a steel mill there that was vitally needed in the conduct of our war effort.

In the fall of 1940 we all enrolled in a cram course preparing to take the District of Columbia bar examination, even before completing the coursework for a law degree. One was permitted to take the examination after three years at law school. We took the bar examination in December and had to wait until February or March to get the results. They were not kind enough in those days to send you a letter. You read about it in the newspaper, and if your name was not there, it was sudden death. Fortunately, Ellison and Olson and I found our names in the *Washington Times* and were able to get ourselves admitted to the District of Columbia bar. There was some small examination of our character, but we all thought we were well enough behaved to be able to survive the test. We were correct. If my memory serves, there were about 800 people who took the bar examination that December and about three hundred of us managed to pass.

By 1942 Covington and Burling had decided that they could afford to pay the boys in the back room a little better wage and as a consequence, just before everybody had to go off to fight in the war, we got our wages raised to about $250 a month. That was a sufficient sum in those days to let one experiment with a touch of social life.

The most important event of those years at Covington and Burling was not the fact that we could use the library. It was not the fact that the law firm had a very high-priced clientele. It was not the fact that it was the Cub Scout den of ex-supreme court clerks and Harvard graduates who were associates and junior partners. The most important event was that I met Lucille Irwin. Lucille Irwin was Mrs. D. Worth Clark's sister and Judge Covington's secretary. Judge Covington was by that time well advanced in years and didn't do a great deal of work, so Lucille did not have much work to do either. We boys in the back room didn't have any secretarial assistance and had to scout around and find somebody who would do some typing for us. By a happy circumstance, I found Lucille. She seemed to like me and drew a map of the office and told me who was important and who wasn't and which bells should be answered immediately and which bells could wait.

Sometime in 1941 I mustered enough courage to ask Lucille to go to a party put on by the Idaho Association (a social organization for individuals with Idaho ties) at the Wardman Park Hotel in Washington. This was an event that was scheduled about twice a year and cost some tremendous sum like ten dollars, but I had just received a pay raise and could afford it. We went to the party, paid not much heed to anybody else who was there, danced all evening, and enjoyed ourselves tremendously.

Having had courage enough to ask her to go to the Wardman Park event with me, I began to ask Lucille to have lunch and go tea dancing at the Carleton Hotel between five and seven in the afternoon. Our enthusiasm for those tea dances was so splendid that they were almost fatal to my career. But if the law, always a jealous mistress, had to take a backseat momentarily so that I could dance with this fine lady, I felt good about the sacrifice.

Carmen Cavallero had one of the biggest bands of the forties and fifties, and Cavallero played at the Carleton in 1941 and 1942. He was a good musician and he became a good friend because Lucille and I were sitting there almost every afternoon even before he started the program. When he finished at the Carleton he went on to the Roosevelt Hotel in New York City, and the last time I saw him Carmen was playing at the Peacock Court at the Mark Hopkins Hotel in San Francisco.

Through most of 1941 and 1942, Lucille and I were courting. We lunched together at a German restaurant on 15th Street that we laughingly referred to as the bomb shelter since it was in the basement. In June 1942 I received my law degree and Lucille attended my graduation in Constitution Hall. Lu went to the commencement with James Ellison and Murial Faherty, another one of the women who worked at the law firm. Murial would later marry Ellison. After commencement I believe we all went up to Napoleon's Restaurant on Connecticut Avenue to have dinner. Those were great days. I still reflect on them with warmth and joy.

Of course the events of December 7 and 8, 1941, had come and gone. I had been in the House of Representatives' chamber when President Roosevelt asked the Congress to declare that a state of war existed between the Japanese empire and the United States of America, and I knew that sooner or later the war was going to catch up with Robert Smylie. When the letter from the Canyon County Draft Board arrived in June of 1942, I enlisted in the Coast Guard as an apprentice seaman and was assigned to duty in Washington. In September 1942 I was ordered to the Coast Guard Academy at New London, Connecticut, to take training as a line officer in the service. Some months later I was commissioned as an ensign.

Lucille, meantime, had taken a job with the State Department, and sometime in January 1943 I was assigned temporarily to Philadelphia. I came down to Washington on the evening train. Lu and I went to dinner at Napoleon's and I asked her to become Mrs. Smylie.

She accepted and then we had to decide what we would do in light of the events that were under way and well beyond our control. I had been informed that I would be assigned to North Atlantic patrol duty with the convoys that were headed for Britain on a destroyer escort convoy. Lucille had already signed a contract to go to Rio de Janeiro, Brazil, with the State Department, and so we decided to each go our separate ways and get back together as soon as possible.

Before many weeks had gone by, Lucille was en route to Rio and the Coast Guard had discovered that I was a lawyer and had assigned me to duty in the district Coast Guard officers' headquarters in Philadelphia. I would remain there until Lucille came back from South America in November 1943. When Lu returned, we decided that we should be married in New York City. We did this on December 4, 1943, at the little Church of the Transfiguration. We spent the next week in New York, where we saw the first anniversary performance of *Oklahoma*, which was entirely fitting because Lucille was a Democrat-Baptist from Oklahoma when I rescued her, and now she had turned out to be a Methodist and a Republican.

We returned to Philadelphia and set up housekeeping in a single-room apartment in the Walnut Park Plaza, a hotel of sorts at 63rd and Walnut Streets in West Philadelphia. The apartment was two blocks from the Upper Darby elevated, putting us within easy reach of all the marvelous opportunities to be found in downtown Philadelphia. There ensued a glorious fifteen months before the orders came that sent me to the Philippines and Lucille to San Francisco and Los Angeles.

The years of World War II were not especially exciting for me. When the personnel machinery found that I was a lawyer and could offer some training to the administrative branch of the service, they decided to use me in that fashion and I set about on a career that was serviceable, unspectacular, and in many instances excruciatingly boring.

In 1945, after a blissful first year of marriage, I was assigned to Tacloban, the naval headquarters in the Leyte Gulf in the Philippines. By that time ninety percent of all personnel of the Coast Guard were in the Philippines, and they had no table of organization that would permit an orderly operation of the service. Our unit was given the task of setting one up that would permit the supply services to utilize the Coast Guard freighter fleet in order to put supplies ashore on Honshu Island in southern Japan. We completed the table of organization, had it approved in General McArthur's headquarters, and two days later the Japanese surrendered. The powers that be immediately began to disband the service, and we never found out whether or not our plan would work. At a very famous celebration in San Francisco on Thanksgiving Eve in 1945, John Crean, my commanding officer, myself, and a few others declared that our plan was a famous success, that we had scored a famous victory, and that we had, indeed, helped to win the war.

Lucille had come up from Los Angeles to join me in San Francisco after my long trip across the Pacific. We spent about a week together there and then took the old Western Pacific train up the Feather River Canyon to Winnemucca and a bus from Winnemucca to Caldwell. We had come back to Caldwell to touch base with my aunt and uncle and to scout out the possibilities of perhaps returning to Idaho to practice law.

In Caldwell, I caught up again with Bill Young. He had spent the war years in a POW camp in Japan after being taken prisoner on Wake Island. He had been working for Morrison Knudsen Company in the construction of the naval outposts on those islands when the Japanese attacked on December 7, 1941. Bill had had difficult years and looked considerably the worse for wear. He was planning to return to Washington to finish law school, and I told him to look us up when he got there.

Lu and I returned to Washington in time for Christmas with D. Worth and Virgil Clark in 1945. The lease on Lucille's old apartment at 1735 New Hampshire Avenue, N. W., had been retained and Lu and I moved in there in January of 1946. We moved in April 1946 into an apartment in a village called Park Fairfax in Alexandria, Virginia. We lived there on Martha Custis Drive until the decision was made to return to Idaho.

We boys in the back room had labored under the illusion that after having sailed off to do our patriotic duty, Covington and Burling would surely have a job for us when we returned. However, it apparently had been determined that anybody who was somebody or wanted to be somebody would have to have been educated at Harvard. There was no place for persons graduating from schools just a few blocks away. One after another we were taken to lunch at the Metropolitan Club and were told that the firm took a position that they had no obligation to us under the Soldiers' and Sailors' Act and that they hoped we would do well and come to see them from time to time. It was probably just as well. If they had offered me a job, I would probably still be there in a more or less menial professional position. Years later Mr. Burling told me that having left them had permitted me to be the only one who had any fun in life.

In the politics of 1946, the Republican party enjoyed a spectacular victory and filled nearly every elected office in Idaho. C. A. Robins was elected governor and Robert Ailshie was elected attorney general. Ailshie was busy staffing his office, and he called me in late November 1946 and offered me a job as assistant attorney general. The job paid a puny wage, but I had not been very successful in getting located in anything except the government job in Washington. I had taken the Idaho bar in June and flunked it. I took it again in December and passed. This made it possible for me to seriously consider Ailshie's offer.

I would have to confess that the decision to come home and be assistant attorney general was an important turning point and that it was probably the most important decision in my life, other than the delightful, delicious decision to marry Lucille—which was the most important and most wonderful thing I ever did.

Early in 1946 I had bought a Pontiac two-door convertible from a friend named William Dolph. The car had once belonged to Jimmy Johnson who was, in those days, a tailback for the Washington Redskins football team and a very famous bon vivant around the

Capital City. He had sold the car to Dolph when he bought another one, and I managed to get the car for $750, the price then allowed under the Office of Price Administration. The convertible had a cloth top, but it would keep the weather out and we decided that we would drive it to Idaho.

In December we set about closing up the apartment in Alexandria, spent Christmas Eve and Christmas Day with Virgil Clark on Massachusetts Avenue in Washington, and, on the morning of December 26, set out for Hagerstown, Maryland, and the West. We traveled for five days through a couple of continental snow storms and some reasonably miserable weather. We arrived at the eastern border of Idaho at a little town called Pegram, and, traveling old U.S. 30, we began to hear the Salt Lake radio discussing the weather and saying that there were snow showers over and against the mountains. By the time we reached Soda Springs, the snow was falling so hard it was difficult to see. When we reached Pocatello, we decided that we probably couldn't get to Boise or Caldwell that night, so I sent a wire to the Coles telling them that we would be delayed. We started out across southern Idaho and got as far as Twin Falls and spent New Year's Eve of 1946 in the old Park Hotel.

The next morning we took off for Boise. When we arrived in the Boise Valley the clouds were lowering across the front range. Shaffer Butte and Deer Point were not visible, and only occasionally could you see the outline of Table Rock. We stopped at Warm Springs Avenue for a brief visit with Bill Langroise and his wife, who were friends of the Coles, and then went on to Caldwell.

We didn't know it then, but this was the beginning of a great adventure and one that we would take together.

CHAPTER FIVE

EIGHT YEARS IN THE ATTORNEY GENERAL'S OFFICE

TWO DAYS LATER we returned to Boise and began the task of organizing a brand new way of life. Two things were essential. One was transportation, for which we had the rusty, trusty transcontinental Pontiac convertible; the other was a place to live, but there we were fresh out of luck.

Housing in Boise was at a premium. Arnold Williams had lived over a garage during his tenure as governor, and Dr. C. A. Robins was unable to find a place to live and had to leave his family in St. Maries when he became governor. Lucille and I lucked out by renting the bottom half of a house at 15th and Hayes Streets, which belonged to Mr. Charles Wayland, and we stayed there for two months. We then bought a house on East Jefferson Street from Mrs. Estella Ayres for $4,000. I am told it was the original house in Boise's first subdivision. The area had been an orchard owned by Mr. Krall before he developed the land. We set about remodeling the place and reconditioning it and spent the next eight, fun-filled, ambitious years enjoying life on Jefferson Street.

A few days later I met Robert Ailshie for the first time. He was the newly elected attorney general, and together we arranged with his father, who was chief justice of the Supreme Court, to get me admitted to practice law in Idaho before I took the oath of office as assistant attorney general. I had, of course, been a member of the District of Columbia bar since 1942 and had been admitted to the Circuit Court in Washington and to the United States Supreme Court, but that would not do in Boise.

Mr. Ailshie suffered from severe asthma, and, except for the first three months of his tenure as attorney general, he was scarcely able to function. He had told Dr. Robins that if he was not able to be in the office and Dr. Robins had need of legal assistance, he should get in touch with me. This was the first significant step up the ladder to appointment as attorney general.

Chief Justice Ailshie, Robert Ailshie's father, and his mother both passed away within six months, and in November Ailshie himself died of congestive heart failure. That Sunday I had to make up my mind in a great hurry about whether I was going to try to become an appointed attorney general. We went to the Arid Club with Dr. and Mrs. Cole for dinner that evening, and I encountered Ralph Breshears and Oscar Worthwine, lawyers practicing in Boise. They both urged me to take a shot at the appointment. That literally made the decision for me, and I was off and running. A week later, after several bushelbaskets of telegrams had been arranged to be delivered to the governor's office and with the very real assistance of Glen Howell, his chief of staff, and Louise Shadduck, his secretary, Dr. Robins decided I was his choice and called me into the office and offered me the appointment. We called Justice Paul Hyatt in from the Supreme Court, and he administered the oath of office marking the beginning of my seven years and forty-one days as attorney general of Idaho.

My first task was to reorganize and restaff the attorney general's office. Robert Holden, who had aspired to be appointed to the office, decided to return to Idaho Falls at the end of 1947. His wife also worked in the office, and she, of course, went with him. John Carver promised that he would stay with me until June 30, 1948, and that left Mr. J. R. Smead and myself as the only staffers. My salary as attorney general was $4,000 a year. The budget required that the assistant attorneys general be paid $325 per month. This made recruitment almost impossible.

Judge Paul Hyatt administers the oath of office as attorney general on November 24, 1947, with Governor Robins in attendance. ISHS 65-48.5.

I decided I would opt for talented personnel who had no experience, and I recruited graduates of the University of Idaho Law School who seemed to have promise. I quickly picked up three or four, and with them we began to build an office staff. I required them to read at least one paperback novel a week, and to report to me that they had done so, and, if possible, to join Toastmasters' International because very few law school graduates had much talent for public speaking.

I did pretty well, I think in retrospect, in picking people to staff that office. There was, of course, John Carver, Jr., and Clint Peterson, Ed Aschenbrenner, Ray Durtschi, Don McClenahan, and Robert Hodge. These people, working with the venerable J. R. Smead, who was then in his seventies, and J. M. Leggat, who was an older lawyer without any particular attachment, became a staff which was talented, accomplished, and satisfying. Blaine Evans came along later and Allan Shepard followed him. All of them were relatively inexperienced when they first came to work for me, but that was no surprise—I was relatively inexperienced myself.

All of these people went on to do greater things than be an assistant attorney general. John Carver was an assistant secretary of the Interior, a member of the federal Power Commission, and ended his career as dean of the College of Law at Denver University. Clint Peterson became a leading member of the California Judiciary and both Ed Aschenbrenner and Ray Durtschi became district judges in Idaho. Blaine Evans became a member of the legislature and prosecuting attorney of Ada County and to this day is one of the leading members of the Idaho State bar. Don McClenahan went on to become a very successful attorney in private practice in Boise. Robert Hodge followed me to the governor's office and then went on to become a vice-president of Intermountain Gas. Allan Shepard, of course, became chief justice of Idaho after a stint as attorney general. This, it seems to me, was a proud record of accomplishment for the little band of lawyers that put together the attorney general's office between 1947 and 1955.

My concept of how to do the attorney general's job best was to treat the task as that of house lawyer to a big corporation. We set about being a service-oriented organization without attempting to interfere in the day-to-day decisions of the administrators, although most administrators, when they got a tough one, tried to make it a legal question so that the assistant attorney general had to decide it. Fortunately, we avoided that most of the time.

We also set about trying to be of service to all of the branches of government that were in our charge. We did not indulge in any of the interbranch warfare that seems to characterize relationships between the attorney general and other areas of government these days. We tried to be of service to the legislature by drafting their laws; and, of course, this was in the days before we had a glorified legislative council to collect and compile information, draft bills, and conduct research for the legislature. This was a real service to freshman members. I think it made it possible for a lot of legislation to originate on the floor of the two houses that otherwise would not have seen the light of day.

The seven years in the attorney general's office, like most law practices, turned out to be relatively dull and mundane and not terribly exciting, with the exception of a few cases that spotlighted that period of time. The last two years of my incumbency as attorney general, I was pretty well occupied with the crazy idea that maybe I should run for governor.

W. Lloyd Adams, the legendary Republican political leader from Rexburg, had been a political guru through four or five generations of Idaho politicians. For that reason alone, his advice about political chestnuts was invaluable. He told me one day that the gambling fraternity would try me on for size and that somebody would try to get me to enforce the state income tax law. He was right on both counts, but I probably disappointed him because I proceeded to do exactly the

The Board of Land Commissioners in 1949: on my right, state auditor J. P. Nielson; on my immediate left, standing, Ed Woozley, commissioner of public lands; Governor Robins; superintendent of public instruction Alton Jones; and Cy Young, secretary of state. ISHS 82-2.14A.

opposite of what he advised, which was to ignore both the gamblers and tax collectors.

Governor Robins had begun to be concerned about what he thought was the proliferation of drug traffic to and through the ski resort at Sun Valley. There had been a couple of unexplained homicides in the area, and they seemed to be connected one way or another with the drug traffic or the gambling enterprises. Casino-type gambling was being permitted almost all over the state and was widely tolerated by law enforcement. Governor Robins asked me if I thought it would be possible to shut the gambling installations down. After some consultation with my staff and a good deal of cogitation, I told him that I thought it could be done, but that we would have to have his wholehearted and unwavering support. We informed the major centers of gambling activity of our intention to shut them down, and, without very much difficulty once they were convinced we meant what we said, they began to shut up shop. There was difficulty with an institution in Pocatello and with some of the Elks Clubs scattered around the state, but by and large it was not necessary to take action except in one instance.

A group of Boise entrepreneurs had built a hotel on the shores of Payette Lake at McCall called Shore Lodge, and they included in their plans a gambling casino that was pretty elegant. They did not think we meant what we said, and it became necessary to set up a raid on the establishment, which was done in due course. Their gambling equipment was seized and burned and the money that was on the tables was contributed to the educational endowment fund of the State of Idaho.

This antigambling activity put me squarely on that side of the gambling issue. This provided very considerable ammunition in the next two or three gubernatorial campaigns.

The Idaho income tax law had been on the books since 1931, styled as the Property Relief Act of 1931, but it had never been enforced, other than perfunctorily. True to Adams' suggestion, the tax collectors came around to find out if we would institute some action to collect the tax. The governor was in favor of a strong enforcement program, largely because he was going to be short of money to meet the 1949 budget.

I set up a small task force in the attorney general's office, and they prepared lawsuits in thirty counties, which were filed simultaneously—all of which resulted in collection of the tax. This sent out the word and resulted for the first time in the existence of a viable, credible income tax law that produced real revenue.

The antigambling crusade and the income tax enforcement program gave me very high visibility in almost every corner of the state; as a consequence, my political prospects appreciably elevated.

In 1949 Governor Earl Warren of California, who was chairman of the Western Governors' Conference, appointed me to a drafting committee and gave us the task of drafting a compact for adoption by the eleven western states providing an interstate cooperation in higher education.

The western states were woefully short on professional education in medicine and veterinary medicine. The governors were attempting to find some method of cooperating that would permit the interchange of excess capacity in some of the schools for a cash consideration paid by the state which was being served. It sounded like a straightforward, very easily accomplished task, but there were various hang-ups that almost denied a good idea any success. These, of course, circled around what to do about the religiously accredited schools and what to do about states like California, which could look down the road a very short piece and see that they would not have enough capacity of their own.

We met in Denver at the Brown Palace Hotel. It was left to Attorney General McCullough of New Mexico and myself to work out some sort of compromise language that could be adopted by the committee and handed to the governors as a basis for their discussion. Sometime about four a.m. McCullough and I thought we had arrived at something satisfactory and took it to Dr. Albert B. Sabin, who was one of the medical giants in attendance at the meeting and who later developed the first polio vaccine. He found our work good, and in due course the committee adopted what we had prepared. It was forwarded to Governor Warren, who carried it to the other governors, and ultimately it was adopted as the Western Interstate Compact on Higher

During the Western Governors' Conference in 1952, Republican presidential candidate Dwight D. Eisenhower joined attendees for a lunch in the attorney general's office. Here I am presenting the general with a bag of Idaho potatoes. Also at his table are Arthur Langlie, governor of Washington, Len Jordan, and Earl Warren, governor of California. ISHS 72-190.73D.

Education. This was a forerunner of cooperation between Washington, Alaska, Montana, and Idaho in furnishing education in medical science to those four states at the University of Washington in Seattle. Looking back, I think I could fairly say that the drafting committee did good work.

Historically speaking, the most important litigation of those seven years was probably the case that involved the validation of the four-year terms for governors and other constitutional officers. A gentleman named Frank Keenan filed a Writ of Mandate to the secretary of state requesting that he accept Keenan's nominating petitions for the office of governor based on the assumption that it was required that an election be held in 1948. The constitutional amendment adopted in 1944 provided that the term beginning in 1946 would last until 1950. Had the litigation been successful, it would have cut Governor Robins' term in two and forced a reelection campaign in 1948, which was exactly what the amendment was designed to avoid. The Supreme Court set the Writ of Mandate down for hearing and ordered briefs on a fast-track basis. We had ten days to file an answering brief and then ten days for the opposition to file a brief, and both of us could respond within five days. The matter was set down for argument within twenty-five days of the time it was filed.

No one knew it at the time, but the case of *Keenan vs. Price*, which was what the litigation would be known as in history, was the first case I had ever argued in a court of final resort, and I was fairly shaken up by the responsibility that rested on my very inexperienced shoulders. About ten days later, Justice Hyatt delivered the opinion of the court, which was a four to one affirmation of the validity of the constitutional amendment. The dissenting justice was the former attorney general Bert Miller, who went on to run for the Senate in 1948 and defeated Senator Henry Dworshak, who had been appointed to that office in 1946 to fill an unexpired term. Dworshak was appointed a second time, in 1949, then elected the next year and reelected for two more terms. The decision was heralded by many as a political decision, but that is often the case with constitutional questions that involve such things as terms of office. Who is elected governor and for how long is a political question and one best answered by the people and not by courts of law.

The case that caused me the most pain and sorrow in all those seven years involved the death sentence in a murder case arising in Ada County. Two teenage lads named Walrath and Powell had robbed the neighborhood grocery store in east Boise, and, when the owner objected, killed him and cut him up on his own butcher block. They carried the remains out to Dry Creek and buried him. They were, of course, very shortly apprehended. Not being very nimble witted, they pleaded guilty to the charge of murder in the first degree, and after a year Judge Koelsch sentenced them to be "hanged by the neck until dead." This sentence involved an automatic appeal to the Supreme Court, and it fell to the attorney general's office to represent the state in that appellant procedure. All of my assistants in the attorney general's office, including the venerable Mr. Smead, recused themselves, and it fell my lot to argue the case in the Supreme Court in favor of affirming the lower court's sentence. I argued the case out of a sense of duty to the state and to my oath of office. I had no particularly fixed ideas about the death sentence, but before these proceedings were over, I knew that I did not approve of the sentence and would have been happy to find some way to avoid its execution. The death sentence is a matter committed to the conscience of the people of Idaho, and they have, of course, spoken through their legislature in favor of carrying it out. It is a harsh, needlessly useless remedy, and one, in my more mature years, I came to thoroughly disapprove of. Death sentences in criminal cases are not for the fainthearted.

When circumstance required me to argue for an affirmation of the lower court decision in the case of Walrath and Powell, I was in effect urging the Supreme Court to impose the death penalty. This was not a task that I took lightly. Admittedly, I was ambivalent in my attitude toward the death sentence when that argument took place, but I would never be that callow again. Twice during my governorship, the legislature considered bills which would have repealed the death sentence provisions of Idaho law. Neither of them passed; but, had they, I would have permitted them to become law without my signature. I had learned in the case of Walrath and Powell that the death sentence provisions of our law were brutal, insensitive, and nonproductive. I would not willingly have cooperated in perpetuating that kind of a provision of the statutes on our books.

One other case of lasting importance involved the sale of public lands to a private citizen in eastern Idaho. He tried to abrogate the contract of sale, and we filed suit to enforce it. The litigation was important because it established the sanctity of those sales and made them serious bidding procedures when people undertook to buy lands at public auction. The case arose in Madison County, and we tried the litigation before a jury in the courthouse in Rexburg. To my rather great surprise, we got a verdict for $5,000 in that heavily Mormon county against a Mormon widow and managed to establish, without question, the strength of the State's bidding procedures in selling public lands.

In 1953, Mountain Bell, the local telephone utility, sought permission from the Idaho Public Utilities Commission to dramatically increase its rates for residential service. The company asked for permission to institute collection of the new rates immediately. The commission, in my view, properly denied the increase for immediate institution of the new rate structure and set the request for an increase down for hearing before the full commission. Mountain Bell went to the District Court and secured an injunction against the commission's interfering with their collection of the new rate. We filed an appeal from the order granting the injunction and then proceeded to hearings before the Idaho Public Utilities Commission

As might have been expected, there was a substantial public outcry at increases in residential service rates for telephone service. There were some very substantial objections to the manner in which service was being provided by the telephone company, and it seemed to the commission that it would be proper to take the case to the people rather than requiring rate payers to come all the way to Boise to be heard in the matter of their grievance over telephone service. Accordingly, they set down seven hearings where the public could appear and testify concerning their problems with telephone service and their attitudes toward a rate increase. These regional hearings about telephone rates provided a very excellent vehicle for the exposure of a young attorney general to a wide and interested public whose votes he was going to be asking for shortly. The resident manager of the telephone company, a gentleman named Herman Stommel, claimed the entire procedure was political, and in these latter days, I would be inclined to agree that he had a point. The regional hearings provided a magnificent exposure for me and proved of invaluable assistance in terms of the people whom we met for the campaign that lay ahead.

The rate proceeding was not concluded until after I had been elected governor, and it resulted in a $4-million refund to the rate payers of Idaho and a rollback of the rate increase. This, I believe, was the first time this had ever happened in the history of the state. Mountain Bell had always taken Idaho and its regulatory procedures for granted, but that day was long over and Idaho was no longer treated like a distant province. I believe that the telephone rate case of 1953 and 1954 may well have marked the beginning of the maturity of Idaho's state government.

There were political events in those years that are worth remembering. In 1948 I was elected chairman of the Ada County Young Republicans organization and as such was entitled to attend the 1948 nominating convention in Coeur d'Alene where the state's preference for a presidential candidate was being determined. This was a very significant event simply because it permitted me to meet a large number of people from around the state who would be effective in the political decisions of the next few years.

In 1950 I decided to run for reelection as attorney general. In a very quiet campaign, I was reelected. I had primary opposition and of course opposition from the Democratic party in the general election. The Democratic nominee was Frank Langley, who was the gentlemen who had been defeated by Robert Ailshie in 1946. It was almost impossible to call the 1950 election a campaign. I think we didn't spend more than $400 in both the primary and the general campaign, and, as a consequence, there was not much in the way of exposure accomplished by the campaign except that I got around to a lot of political meetings. Governor Robins didn't particularly enjoy making political speeches, so much of that duty fell into my willing hands. After a very abortive start at political speaking in Pocatello, I finally developed a talent for speechmaking and became fairly adept.

The most important political event of those eight years was the visit of General Dwight Eisenhower, the new Republican candidate for president in 1952. He came to Boise for a meeting with the eleven gubernatorial candidates in the Western states. I had been appointed to be coordinator of the ten Western states (excepting California) and had begun my work in that area on instructions from the Denver headquarters of Eisenhower's campaign. Governor Sherman Adams called me into Denver in late July and told me they were planning the meeting in Boise on August 20 and did I think it would be possible to get a crowd of reasonable size together to hear the general make a speech. I thought it would be possible to do so, and we began planning the visit, which was a one-day operation.

The speech on the statehouse steps was the opening speech of the Eisenhower campaign for president. We had about 30,000 people crowded into the Capitol Plaza Park. The trees had not yet been planted in the park, and you could see all the way from old City Hall and the *Statesman* building through the park to the Capitol steps. It was a splendid occasion. The national press was there en masse, and they were impressed with a crowd as big as that in Boise, Idaho, whose population in 1952 was scarcely 30,000.

For security reasons it was decided to have the entire program accomplished in the Capitol building. The ten governors and the gubernatorial candidate in Montana, Governor Aronson, met with General Eisenhower in the governor's office. In those days, the attorney general's office was right across the hall, and we had a room big enough and tables big enough to accommodate the gubernatorial guests and the general and his entourage at lunch. We served lunch in my office, and I was, of course, entitled to attend. I presented the general with a sack of Idaho potatoes, and the press used that as the lead picture on the wire photo out of the Idaho state capitol. It appeared in something like seventy-eight newspapers around the country. I had quite a bit of notoriety as a result.

The success of the Boise speech established my credentials as a planner and organizer with Governor Sherman Adams, Senator Fred Seaton, and the others in General Eisenhower's staff headquarters in Denver; as a consequence, I had good access to General Eisenhower all through his presidential years. When General Eisenhower was elected there was some discussion about whether I should accept an appointment of some kind in Washington, D.C. When the 1953 legislature met in January, I had already pretty well determined I was going to be a player in the gubernatorial contest that was upcoming in 1954. I began preparation in terms of personnel and planning to spend most of 1954 campaigning for the gubernatorial nomination and for election as governor. No one had ever moved up from cabinet rank in the Idaho government to become governor after an election to that office. I would be the first.

The events of the service in the attorney general's office provided an excellent launching pad, and the visit of General Eisenhower to Boise to open his campaign on our capitol steps presented the opportunity to become reasonably well-known on the national scene as a player of consequence. Certainly, the luncheon for President Eisenhower was the most glittering assembly of political persons in the history of our state. There was the general himself; the governor of California, Earl Warren, who would later be chief justice of the Supreme Court; Douglas McKay, the governor of Oregon, who would later become secretary of the Interior; Arthur Langlie, governor of Washington, who was the chairman of the National Governors' Conference at the time; and Senator Fred Seaton of Nebraska and Governor Sherman Adams of New Hampshire, both of whom were later to be chiefs of staff to President Eisenhower. For me the most important element in the visit of Eisenhower and his staff to Boise on that August 20, 1952, was the fact that it created a vast opportunity for me to assume leadership of the moderate wing of the Republican party in Idaho. Without really realizing it, I had taken a giant step forward in the race for the gubernatorial nomination of the Republican party in 1954. As a matter of fact, the luncheon for President Eisenhower probably placed me in the lead for the first time, and it was a lead which I never relinquished.

During all the years that I was attorney general, Lucille and I lived in the little house on East Jefferson Street that we had bought from Mrs. Ayres in 1947. It was a tiny place, but charming in its way and a house that became full of memories and triumphs and love and family affection.

We had been fortunate to come to Boise well acquainted with a good number of the leading citizens, and, as a consequence, we entertained at 318 East Jefferson with some degree of style and élan. The Leo Falks were there, the Mendenhalls, the Langroises, Mrs. James McDonald, the Davidsons, and Ham and Bunny Burroughs, among others. We were usually invited to dine with Mrs. McDonald on New Year's Eve, and occasionally we were asked to take tea with Mrs. Laura Cunningham on Sunday afternoon at her historic old mansion at the corner of Walnut Street and Warm Springs Avenue. Midway through these eight years, we had the great good fortune to have two young men come to live with us, our sons, Robert William and Richard Steven. They have been a source of great satisfaction to Lucille and me. In a very real sense, the first years were the best years.

CHAPTER SIX

THE FIRST CAMPAIGN FOR THE GOVERNORSHIP—1954

"WHEN DID YOU first think about running for governor?" and, then, almost inevitably, later, "Why?" I have attempted to give reasonably honest answers to those questions at least a thousand times. They are apparently a source of endless public curiosity and were asked in town hall meetings, in central committee inquisitions, and in classrooms from grade schools through high school and college. The questions were even asked at the Columbian Club when they still held their meetings in the old clubhouse at the corner of 9th and Washington Streets. So here, as best that I can remember it, is how the idea of becoming governor of Idaho came about.

I may have had some thoughts about running for governor when I was in college, but they could not have been very serious because I had no plans for returning to Idaho after I went east to law school. When I did return to Idaho, it was to make it my home and to begin my work as an assistant attorney general. The location of the attorney general's office across the hall from the governor's office was probably an infectious circumstance. Sometime in the years before 1950, I seriously began to consider that it would be worthwhile to at least scout out the proposition of a run at the governorship.

The question of why one runs for governor is a little more complex. One thing is certain, it was not the salary that led me to seek the office. I doubt that anyone runs for governor, even today with the elevated salary levels that are now in effect, solely because it pays much money. In any event, the $10,000 per year that the governorship paid in 1955 was not much reason to seek that office. Even in the days of the postwar economy, it was not enough of a sum to really attract attention.

In the eight years that I served in the attorney general's office, we were never farther than forty feet from the office of the governor. Most of the time you could almost hear the hum of those wheels of power, and, if you listened very closely, you could sometimes hear them whir when they got out of gear. I think it was the knowledge of all of that power just forty feet away that finally led me, almost inexorably, to the decision that I had to try and get my hands on those levers and learn how to run that power for the benefit of the people of the state.

It would be fair to say that I had been quite disappointed in the performance of Leonard Jordan's administration in the matters of public school education, higher education, parks and recreation, and conservation generally, except in the field of water conservation. Jordan had been elected governor in 1950 after serving in the state legislature for one term, and he was subsequently elected to the U.S. Senate. As it became known that I did have some differences with the governor, I began to attract the friendship of other people who were similarly disappointed. I suspect that the real reason I ran for governor was that I had an unquenchable thirst to start doing the things for Idaho that I thought needed doing in the field of education (both public school and higher education), in the matter of highway transportation, in economic development, and in the development of a system of parks and recreation.

I never quite decided that I would run for governor until early in 1953 on the theory that if it became generally known that I was available and willing, it would attract the enmity of the establishment of the Republican party in a greater degree than already existed. They had a tendency to be opposed to anybody who was not Len Jordan, and it was a good idea to keep one's ambitions to one's self. I had been helped toward my decision by some loyal friends in Ada County who were similarly disenchanted with the record of the Republican administration. We realized that it would be necessary to run against the Republican record, and this presented some difficulties, but Bill Jonasson and Charles Link and Claude Marcus, who formed the nucleus of my original campaign organization, were equal to the task. Finally, one day in 1953 I went home in the evening and told Lucille that I was going to have to give the campaign a try—that its outcome was an answer that I really had to have. Loyal and loving, Lucille said that if I had to know the answer then that was what I ought to do; and, with that support, unflagging and unremitting, I went forward into the campaign with more optimism than was justified by the circumstances then prevailing.

At the 1954 Lincoln Day Banquet in Boise, we received the endorsement of my candidacy by J. H. Gipson, Sr., President of Caxton Printers, Ltd., a political leader whose counsel stretched all the way back to the Bull Moose campaign of 1912. He called a meeting of Young Republicans to proclaim his support.

The 1950 campaign for attorney general was not a very active event, but it did provide the vague outlines of what might be necessary in the way of a campaign for the governorship. One could deduce from those outlines the logistics of a campaign and the political dynamics that might drive it to success. It was apparent that one would have to distance oneself from the record of the Jordan administration in some key areas. My own personal study of election results had indicated to me that to win a Republican primary, one had to carry at least six of the ten northern counties, win quite well in Ada and Canyon Counties, and run about even in the rest of the state. We had also concluded that in the general election campaign there were really only ten counties that were important, and that a good campaign would concentrate on those ten counties. They were Kootenai, Nez Perce, Canyon, Ada, Twin Falls, Cassia, Bannock, Bonneville, and Madison. This did not mean that you neglected the rest of the counties, but you had to—if you had good political sense—try and gather the grapefruit where the trees grew.

The original campaign car, ready to roll, in 1953.

A political campaign in 1954 was a considerably different enterprise than it is today. There were three TV stations in the state and only one of them was as old as a year. All of their equipment was pretty primitive and no one in the advertising business knew how to use television for the dissemination of political ideas, arguments, and rhetoric. There were only fourteen radio stations in Idaho in 1954, and, if my memory serves correctly, forty-four or -five weekly newspapers. There were daily newspapers in Kellogg, Coeur d'Alene, Moscow, Lewiston, Caldwell, Nampa, Boise, Twin Falls, Pocatello, Blackfoot, and Idaho Falls. Prior to 1954, I don't believe anybody had ever used single-engine airplanes as a convenient mode of transportation in a political campaign. We did, and it worked out very well. There were no polling services available in the state, and the one that you could employ if you had enough money was located in Iowa. It was far too expensive for any campaign that we could have mounted.

We tried to develop a means of ascertaining what the issues really were that would move and shake the people. Based on my travels around the state and a very extensive schedule of public speaking on my own part, I finally decided that there were four issues which could be profitably explored that might turn the campaign one way or another. These were public school education funding, economic development and diversification, water conservation policy, and tax reform policy. I decided that I would prepare formal addresses on these subjects, find someplace where I could use those speeches, and turn them into campaign documents. They did provide the basis for a later-to-be-developed campaign platform. One of these speeches was made at a junior high school PTA meeting in Caldwell. Another was made to a Chamber of Commerce meeting in Grangeville. A third was made to an economics fraternity dinner at Idaho State College, and the final speech was made at a Rotary Club meeting in Twin Falls. As I had surmised, the education speech attracted the most attention. We sent copies to all of the newspapers and radio stations, and I think some of them read the documents. In any event, they proved to be what I had hoped they would be—a gauge of public sentiment about what the campaign should be.

By this time, we had people in most of the major counties who were unqualifiedly in support of my candidacy and were out working to further our aspirations. The big question was when to announce my candidacy and when to find out who the opposition was going to be in the primary election. After some hesitation, we decided to make a public announcement on the second Thursday of March 1954. You did things on Thursday in those days because that was the day the weekly newspapers were published, and you wanted to get coverage in all of them. I remember being quite impressed because some of the weekly newspapers took our candidacy quite seriously.

We had about $9,000 to raise if we were going to spend as much money as we had planned. We had received nothing in the way of contributions from the traditional sources of Republican nominating money and were at a place where small amounts of contributions would not carry the day. With the help of a couple of more liquid friends, I was able to raise $5,000 in cash, and we called a meeting in the attorney general's office that was attended by Bill Jonasson, Chuck Link, Claude Marcus, Fred Charlton, myself, and maybe two or three other people. I got the reports from all of them about how things were not going well financially, and finally I pulled out a roll of bills from my pocket, and tossed them across the room to Claude Marcus, and said that it was $5,000 and for him to get it in the bank the first thing in the morning. He did this and by noon the contributions had started to roll in and the campaign was well financed again. We were on our way.

In retrospect, it seems that from that meeting, the campaign was downhill all the way. The billboards went up. There were fifty of them statewide, and they made a tremendous impact. We were able to let contracts for newspaper advertising and for television time and nobody else had been able to get that done up to that point.

In mid-July in Idaho Falls, W. C. Burns, an influential eastern Idaho contractor, walked into the Rogers Hotel and offered his support to my candidacy, and we went out touring Jefferson County the next day. This was a turn of events almost equally as important as the enlistment of Senator Thomas Heath, former state Republican chairman.

In late July we went north to a series of meetings in Coeur d'Alene, Moscow, and Orofino. These were central committee-sponsored picnics, usually in a municipal park, and we managed to meet a lot of people and to say our say. The mining interests, whose headquarters were at Wallace, Idaho, had Henry Scheideman, Shoshone County Central Committee Chairman, stalk the Moscow meeting to decide who was going to be the winner of the nominating primary. I did not know this, but he told me so after the meeting at Moscow, and he said he was going back to Wallace and tell them I was going to win. He did so and this pretty well dried up Coeur d'Alene Mayor Larry Gardner's support in north Idaho, and was probably highly instrumental in giving us the six northern counties that we needed to win.

The primary election happened at the end of the first week in August; when the results were in, I had been nominated as the Republican candidate for governor. Congressman John Sanborn ran second and Mayor Gardner ran third. The results were about as we had anticipated. I did quite well in Ada and Canyon Counties, carried the six northern counties that were needed, according to my calculations, and did better than we had expected in eastern Idaho.

Meanwhile, the Democrats had been conducting their own primary, and there were four candidates, two of whom were formidable. One was former Governor Charles Gossett from Nampa, and the other was State Senator Clark Hamilton from Weiser. I think the nonpartisan political establishment had planned to have Governor Gossett nominated by the Democrats and Congressman Sanborn by the Republicans, and then they would retire from active combat having won regardless of who was elected. In a surprise finish, Senator Hamilton, who was regarded by the establishment as quite dangerous, although that was a foolish supposition on their part, was nominated by about 4,000 votes. This set the final stretch of the campaign up to the general election as a race between Senator Hamilton and myself. He had been campaigning vigorously throughout the state for nearly a year, and we had to regard him as a formidable candidate. He was.

My first task as Republican candidate for governor was to get our partisan house in order, to make peace, and to arrange for the support of all of the previously visited factions in the party who had either openly or surreptitiously opposed my nomination. Then we could set about planning to defeat Senator Hamilton and his Democrats.

I had expected that Governor Jordan might come across the hall to offer his congratulations. When this did not happen, I went to his office and said that I would appreciate his support and that I would like to have any suggestions he might have concerning the campaign. He had no suggestions to offer at the time, but said he would be in touch if he thought he could be helpful.

My next move was to get in touch with Smoky Pugmire, chairman of the Gooding County Central Committee, who lived in Hagerman, which was Congressman Sanborn's hometown. I asked him to set up a meeting of the central committee in the grange hall in Hagerman, and then I phoned Congressman Sanborn and asked him to introduce me at that meeting. He did so and called me Idaho's next governor. This was a peacemaking mutuality that was very important. Next I repeated this procedure in Coeur d'Alene, where I asked Larry Gardner to introduce me again as the candidate for governor.

Meanwhile, William Campbell, who was the state chairman of the party, had resigned. He had not supported me in the primary campaign and thought it best that he be replaced. I asked W. C. Burns of Idaho Falls, who had helped in the primary campaign, to accept the post of state chairman, and he accepted. The position of state vice-chairman, which traditionally had been a post occupied by a lady, was vacant, and I asked Phyllis Loehr from Moscow to become state vice-chairman. It was only a coincidence that she was John Sanborn's stepdaughter. Without being offensive to her stepfather, Mrs. Loehr had been helpful to me in many ways during the primary campaign. The upper echelons of Idaho's business community had become increasingly upset with Senator Hamilton and his proposals. They decided that they needed to take steps to prevent Hamilton from winning the election. I think that they really didn't think too much of my capabilities as a candidate.

Accordingly, they sent two of the crown princes of the establishment—Robert Elder and Robert Brown from Coeur d'Alene and Kellogg, respectively—to Boise to meet with me. We met in Lynn Driscoll's office in the First Security Bank, and the sole important question was how much money did I think I would need to win the election. I had thought maybe something like that was coming, and I told them $40,000. Arrangements were made for that sum to be available if needed, and with that we were off and running. I assured them that they had not acquired anything except peace of mind, and that no commitments of any kind on anything were implied or given.

A week later the state platform convention was held in Boise. It elected Mr. Burns and then Mrs. Loehr as chairman and vice-chairman, respectively; drew a platform which was modeled after the speeches that I had been making for the last five or six months all across the state; and laid plans for some joint campaigning for other members of the ticket. The campaign had begun.

It had been my belief that issues were important, and that if one could find an issue of substance to a majority of the people, it could be ridden home to a victory. The state Chamber of Commerce had arranged for a poll based on issues, and to a certain extent on candidates, that they gave us the privilege of seeing and copying. It confirmed the belief I held all through the campaign for the primary election that education funding for the public schools was the most important single issue to voters. Sixty-seven percent of the people identified that issue as of major concern to them. Economic development ran second and tax reform was a poor third. It was obvious that the public wanted more money spent on public schools and they were willing to pay for it. Other than that, the poll did not tell us much about who would win the election ultimately. The poll was done by Central Surveys in Shenandoah, Iowa, and was about as professional as anything that could be purchased in those days. I believe that the issues poll was quite accurate. In checking back with legislative candidates later in the year, my belief was confirmed.

The first speech of the campaign was delivered in Smoky Pugmire's grange hall in Hagerman, and based on my own intuition and the polling results that we had received from Central Surveys, I made education the major thrust of that first address. I used the same phrase I had used during the primary campaign: "We will appropriate the full requirements of the public schools equalization formula." The phrase became a sort of mantra for the campaign and was repeated by almost everybody who was making speeches anywhere in that fall of 1954.

The newspapers took note of the emphasis on public school funding in this first address and accorded it even more space than the fact that I had been endorsed by my erstwhile former opponent, Congressman Sanborn. In *The Idaho Statesman*, John Corlett, the political editor, called education "the defining issue of the campaign."

Senator Hamilton took the issue a little differently. He didn't quite oppose what I had said, but he did try to waffle by saying that it was a great idea, but Idaho would not have enough money to fulfill the promise. I think this waffling on the education issue was his principal mistake of the campaign. He might well have been governor had he faced the issue head on, but it was quite unlike him to do so. He was one of the last of the wool-hat Democrats (i.e., Democrats who were often more conservative than Republicans), and his theory of government was that it was better to do nothing than to spend very much money. Almost all of his solutions involved diminishing appropriations for the things that people wanted. Hamilton failed to recognize the fact that there was a new generation abroad, and that the baby-boom parents wanted a place for the children to go to school. This, I think, was crucial to the decision in 1954 to attempt to move onward and upward toward a mature approach to government and a mature manner of handling both our economic and our social problems.

After the speech in Hagerman, it was just sixty days until the general election, and so we set out on what was then regarded as an almost obligatory and traditional campaign trail. In those days, Idaho elected six other candidates statewide in the same election. It seemed just common sense to invite these six people, who were candidates in their own right and traveling the lonely campaign road, to join us when they could and become a part of the mainstream campaign effort. This was not graciousness per se on my part. It simply was a method of conveying to what I hoped would be my elected cabinet the fact that I planned to be of help to them and they to me in the years to come. Governor Jordan had been a loner, and not many of them felt very close to the governorship. For that reason, it seemed important to ask them to travel with us whenever we could manage to arrange it.

In the early spring of 1954, Don Watkins of Pocatello had signed on as advertising advisor and television scheduler for the campaign. His help was crucial and invaluable. I knew nothing about how to attended to such matters or how and where you bought time and billboard space or how you placed advertising in the newspapers on a fairly large basis. Advertising was Watkins' business, and he very shortly was devoting a disproportionate amount of his time to our problems. We moved into the general election campaign without missing a stitch, and soon we were meeting television schedules when and where we needed to.

Television was in its infancy, and we spent a good deal of time shuffling between Idaho Falls, Twin Falls, and Boise in an attempt to utilize as much available prime time as we could manage to pay for. I do not remember that any of the television stations had more than one camera in those days, and, as a consequence, our ability to do television advertising was limited. The stations would sell us one-minute spots or five-minute spots or longer, but we decided that five minutes was about as useful a slot as we could manage. I began ad-libbing five-minute programs that were devoted to a single topic of relevance in the campaign, and these were produced on camera with a system of signals that we had worked out and that I gave by hand to the cameraman. The Boise stations were a little better equipped and more capable than either Idaho Falls or Twin Falls, but the entire television business was still pretty primitive in 1954. I think, however, that my ability to handle the media was crucial to our success. I know it finally drove Senator Hamilton to attempt to use television, and he was a plain disaster when he tried to appear on camera. He was a fairly effective public speaker in person, but somehow the television cameras did not treat him very well. Scurrying back and forth between Idaho Falls and Boise required the use of airplanes. Not only was the 1954 campaign the first airborne political enterprise in Idaho history, but it was the first time billboards were used extensively for political purposes. We used them especially in the northern counties, where television on the Spokane rate card was just too expensive. The Markham Advertising Company in Pocatello arranged for most of our billboard bookings and also ordered the paper to cover them. They managed to construct a picture of me that was about eight feet tall, and it was an effective tool in the campaign.

Attendance at the Eastern Idaho State Fair in Blackfoot was almost mandatory in any political campaign in those days. Lucille and I went to Blackfoot and rode in the parade in the back seat of a touring car of ancient vintage, and then went to the fairgrounds to see if we could do a little political business. It was Lucille's first adventure in political campaigning. We got inside the gate, and she asked me, "Now what do I do?" I handed her a stack of campaign brochures, headed her into the pavilion where the food displays were being shown, and told her to start saying hello to people and handing out brochures. I thereupon walked off and left her. I don't know what she really thought at first, but, by the time the day was over, she rather liked it. The Twin Falls County Fair at Filer was also obligatory, as was the Western Idaho Fair in Boise.

To be utterly candid, I do not know how we got to so many places and did so many things in that sixty-day campaign. I believe we traveled more than 25,000 miles and visited thirty-five of the forty-four Idaho counties. This was a very exhausting enterprise, but somewhere along about mid-October I caught my second wind, and from then on I never did get tired.

Toward the end of October, there was a day to spare and the weather was good, so we decided to answer the call of the north Idaho county chairmen who thought they had been neglected. Until then we had stayed down in southern Idaho where the votes were closer together and could be gathered with greater ease. We scheduled stops in Coeur d'Alene, St. Maries, Moscow, and Grangeville, and started off one morning on a green and golden October day with bright blue sky all the way to Coeur d'Alene. I don't think there was a cloud anywhere in northern Idaho that day, except just over the airport at Coeur d'Alene, so we landed at St. Maries and arrived an hour early. We caught a ride with a lady passing by and drove into St. Maries. She was hauling a cow to market. She let us out in front of the newspaper office, and I stuck out my hand and said, "Ma'am, I'm Robert Smylie and I'm running for governor." She looked at me and she said, "Well, you are aren't you?" I said, "Yes, ma'am." She said "Well that's one vote you'll get." When we counted that precinct she was exactly right. This is a true tale, and I have told it many times in public speeches since and always to hilarious applause. I do not know what the lady's name was and never did get it. The editor of the St. Maries *Gazette* could not get it for me either.

By now, we were bearing down on October 31, my fortieth birthday and only four days away from the general election that would make me governor. The Canyon County Central Committee had scheduled a potluck picnic for noon of my birthday in the courtyard of the Kirkpatrick Memorial Church in Parma. There I confided in my closest associates that I thought we were going to win and finally said so in public to the assembled central committee members and their friends.

I had always maintained a voting residence in Canyon County in the third precinct in Caldwell. On Tuesday, November 4, we went down there to vote, had our picture taken by the local newspaper, and then called on my aunt, who lived around the corner and up the street one block. We returned to Boise and home and waited until eight o'clock when some returns started coming in. There was one precinct in Franklin County which always voted early and counted early. It was a power station on the Cub River, and we carried the precinct twelve to six. Our calculations were that if we could break even north of the Salmon River, we had the election won. We could afford to lose it by some margin, as long as that could be swallowed up in Canyon County. As it

Lucille and I get word of my election on the night of November 2, 1954.

turned out, we did not need to worry about northern Idaho; the Ada and Canyon County margins provided sufficient voting power to overcome the loss that we sustained in the Magic Valley. The Twin Falls newspaper had done a job on us, and it really showed. The Magic Valley was supposed to be the deep heart of Republicanism in Idaho, but that night it was not. Finally, at four minutes after eleven, Mountain Standard Time, the Associated Press called and said that they were predicting my victory on their morning wire and did I have any comment. A little after midnight, Mr. James R. Brown, the publisher of the *Statesman*, who was unofficially designated as the person who could finally say that an election had been won or lost, called and made the Associated Press prediction a fact. I don't know who got me on the phone for Mr. Brown's call, but he came on the line and said, "Governor, we are going to call you the winner in the morning paper." It was the first time that anybody had called me governor. I still have a picture of Lucille and me receiving that telephone call.

We had been receiving the returns in the little house on East Jefferson Street, and, by the time another thirty minutes had gone by, the joint was jumping. I can't remember exactly when it was we got to bed that night, but it was not early.

Now I began the task of organizing the government and making the changes I thought were absolutely necessary. I had already decided that most of the people who were in the Jordan administration were staying—at least for awhile. I knew that most of them were at least as loyal to me as they had been to Governor Jordan. For that reason, I thought they were entitled to consideration for reappointment. I had done a lot of talking about revitalizing the Department of Agriculture, and I began a search for somebody to fill the position of commissioner of Agriculture. One change was mandatory, and that was the chief budget officer in the governor's establishment. The position was held by a young man who I thought had been purposely putting rocks in front of our vehicle and was not entitled to any consideration for reappointment.

I decided that since I was regarded by the Boise power structure as a young fellow who did not really know what he was doing, it might be advisable to surround myself with a little gray hair. James Young, a former state senator from Payette County, and the unsuccessful Republican candidate for secretary of state in the recent election, had been chairman of the House and Senate Joint Finance and Appropriations Committee for two or three terms. He had an impressive knowledge of the fiscal workings of the government, and I called him up and asked him if he would be my budget director. His answer was yes, and he reported for duty the next morning.

Lu and I took off for a short vacation in San Francisco and southern California and were gone for about five or six days. I returned to the serious business of building a budget, preparing a program for the legislature, which would convene on January 7, and otherwise completing the arrangements for taking over the reins of office as governor of Idaho. In those last twenty days, we had met with everybody who had prepared a budget for their functions in the government of Idaho, and I had reduced the budget to two columns of figures on a four-by-five card. By then I realized that Governor Jordan had left me a $50 million government with resources of about $40 million. This was going to make it necessary to write a fairly rigorous message on fiscal requirements when we got to that point in the establishment of the new government.

Christmas came and went and Judge Chase Clark brought a wreath for the door of the house on East Jefferson Street, which he presented with a little ditty that was popular at the time—"You ain't' gonna need this house no longer."

As many people know, I wrote most of my own speeches, including the speeches on the state of the state and the addresses to the legislature at their opening session, which were completed on New Year's Eve. We didn't celebrate that occasion, but I was glad to have it finally on paper. There is one amusing story on that first message on the state of the state. Lloyd Adams, an attorney at Rexburg and a lobbyist for the First Security Corporation, had asked me if he might make some suggestions about the speech. I said that he certainly could, although I had no intention of using any of it. Adams put together a half-dozen paragraphs of reasonably good material, none of which was provocative or urged any particular course of action, but he did have some good prose which I used to wrap up the speech. Adams had intended that language to be used at the beginning of the speech, and he was terribly upset that he had been relegated to the end.

Carroll Sellars had already outfitted Lucille with an inaugural ball gown, and I had a skinny tuxedo that set us up for that event. Between Christmas and the new year, I went downtown and had Frank Lorance trim my hair, and then I went across the street to Ralph Davis' store and bought a sincere blue suit and two light blue shirts—the better to be televised in. With that, I was ready to face up to the swearing-in ceremony on the first Monday after the first day of the New Year.

CHAPTER SEVEN

THE FIRST GOVERNORSHIP 1955–59

THE INAUGURAL CEREMONY in 1955, which would make me governor of Idaho, was simple and straightforward. It took place in the House of Representatives Chamber in the well before the Speaker's Podium. My old college classmate, R. H. Young, Jr., a representative from Canyon County and Speaker of the House of Representatives, presided. I was introduced to the Speaker by Governor Jordan, and the oath of office was administered by Chief Justice C. J. Taylor of the Idaho Supreme Court. The Twenty-fifth Army Band, which was assembled in the rotunda of the capitol, struck up "Hail to the Chief," and in Capitol Park across from the statehouse there was a nineteen-gun salute. It was an intense, emotional moment. Now I had my hands on those levers of power and was going to try to do what I had striven so long to accomplish.

My family and friends were in the gallery. There was Lucille and my two sisters, Dorothy and Frances, the two boys, Bill and Steve, the aunties from Caldwell, my father and his brother, and cousins Ike and Lola Wescott.

I noted that George Greenfield, who had been Democratic state chairman that year, was in the gallery. I reflected on the fact that he and Young and myself were all in the class of '38 at the College of Idaho, and that Bill Rankin, who was directing the Twenty-fifth Army Band, had been in the class just behind us. It was a great day for the Caldwell institution.

With the ceremony concluded, Governor Jordan and I returned to the governor's office and he handed me the keys to the automobile that he had used and the keys to the residence on 21st Street where Lucille and I would live for the next twelve years. With that, he took his leave and flew to Washington, D.C., that afternoon. He did not participate in any of the rest of the inaugural festivities.

My family came in just then and we took some pictures of the group, and then I took them over to the Hotel Boise where I had arranged a luncheon for the entire family and some friends. About mid-afternoon I returned to the governor's office to meet with Robert Hodge and Bernice Callsen. Bernice Callsen had been my secretary all

I am sworn in as governor by Chief Justice C. J. Taylor on January 3, 1955. Bill Young, Speaker of the House and college friend and classmate, is at the far right. ISHS 0-142.19.

through the attorney general years. Hodge, of course, had been a big hand in the campaign. I asked both of them to stay on and become the nucleus of the new governor's staff. Hodge occupied the title of administrative assistant and what is now termed the chief of staff to the governor. Earlier we had secured the services of Nadine Dean to be Senator Jim Young's assistant in the budget office; with that our staff was, for the time being, complete. Later we asked Phyllis Spinharney to be a receptionist and general social secretary to both Mrs. Smylie and myself.

To our very great surprise, the file cases were empty. There was no unfinished business lying on the governor's desk and no calendar of events for the coming year. We started with a clean slate and any marks that we made upon it would be ours and nobody else's.

My first speech to the legislature on the state of the state was

Family members gathered in the governor's office after I was inaugurated on January 3, 1955.

Lucille and me at the inaugural ball on January 3, 1955.

tentatively scheduled for Wednesday morning at 11:45. We were now about forty hours from the first major challenge of the new administration.

With a day to spare before we had to go back to the House of Representatives, we plotted to steal the march on the lobbyists of the town. We hand-delivered a message to each of the legislators with an invitation to five consecutive breakfast meetings at seven o'clock in the morning in the Crystal Ballroom at the Hotel Boise. The groups were divided into guest lists of twenty-one members, and it was a great pleasure to learn that they all planned to attend and did. I greeted the guests at the door, called them by their first names, to their great surprise, and scored heavily in the field of influence making. I think in the course of those five breakfast meetings we picked up at least ten votes that we could always count on.

On Wednesday, January 5, 1955, Speaker of the House Bill Young and Lieutenant Governor J. Berkley Larsen appointed committees to wait upon me and tell me that the legislature was prepared to receive any messages that I might care to send them. With the escort committee, we trooped up the stairs and approached the doors to the chamber of the House. The sergeant at arms swung the doors open and sang out in a loud voice, "Mr. Speaker, ladies, and gentlemen, the governor of the State of Idaho." It was a thrilling moment. I began to deliver what turned out to be the most crucially important and most effective speech of that two-year period.

The address was received with almost universal approval by Democratic and Republican members of the legislature and scored well in the editorial columns of the newspapers of the state. In general, the public thought well of the speech, and I received many laudatory telephone calls and written commendations. There is an amusing anecdote having to do with that speech that involved J. R. Brown, the publisher and editor of the *Statesman*. Brown had not liked me when I was attorney general and was only now beginning to learn how to get along with the idea that I was governor. He had graciously conceded my victory in November, but the speech on the state of the state was another thing altogether. I am told by an Associated Press reporter that he tried for three days to find some justifiable reason for bashing the speech and giving me the benefit of his spleen. After trying hard, he gave up. He finally wrote an editorial which he titled "A Splendid Address" and treated me to almost a full column of complimentary prose. This was the beginning of a long and effective relationship with the *Statesman* and its publisher, which was very important. In those days, *The Idaho Statesman* had immense political clout and its endorsement of my first message to the legislature was of major political consequence.

There were few surprises in the message because I more or less repeated what I had been saying all through the summer of 1953 and all through 1954. We spoke about the fiscal situation simply because it was necessary in light of the financial condition in which we received the reins of government. A potential $10 million deficit was no small item in Idaho's government finances in 1955. When we sent the budget up to the legislature, it was in balance, but it also required the enactment of $10 million in taxes that had not previously been imposed. These were mostly so-called "sin taxes" on booze, beer, cigarettes, and similar items. This made them a touch more tolerable.

I asked the legislature to create a Department of Economic Development, and they did so—although it was funded miserably because of the shortage of financial resources. There had been a constitutional department of commerce in the original days of statehood, but it had never been activated and had been generally ignored.

We asked the legislature to appropriate $15.2 million, the full amount necessary to make the public school equalization formula work. This was a major portion of the general fund budget, and my promises in the campaign brooked no waffling on that undertaking. I made it quite clear to the legislature that I would not settle for less than

I laid out my plans for Idaho in a speech to the legislature on January 4, 1955.

$15.2 million. This did not seem to dismay them; they apparently had been feeling some of the same heat in their legislative districts from the local parent-teacher associations as we had seen reflected in the Central Surveys political poll. As I expected, the leadership of the Idaho Education Association tended to be critical of my approach to education, largely because it did not reflect support of the Teacher's Retirement System, which had been created in 1946 but was still unfunded. I would have to confess that my decision not to spend money on sterile retirement reserves and to expend it first in the classrooms of Idaho was an entirely political response to the pressures that were being felt in the school districts of the state. The secretary of the Idaho Education Association, Dr. John Booth, was a professed member of the Democratic party, and the thought occurred to me that his Democratic affiliation may have colored his failure to support what we thought were pretty adequate approaches to public school financing.

The message asked for additional funding for the dedicated highway funds, and this resulted in abandonment that year of the five

Republican officeholders, on May 10, 1955: Senator Herman Welker, myself, Senator Henry Dworshak, and Second District Congressman Hamer Budge.

dollar license plate fee, which had become a kind of political albatross on our attempts to improve the highway system generally since it produced insufficient revenues.

I also asked to have the Employment Security's Employment Compensation Benefits modernized and brought more into line with current pay scales in private industry.

The only thing that could be called a major surprise in that first message was a request for the people to ratify a constitutional amendment that would permit the governor to succeed himself in office. In 1944, the legislature had submitted the constitutional amendment that had been in effect for the last two gubernatorial terms. It limited the governor to one four-year term until a full four-year term had expired after he left office. I had watched the legislature literally destroy two governorships because they knew the governor would not be around to defend his course of action, and it seemed entirely appropriate to me and consonant with the tenets of good government that the governor be permitted to test his programs and policies in the cauldron of political decision. This proposal provided one of the focal points on which the business of the 1955 legislature turned.

The legislative organization had been completed, the message had been received, and, even in 1955, there was a tradition of going home on that first legislative weekend. Although legislators did work on Saturdays, returning home permitted them to find out that all-important piece of political information—what the people thought. They would return on Monday to begin a new week and to receive on Wednesday what my staff was referring to as the "blue-back monster"—the budget.

Anyone who has attempted to move a household knows that it can be frustrating business. If you add to that frustration the difficulties of organizing a state government in the same week that you are trying to move, you know what problems the Smylies encountered. The house on Jefferson Street had served us well, and it was wrenching to have to leave it even to move to the governor's residence. By mid-week, I had given up and Lucille had called the moving vans to transport the contents of 318 East Jefferson Street to the governor's mansion.

Actually, the new residence was no mansion. That was a euphemism that was adopted by the minority of the legislature after we had tidied the place up a bit. The residence did not have a staff and was not furnished, except in a very minor way. There was a beautiful dining table and a grand piano, but not much in the way of occasional chairs or other furniture for comfortable living. Both Lucille and I had our work cut out for us. I was attempting to master the intricacies of leading a legislature into substantial accomplishment, and she was going to have to master living in what we quickly dubbed "The Governor's House." I came home to dinner there on Friday night. We ate in the kitchen with the two boys and began life as Governor and Mrs. Robert E. Smylie.

The legislature came back to town on Monday with pleasing reports of popular acceptance of my proposals and the state of the state message. We put the finishing touches on the budget, and I readied my speech to accompany it for presentation to the legislature on Wednesday. I was under no illusion that this would be a different sort of a speech than the one that I had given at the opening session. I would have to recite the bitter truth about the condition of our finances and the difficulties confronting us in fulfilling our campaign promises. Legislatures, like Mohammed, tend to beat the bearer of bad tidings.

In the speech that accompanied the budget I was obliged to inform the legislators that we were now operating in the red, and that the previous administration had left us a revenue structure that would produce a deficit of somewhere between $600,000 and $1 million by June 30 of 1955. I told the legislature that we would institute heroic measures designed to avoid that result, and that I had some confidence that if we were fortunate, we would be able to do so. However, I told them they should bear in mind that it was touch and go all the way. The remainder of the bad news had to do with the upcoming biennium. The departments had proposed a budget of about $55 million. I had managed to trim $5 million off of those estimates and was proposing to spend $50 million, but the bad news was that Governor Jordan's revenue structure would only produce about $40.5 million. We thus ended with a $9.5 million shortfall that would have to be covered by new taxes or increased taxes or both. The alternative, of course, was to dramatically slash the expenditure estimates of the departments and institutions, including the universities and public schools. I was prepared to do neither and to proceed with plans for an increase in various taxes. The legislature received this news with laudable stoicism. My proposal for a $50 million budget was immediately attacked by the Idaho State Chamber of Commerce as an unrealistic and almost profligate expenditure. Fortunately, the *Statesman* did not take such a bold stand. The editor tended to think that we ought to move forward to solve some of our problems.

The legislature began examining the budget and making preparations for consideration of the proposals which had been made to them in the state of the state. The Thirty-third Session of the Idaho Legislature was off and running.

For my part, I began to try to find ways to get the budget back in balance by the end of the biennium on June 30. We put a stop order on any new expenditures for capital goods and called a halt to all new hiring or filling of vacancies until that date. About a week later, Fred Charlton, whom I had appointed to be superintendent of the State Liquor Dispensary, came into the office with a suggestion. He had been Judge Chase Clark's referee in bankruptcy and was used to presiding over the liquidation of failed enterprises. He had immediately spotted the fact that we had an inventory of about $6 million in the warehouses of the liquor dispensary, and he could see no reason for maintaining an inventory of much more than $3.5 or $4 million. As the law then stood, it gave the executive tight control over management of the liquor dispensary, and so we immediately commenced liquidating the inventory and converting it to cash. We did this by failing to order new supplies until we had reduced the inventory to what we thought were reasonable proportions. The money then was credited directly to the general fund and assisted greatly in meeting the needs of the projected deficit. It may have been the only occasion in the state's history when booze served a totally good purpose.

The Joint Finance and Appropriations Committee set to work on the budget. Representative Elvon Hampton told me that he thought it might be possible to reduce my estimate of $50 million by a minor amount, but that he thought that we would end up pretty close to that figure. I told him that if anything could be trimmed without harm to programs that we needed, I would approve of their action. They set to work and were able before too long to tell Ralph Wickberg of the Revenue and Taxation Committee what would be needed in the way of revenues. They finally ended by spending $49.1 million in opposition to my $50.1 million proposal. That's about as close as legislatures and governors ever get.

For the first four weeks of that Thirty-third Legislative Session, Wickberg and his committee wrestled heroically with the problem of finding appropriate, politically acceptable ways of raising the revenue that would balance the budget. While they were performing that thankless task, Hampton and his Appropriations Committee were finding very acceptable methods of spending the budget. Progress was being made in that wonder world of public finance, but there were still three gridlocked issues which would require solutions before much could be accomplished.

The delegation from the Clearwater Valley, led by the members from Lewiston, Howard Hechtner and James Monroe, were busy attempting to find some way to reopen the closed college at Lewiston. Lewis-Clark State College (also named, at various points in its history, North Idaho College of Education and Lewis-Clark Normal School) had been established at Lewiston in 1893 offering two-year degrees in education. In 1947 it was authorized to issue four-year de-grees, but closed in 1951 when the legislature failed to appropriate funds for it. When Governor Jordan's budget decreed its death, it was assumed that most of the students would troop up the hill to Moscow to attend the University of Idaho. A reasonably reliable study indicated that of the 880 students attending in 1951, only about 100 went anywhere else to school. Quite a few did go to the University of Idaho in Moscow, but the vast majority just seemed to disappear from the college scene. This was a damning statistic in the days of the GI Bill of Rights.

The second issue involved the University of Idaho, which had been trying since 1927 to secure an appropriation to build a library. At the time the library collection was inadequately housed in part of the administration building on University Hill. The facilities had probably occasioned frowning comments from accreditation people from 1927 onward. In 1927 a representative named Chris Hagen asked to appropriate $27,500 for a library building at the University, but the request was rejected because there was no money. This insupportable reason had survived many legislatures and several governors. In my budget message I had asked for approval of a $2 million bond issue, which would be off-budget and which would be spent in various capital projects located strategically around the state in order to secure approval. This is a process known as pork-barrelling. One of the projects was $1.3 million for the University's library building. The bill to accomplish that result had been written and filed with the legislature and was pending for action.

The third gridlock issue centered around the so-called succession amendment permitting the governor to succeed himself in office beginning in 1958. The resolution had passed the House with ease with the necessary two-thirds majority and was pending in the Senate. The Senate was composed of twenty-four Republicans and twenty Democrats, and without substantial Democratic help, the resolution could not hope to secure the two-thirds majority that would be required.

In the sixth week of the session, these three measures were locked in a whirlpool at the vortex of legislative power. At any given point in time, it could have been assumed that none of them had a chance. The Lewiston college bill had been dubbed the Lewis and Clark Normal School Proposal. It passed the final house on a Saturday morning, and on Monday, it was delivered to my office for review. When the bill arrived, I placed it on the corner of my desk in plain view of visiting legislative delegations, and it lay there untouched and dusty for five long days. Mr. Hechtner and Mr. Monroe visited almost every day in an attempt to bring me some new argument in favor of opening the college. I think they were quite sure that I really wanted to be of assistance, but I think they were also quite sure that somehow their proposal's fate was tied up in the consideration of other matters.

They first brought up the question of the gubernatorial succession resolution, which was locked up by the Democrats in the Senate, and I said its enactment would be helpful but there was no deal. I assured them that the college would have to rise or fall on its merits. When they visited me on Wednesday, Hechtner and Monroe both suggested the possibility of securing approval of the bond issue proposal for the University library. Once again, I gave them no assurances, but pointed out that their bill was in the same location on the corner of my desk.

Tom Boise was a lobbyist and a political leader in the Clearwater Valley, and he was also a leader of the Chamber of Commerce movement in support of the Lewis-Clark Normal School Proposal. For a generation he was the most influential Democratic politician in the state, and I counted him as a close friend. He came to call on Thursday on behalf of the Lewis-Clark Normal School Proposal. Boise was politically astute, and he was aware of the difficulties I could be in if I permitted approval of the bill. He knew of my conversations with Hechtner and Monroe, and he wanted to know flat out whether there was any connection between the Lewis-Clark bill and the succession resolution and the university library bond issue. I told him there was no connection, but that it would be much easier to approve the Lewis-Clark Normal School Proposal if the other two measures had both been successfully passed by the legislature. He said he thought he understood and took his leave to go and see what could be accomplished among his Democratic stalwarts. Boise correctly assumed that while we could live without the University library bond issue and without the succession amendment, that all of the Lewis-Clark Normal School eggs were in one basket on the corner of the governor's desk.

Late Thursday afternoon, Boise called to say that he thought it might be possible for the logjam in the Senate to be broken and asked when it had to happen. I said prior to the time that the possibility of a veto of the Lewis-Clark Normal School bill expired sometime Saturday morning. Later he called back to say that he thought the project was doable. I had learned through clandestine sources that Senator Al Derr from Bonner County, the Democratic whip, had requested a Democratic caucus at noon on Friday and that he would then propose adoption and passage of the gubernatorial succession resolution and a commitment to support the University library bond issue.

I confided this information to Senator Ted Hoff, who was my de facto leader in the Senate, and told him to confide in no one else. I asked Speaker of the House Bill Young and Majority Leader Charles Cook to be sure that the House was still in session at four o'clock on Friday afternoon and told them it was possible that the logjam was going to break.

On Friday everything worked exactly on schedule. Tom Boise was a magnificent political architect. The Democrats held their caucus at noon and the resolution approving the gubernatorial succession amendment was approved. It was introduced in the Senate at about 2:00 P.M. and was enacted unanimously at 2:30. It then went to the House, where it was rapidly brought forward under suspension of the rules, and passed again with an almost unanimous vote. The state Senate had approved the University library bond bill, and the logjam was broken. On Saturday morning, I signed the Lewis-Clark Normal School Bill, and the legislature began a racehorse performance to end the session in sixty-one days. As I noted earlier, they appropriated almost exactly the amount I had asked for, imposed new taxes to pay the bill, and went home to almost universal applause.

The only sour note in the whole proceeding was the voice of the *Times-News*, a Twin Falls paper that had led the fight against the school at Lewiston for no good reason that I could imagine. Nonetheless, they editorialized at length that the solution of the gridlock was some kind of deal. In the sense that all political progress in legislative halls is the result of deals of one kind or another, there was a deal, but no promises were made. It would be much fairer to say that the proponents of the Lewis-Clark Normal School Proposal had found themselves in a position where their pet project was being held hostage to the enactment of the gubernatorial succession resolution and the bond issue that made the University library a possibility.

In political affairs, it is usually what happens after the fact that is the best proof of what was the proper thing to do. Forty years later,

Lewis-Clark Normal School is the thriving Lewis-Clark State College performing yeoman service to the students of the Clearwater Valley. The $1.3 million library building at the University was built, oc-cupied, used, and forty years later has doubled in size and usefulness. This was accomplished at the cost of another $5.5 or $6 million. The gubernatorial succession amendment was approved in the 1956 election by seventy-one percent of the electorate.

The *Times-News* did have its revenge. It stands as a political reality that I never carried the Magic Valley counties in any general election—even the election of 1954. Although I know of no reason why that should be so, it had a great deal to do with the fact, I think, that we brought Lewis-Clark State College back from the dead and restored it as a useful instrument in the educational arsenal of Idaho. It is a curious fact that the College of Southern Idaho, now located at Twin Falls, a community college of extreme excellence, has a population of about 3,000 students. I think this proves that when we need something, we can afford it and we ought to be about accomplishing the task.

The legislature finished up its work and returned home with a favorable verdict on those first sixty days. At the Capitol, when the quiet of legislative adjournment had settled over the place, we began to tidy up the administrative reins of government. Fred Charlton had already taken complete charge of the State Liquor Dispensary and was busily engaged in liquidating that immense inventory. Harold West was busily engaged in reinvigorating the Department of Agriculture and realigning and streamlining his activities. Ted Kramer took over the State Purchasing Agency and instituted with ironclad effectiveness our "don't buy until July" policy, which was designed to erase the red ink left over from the previous administration. Bill Jonasson took on the task of organizing the new Department of Commerce and Development, and, with very little in the way of resources, did what I regarded as a creditable job. Most of the rest of the departments were left in the hands of the people who had been running them under Governor Jordan, and they continued to do a satisfactory job. The Department of Public Health showed some weaknesses that would later appear to be real and would provide a problem when the next legislature convened.

In the summer of 1955, President Eisenhower suffered a heart attack and the political wheels began to grind. Whether or not he would be a candidate in 1956 was the principal object of political speculation. I had been scheduled to make a fund-raising swing through California on behalf of the several committees there and make speeches in Los Angeles, Modesto, San Francisco, Richmond, Santa Clara, San Rafael, and Sacramento. Leonard Hall, the Republican National Committee Chairman, knew of these fund raising speeches and called to ask if I would have any difficulty proclaiming my belief in the complete recovery of President Eisenhower and the fact that he would be a candidate for reelection. I said no and became a great friend of the chairman as a consequence.

Along about the end of 1955, Sherman Adams, former governor of New Hampshire, who was Eisenhower's chief of staff in the White House, called to inquire about my estimate of Senator Herman Welker's chances for reelection. Welker, a rightist from Payette, Idaho, was no friend of the administration, nor they of him, but the administration wanted to be able to count that vote when they organized the Senate in 1957. After conferring with people around the state and after some study, I concluded that it might be close, but I thought Welker could be reelected. It would be difficult to deny him the nomination without a pretty rugged political bloodletting. None of us knew it at the time, but Welker was suffering from a brain tumor, which was to take his life within about a year and a half. He was sometimes subject to aberrant behavior, which led people to think he had been indulging in either dope or liquor. I had seen enough of him to believe that neither of those charges was true, but rumors persisted and did him substantial harm in the general election campaign. He ran against Senator Frank Church in 1956 and was the victim in part of one of the first negative ads I have ever seen in Idaho politics. The Democratic state central committee used some billboards that suggested that "Idaho could be PROUD" of Frank Church in the United States Senate, implying that Idaho was not proud of Welker. That was a milquetoast ad and was a forerunner of some of the outrageous stuff being used in political campaigns these days.

The Democratic nomination in 1956 for United States senator had been contested between Frank Church and former Senator Glen Taylor. It was a nip-and-tuck election and finally came down to Church's winning by not more than 200 votes. The contested votes were in Elmore County, and there was some evidence that they had been recounted to achieve the result. Senator Taylor wanted a full-scale investigation which, of course, was impossible. There was no authority for the State Board of Canvassers to undertake such an investigation and no machinery for doing an official recount. Legislation was later enacted to provide for recounting contested elections. In the meantime, Senator Taylor was loud in his lamentations about how the election had been stolen from him. I think he just lost by a few votes and couldn't really tolerate the idea. In any event, he complained to the State Board of Canvassers; he complained to me as governor; and he complained to anyone he talked to who would listen. The State Board of Canvassers declared Senator Frank Church to be the nominee of the Democratic party, and he went on in the general election to defeat Senator Welker rather handily.

This little by-play in the political history of Idaho is not really worth noting, except for the fact that years later at a luncheon in the White House, President Lyndon Johnson told me that he was not particularly fond of Senator Church, which of course was not news, but he said they had one thing in common. They had both stolen their first election.

At the conclusion of the 1955 legislative session, an interim committee had been authorized to study and report on our tax structure in response to a suggestion in my budget message that we should find a solution to our always recurring revenue shortfalls and ascertain whether some new revenue structure would be required. Unspoken though it was, this was probably the first time that there had been a direct move to enact a modern sales tax. The committee was organized under the leadership of Ralph Wickberg, chairman of the House Revenue and Taxation Committee. The committee did come in with a

The tax structure committee so critical to my first administration. From left, Robert Doolittle, Jim Young, Ralph Wickberg, Charles Tilford, myself, Carl Irwin, Ellis Shawver, Ralph Jones, Jr., and Fred A. Miller. ISHS 80-2.86

---

report that recommended the enactment of a sales and use tax and replacement of several other sources of revenue, which were thought to be onerous and unkind to various business interests and individuals. That report, coming just before the election, coupled with the candidacy of Senator Herman Welker, was pretty heavy luggage to carry into the general election of November 1956. President Eisenhower did recover and was a candidate. He had been renominated in San Francisco and went on the defeat Governor Stevenson of Illinois handsomely for the second time around the track.

Republicans lost badly in Idaho; they were held responsible for the tax reform proposal. Ralph Wickberg was defeated in Shoshone County and Perry Swisher, a strong civilian supporter of the sales tax, was defeated in Bannock County. These were two people we would have relied on to carry forward any proposals for new taxation. The net political result of the general election in 1956, as far as legislation was concerned, was that we were being told that the people did not want a sales tax—at least in 1957. The budget figures that were reaching the governor's office from the departments and institutions indicated that we would have to face a budget proposal that was badly out of balance. This was the shape of things to come for the next six or eight years.

The 1956 elections produced a mixed bag of political winners. The gubernatorial succession amendment to the Constitution, which permitted the governor to run for office to succeed himself, was approved by the people by about seventy percent of the vote. Rightly or wrongly, we took this as something of an endorsement of our first two years in office. President Eisenhower carried Idaho by about seventy percent. Both of the incumbent congressmen were reelected. They were Gracie Pfost and Hamer Budge. Senator Herman Welker, whose illness was becoming more and more apparent with each passing week, was handily defeated by Senator Frank Church, who began his twenty-four years in the Senate.

The Republicans decreased their majority in the House of Representatives by three seats, but the Democrats carried the state Senate by a margin that I now remember to be twenty-five to nineteen. The new Democrats were mostly young lawyers very lately out of the University of Idaho Law School who were more inclined to be mischief-makers than policymakers. They had one shared conviction, and that was that anything that I suggested should be opposed. These mischief-makers did not contribute much to the legislative program in 1957, but we managed to craft a bill of particulars that the legislature approved by about ninety percent. The principal item was an increased appropriation for public schools—once again meeting the full requirement of the then-existing equalization formula.

When we met the full requirements of the formula in 1955, the educators quickly set about determining that the formula was somehow inadequate. The inadequacy, of course, was that it didn't spend enough money. They worked out a proposal which would put educational opportunity on a more equal basis. The formula that was devised almost inexorably increased costs above the levels of money that were

In Richard Nixon' s vice-presidential office in 1956. ISHS 77-163.28.

available. This had the effect of making educational equality across the entire state an ever-retreating goal and provided a basis for those involved in education to be continuously and regularly unhappy. It did seem to me, however, that the customers of the education system—the members of the Parent-Teacher Association—had a little different slant on what we were trying to do, which was, of course, the best we could for the children in the classroom.

We also began to restructure the Department of Health. With the end of World War II and the passage of a little time, medical doctors had become available to staff the public health agency, which made possible a much more sophisticated endeavor in the field of public health. We set about creating that sort of agency. Dr. Fred Graeber came on board and Dr. Terry Carver reported for duty. This began to create stresses in the administrative management of the department, which had been confided for many years to a nonprofessional administrator.

We also began to undertake a modest effort in the field of preventive mental health and began to reestablish the state residential hospitals for the mentally ill as well-equipped and well-staffed operations. The location of these two hospitals at Blackfoot and Orofino made this extremely difficult because trained personnel hesitated to go to those back country places after they had "seen New York."

This legislature did not get out of town in sixty-one days. It took them, as my memory serves, sixty-nine days to create a balanced budget and to achieve at least a portion of the legislative goals. To attempt to get the Senate Democrats to embark on any new departure in the field of revenue enhancement would have been futile. As a consequence, our increased budget had to be accommodated within the framework of the then-existing revenue legislation. We had to tinker with the rates of imposition of the income tax and make it really into

At my desk in the governor's office. ISHS 72-190.83B.

a more graduated tax than had been the case theretofore. We did increase the taxes and increased some of the bits and pieces of patch-and-scratch taxation that we had been relying on two years earlier.

Meanwhile we put the report of the tax committee on the shelf where it could be studied by anyone who wanted to inform themselves in the field of tax reform, tax balance, and new forms of taxation. The House of Representatives would have been fairly amenable to new departures in taxation in 1957, but we would have faced opposition that was impossible to overcome.

The legislature finally scraped together enough money to balance our skimpy budget and adjourned to return home to determine the peoples' verdict. It seems safe to say that nobody saw the economic storm brewing on the horizon; not Republican, Democrat, legislature, or governor. In those first four years, it seemed that the City of Lewiston always wanted something. Congress had authorized and commenced construction of the four dams between Pasco, Washington, and Lewiston that would make slack water navigation to tidewater a reality for barge traffic originating at the Port of Lewiston. The first dam at Ice Harbor was nearly complete, and the Lewiston Chamber of Commerce began to thump for construction of the road they called the Lewis and Clark Highway, which would run roughly parallel to the old Nez Perce trail over the mountains to Montana. At the insistence of Senator Church, the chairman of the Senate Transportation Committee, the Honorable Albert Gore of Tennessee, held hearings in Lewiston to study the feasibility of the road. Feasibility had already been studied to death, but the Gore hearings finally set things in motion, and it was possible to ultimately get funds appropriated for the highway due to the real efforts of Senator Church and Senator Henry Dworshak. I attended the hearings that Senator Gore held and coined a phrase that was useful in the speechmaking that followed. I thought we ought to "tie a road to the river" so that transportation could come from the wheat lands of Montana all the way to the sea. As it developed, the highway was completed before the dams were completed, and I remember going up to a place called Packer's Meadow to join Governor Tim Babcock in sawing a log with a crosscut saw that would officially open the highway, now known as U.S. Highway 12.

This little incident was of great significance to me because about five generations ago a frontiersman from St. Louis named William Clark had passed that way in company with Meriwether Lewis. William Clark was the brother of my great-grandmother to the fourth degree. There is another bit of history about that little patch of land on the top of the Bitterroots between Kooskia and Hamilton, Montana. It is that no flag but that of the United States had ever been unfurled up there, and that makes it unique. It was not in the Louisiana Purchase. The British never really claimed it. The French really never got that far south in their trek across Canada. It is country that we love, and it is interesting to know that it never belonged to anybody else except the Nez Perce Nation.

There are no universities that have a school of political science that tells you how to become a governor or what to do after you become one. It is an office of such lonesome elevation that there is hardly anyone you can ask for advice, and you tend to turn to those who have been there before you. I would like to take this opportunity to pay tribute to Governor C. A. Robins and to Governor Charles Gossett—one a Republican and the other a Democrat—on whom I relied fairly regularly for advice in the loneliness of high office.

Midway through 1958, Bill Jonasson decided he would return to private life and the operation of a business which he owned. He brought his resignation in as secretary of Commerce, and I was happy to appoint in his place Miss Louise Shadduck, who was, I believe, the first cabinet-rank female appointment in the history of the United States. She remained in that office for almost a dozen years through two governors and did a superb job.

I had occasion during those years to face my first judicial appointment and to learn what I had already suspected—that the organized bar associations were not going to be of much help in choosing judges. On this occasion, they wished to have me appoint a gentleman who was eminently qualified, but whose age was such that the average age of the justices on the court would have been in excess of seventy years. This, I thought, was insupportable. I therefore found another appointment, Henry McQuade, that would fill the bill. I think that the only times I ever followed the bar association's suggestions in appointing judges were two, and those two were two of the three mistakes that, in retrospect, I think I made in the selection of judges.

Lucille and I had a lot of fun outside of Idaho in those years. We went down to San Diego to join Goodwin and Virginia Knight, the governor of California and his wife, at the opening ceremonies of the Fiesta del Pacifica, which San Diego used to mark the discovery of Point Loma, the peninsula that guards San Diego harbor. We rode in the parade with Leo Carrillo, and one evening during the Fiesta we went up to the Goodwin mansion on Point Loma and listened to Meredith Wilson play the entire score of the *Music Man* on Goodwin's grand

Our hosts at the Fiesta del Pacifica in San Diego in 1955 were California governor Goodwin Knight and his wife Virginia.

Lucille and me with Steve and Bill in the backyard of the governor's house, June 1955.

piano. He was going to leave the next morning for New York to put the musical in production. We later saw the play at the theater where it opened in New York.

Largely because we had two children of our own and because it was my birthday, we made quite a celebration of Halloween in those years that we were in the governor's residence. Mr. C. C. Anderson, one of Idaho's merchants and founder of C. C. Anderson Department Stores, which was later purchased by the Bon Marché, had always entertained the youngsters on Halloween at his house on Warm Springs Avenue, and it was one of the jokes of the times that he had left the Halloween celebration to me in his will. In any event, we used to get 500 or 600 at the front door Halloween night, and every once in a while they would sing "Happy Birthday." Once when I was listening to their young voices, an egg came sailing across the street and smacked me right in the forehead. About four days later the doorbell rang at 5:30 p.m. I said hello, and a young man said, "I'm the boy who threw the egg." I invited him in, and we visited. The next time I saw him, I was standing on the bridge across the Washoe River in Reno, where he had grown up. He told me who he was and we had a little visit. He had turned out to be quite a basketball player and was six foot six at the time we met again. He was one of the basketball players at UCLA who won national championships in the fifties. I told the young man that when he was fourteen he had an arm like a whiplash, and that he was the only teenager that had ever hit me with an egg. It was a rather splendid Halloween birthday remembrance.

It seems appropriate here to mark the passing in those years of former Senator D. Worth Clark, who was the person who gave me a little preferment for political patronage in my first trip to Washington and made it possible for me to enter George Washington Law School. Without that help, it is unlikely that I would have been in time to get back to Boise to become attorney general and later governor.

As 1957 ended we began to prepare for a campaign for reelection in 1958. The economy was not yet weak but was worsening. Unemployment figures were climbing, but not dangerously, and we thought the referendum on our performance that constituted approval of the constitutional amendment for gubernatorial succession boded well for the campaign that lay ahead.

CHAPTER EIGHT

SECOND CAMPAIGN FOR THE GOVERNORSHIP

THE IDAHO GUBERNATIORIAL campaign in 1958, in retrospect, resembles nothing quite so much as President Bush's unsuccessful campaign in 1992. The only difference was that we managed to squeak out with the narrowest of margins and win.

We were overconfident in the beginning and quite misjudged the economic condition of the state. Statewide editorial comments in the small newspapers had been generally positive, and the daily news papers, with the exception of the *Times-News* in Twin Falls, were reasonably favorable. Our contacts in the counties indicated that the voters were inclined to our reelection, and that was as close as we could come in those days to a poll.

We should have recognized that the economy was getting tight by the fact that campaign contributions were extremely slow in coming. We had to cut back on planning on that account, but we were not overly concerned with the Democratic opposition. It did not seem to be formidable or very well known around the state, and that was a reason why we postponed commencing the campaign until it was almost too late.

W. C. Burns had resigned as state chairman to accept an appointment to the State Board of Highway Directors, and it became necessary to find someone qualified to take the job. This proved difficult, which should have been another straw in the wind.

We finally drafted a two-term state legislator from Minidoka County named Ray Robbins to take the job, although he made it quite clear that he was not going to be able to devote much time to it. This was satisfactory because it allowed my campaign people to take over the state headquarters, which we were financing and had every right to have in our corner. Having endured twelve years of Republican governors, the Democrats thought 1958 was certainly their year. The two major candidates in the Democratic primary were State Senator Alfred M. Derr of Bonner County, who was the member of the legislature that submitted the succession amendment to the people for ratification in 1955. The other major candidate was John Glasby, a precinct and county chairman in Elmore County in 1956. He had engineered the recount of the Church-Taylor ballots in that precinct that changed the outcome of the official canvass. Glasby had also been a member of the Basler-Page football teams at the College of Idaho in the mid-thirties. He played alongside me as tackle when I played guard in my freshman and sophomore years. (There are times when I dictate this that I think I have been followed about by the alumni association of what is now known as the Albertson College of Idaho.)

When the campaign began in the spring of 1958, neither Senator Derr nor Mr. Glasby seemed very formidable, largely because neither of them had any statewide organization or statewide identification. These facts tended to nourish the overconfidence that was later to almost prove my undoing.

Like Mr. Bush thirty-five years later, what we had neglected to pay attention to was the economy, which was already beginning to slope off. At the end of the first quarter of 1958, Fred Charlton, superintendent of the liquor dispensary, came to me with some disturbing figures. We had developed a method of ascertaining the confidence of the consuming public in Idaho. In those days the Federal Reserve Board had no statistics based on retail sales in Idaho that didn't include Salt Lake City and Spokane, and these were not much use in forecasting revenues. Charlton had discovered a correlation between bottle sales and dollar volume in the liquor dispensary that was an almost fail-safe method of ascertaining how people felt about their money. In the first quarter of 1958, the bottle sales of whiskey, which were ninety-five percent of the volume of the dispensary in those days, were increasing rapidly, while the dollar volume of sales was declining. This was an early-warning signal that people were buying "old fruit jar" instead of Old Forester and Old Grandad. Their taste for cheaper whiskey was indicative of the fact that they didn't feel they had much money.

In my judgment, there has never been a time in Idaho, or elsewhere, where a shift in the economic circumstances of the voting public did not portend political sentiment when the vote came to be taken. This same early-warning signal was confirmed on June 30 and again on September 30, and we didn't really give it much credit until sometime in the middle of the summer. By that time the Democrats were beating us to death with the right-to-work issue (the intent of which was to eliminate mandatory union membership where employees had voted to have a union shop) and something they called "lack of leadership." This latter issue was a synonym for failure to pass a sales tax and thus commit hari-kari. It also referred to the uneasiness within the body politic concerning the state's economic situation. The polls that we took in mid-August indicated that we had a reasonably safe margin, that is to say about fifty-four to forty-six percent, and that the Democratic campaign was not hitting us too hard.

About two weeks before the primary election in which he defeated Mr. Glasby, Senator Derr had announced a plan to legalize casino-type gambling in Idaho as a means to raise revenue and thus avoid a sales tax. This gave him temporary momentum in the northern counties and border counties. Glasby took the position that casino gambling would not solve any problems, but he never survived the primary. Derr continued to proclaim the validity of his plan all through the election campaign, but was muting it toward the end of October because it was costing him votes in what he hoped would be his heartland—in eastern Idaho.

The real sleeper of the 1958 campaign was an initiative proposal to enact at the general election a so-called right-to-work law, which was a favorite campaign tactic of the conservative wing of the Democratic and Republican parties. A wool-hat Democrat, W. Clay Sutton, representative from Washington County (Weiser) was always the person who introduced a right-to-work bill in the legislature. He had done so in 1955 and again in 1957. In 1958, the business community got the agricultural groups excited with the idea that Cesar Chavez was going to come north and organize the onion and potato fields. Chavez never came to Idaho for that purpose, but he did come to Sun Valley to a Democratic convention, where I am told he ate a green salad. The labor movement in Idaho in 1958 had some real substance, and they brought in some very talented organizers who concentrated in Pocatello and Lewiston where the union vote was normally pretty heavy. The union vote in those days was also of consequence in Ada and Canyon Counties. The organizers did not tend to debate the issue of right-to-work. They simply worked at getting out the vote that they could count on. It was an almost fatal arrow aimed at the heart of the Republican cause. The effect of this organizing effort was to just about double the union vote in both Nez Perce and Bannock Counties, and that was a formidable number.

Meanwhile, Mr. Derr had developed what he called a "potato plan," which was designed to get a decent price for field-run potatoes in eastern Idaho. They were then selling for about $1.25 per hundred-pound sack and farmers could barely afford the expense of harvesting them. Derr was an agile campaigner and very adroit at picking up issues, using them for a spell, and then dropping them. With the potato plan he got into the Republican stronghold of Madison, Jefferson, Bonneville, and Fremont Counties and was able to tear votes away from us in those places.

When we counted the votes on election night, I was the only Republican who survived as late as ten o'clock in the evening. Every constitutional officer, except the Governor, had gone down the drain. Both houses of the legislature had been returned with Democratic majorities that were veto proof, and Senator Derr and I walked past the midnight hour creating the lead by very narrow margins. At about two o'clock in the morning, I pulled even with him with some votes in Ada and Canyon Counties and then began to build a very minor lead. At four in the morning, James Brown from the *Statesman* called to tell me that I had a margin unofficially of about 4,000 votes and that he was going to declare me the winner. I was the only Republican to survive the Democratic landslide in 1958.

There were no historic parallels for that 1958 Idaho election. In the new government, the governor would be a minority of one on the Board of Examiners, on the State Board of Canvassers, and on the State Land Board, and any veto of legislation enacted by the legislature could be overridden with a purely partisan majority.

The press corps found this hilarious. They predicted all manner of political disasters, and, as a matter of fact, called it today's equivalent of political gridlock, or deadlock in their judgment. One commentator (he was no friend) even went so far as to suggest that I should take office and resign, making the newly elected lieutenant governor the governor of the state. I quickly realized that it was not a time for political high-jinks, but for adroit management of whatever assets were at hand. I was still going to be governor and in charge of the administration of the state, and that gave me leverage at all levels of government, with the possible exception of the attorney general's office, which was presided over by Frank Benson, who was almost paranoid in his feelings about Republicans.

The newly elected secretary of state was Arnold Williams from Rexburg, who had served as governor in 1945. I surmised correctly that as a result of his service in the governor's office he could be depended upon not to wish to dismantle the institution as an instrument of power. Joe Williams of Boise had been elected state auditor after a long career of having worked in that office and then leaving it when the Republicans took over in 1946. He was a friend of mine, and it was never difficult to work with him. He was, as a matter of fact, more often than not, a stalwart on my side of an issue. Delmer Engelking was the newly elected superintendent of public instruction, and he tended to be what he was elected to be and not to be very partisan about what he did. He always voted with the Democrats on the State Land Board but, other than that, was reasonably cooperative with the governor's office.

The newly elected lieutenant governor was William Drevlow of Craigmont, and his cooperation would be crucial to the success of my second governorship. I determined to reach out and try as best I could to accommodate his ambitions and desires and still have him be helpful in my conduct of the governor's office. Drevlow was a two-term state senator whose service in the upper house of the legislature had been relatively undistinguished, although satisfactory.

The test of our ability to cooperate was to come sooner than I thought. In late November of 1958, I was invited to address the fall meeting of the North Idaho Chamber of Commerce in Moscow, Idaho. As is still the custom, most of the legislators were the guests of one or another lobbyist at this annual dinner event. The lieutenant governor-elect was also in attendance. It seemed an excellent opportunity to do a little exploring of what the legislative attitude and the attitude of the lobbyists would be toward my new exercise in gubernatorial control.

I was introduced to speak at the banquet that evening by a young lawyer from Orofino named Ray McNichols. He was later to become a distinguished federal district judge under the patronage of Senator Frank Church and President Jack Kennedy. McNichols introduced me as the Crown Prince who was being held captive in his own capitol by a group of political enemies and who would not be able to accomplish much because he was in political deadlock with those who had won the election. McNichols, of course, was a Democrat. When I took the floor, I responded by relating a fable from Mr. James Thurber's book of cartoons which had originally appeared in *The New Yorker* magazine. I told McNichols and the crowd that the Crown Prince could identify foxes when he saw them even if they were roaming in the peach orchard that was occupied by his friends the orioles. The foxes decided that the orioles did not know how to run their business and savagely attacked them and destroyed the oriole covey. I told McNichols and the assembled audience that the moral of the story was the motto that would guide the Crown Prince in his conduct of their government—

that government of the orioles by the foxes and for the foxes must perish from this earth. The fable was greeted with hilarious laughter and was an excellent beginning for a speech that paid almost unending tribute to the loyalty and patriotism of the new lieutenant governor. I said I anticipated no difficulty in working with him or with the other elected officials, and that I would predict a successful tour of duty for all of us for the next four years. The headlines the next morning said that "Smylie Lauds Drevlow."

In mid-December, when Mr. Drevlow came to town to ready the legislative chambers for the convening of the session beginning in January, he came into my office and said that he knew he had been elected to be lieutenant governor and that he did not confuse himself with the governor and thought we would get along very well. It developed that my gamble with oratorical praise had been successful.

Drevlow and I worked out a modus vivendi whereby he would appoint vacancies in county offices but go no further than that in my absences from the state. This freed me up from any worry of adverse appointments originating with him. As it turned out, the only real difficulty with having a lieutenant governor of the opposite party was the count that Richard Charnock of the United Press used to keep track of my absences from the state. Mr. Drevlow had an enthusiasm for collecting paychecks, and, as a consequence, never failed to put in a bill for any time that I was absent from the state. Often this was less than a day when I went to Spokane or Salt Lake City. Nonetheless, in Charnock's diary that counted as a day. The total, especially after my trip to Russia, grew to be quite large. Charnock's calendar of my absences did become an embarrassment. There was a political precinct committeeman (a Democrat of course) who lived up on Hays Street, along which I traveled en route to the residence when I went home in the evening. Whenever I had been out of town or out of the state, he noted it and always hung up a sign welcoming me back to Boise. This grew to be a little tiresome and did have some political repercussions as time wore on.

When the political winds blow with tornado-like force, as they did in Idaho in 1958, it is useful for history to inquire about what happened and why. The newspaper pundits, the political seers, and the politicians in both parties have already ventured their thinking on this. Because I was at the eye of the storm, it seems appropriate for me to give my view of the events of the last six months of 1958.

Certainly there were other issues of consequence, but essentially it was the economy that came close to bringing me down. In 1958, the Idaho farmer did not tolerate potatoes selling at a dollar per hundredweight or cattle prices that made steak a common food staple. We should have heard the economic storm brewing and taken some steps to counter its political effect, but we didn't do it until it was too late.

Idaho people have a tendency to like to balance their government between the parties by making frequent changes. The history of the first hundred years indicates that quite well. There had to be a lot of voters who voted for me as governor and for Bill Drevlow as lieutenant governor, well realizing that we were from opposite parties. This did not make much difference to them. I'm sure they thought one of us would be a check on the other.

Senator Derr was looking for some way to avoid taking a stand on the need for additional revenue, and he hit upon casino gambling legalization as a way of doing that. All through the fifties and early sixties, the Democratic party had a penchant for espousing the cause of casino gambling. Senator Derr took that stand, I think, partly because of his strength in the northern counties where gambling and other forms of open license had been a way of life. Ever since the legalization of liquor by the drink, and the ability to use licensing processes as a means of enforcing the antigambling laws, we forced the issue so that it was one which could no longer be avoided. By 1958, gambling was at a minimum in most of the counties. That is not to say that people favored doing away with it, it was just that if you wanted to have a liquor license from the state, you had to be very careful about whether or not you broke the gambling laws. Derr's casino gambling plan would have given us a few places that would have been like Elko, Jackpot, or Winnemucca, Nevada, and not much more. They would not have attracted the tourist trade and would have simply provided a convenient and easy method for fleecing each other. I doubt that casino gambling ever had more than about forty-six percent support among the voters of Idaho. Therefore, I do not think that issue was determinative in the 1958 election. It was the economy that was dominant.

In my judgment, it was the right-to-work issue which determined the outcome of the 1958 gubernatorial race. Senator Derr had taken the issue more or less for granted. It was political folklore that unless a Democratic candidate for statewide office carried Lewiston and Pocatello by almost immense majorities, he could not win. Derr left Pocatello and Lewiston pretty much to their own devices and to the operations of the AFL-CIO agents who were sent in to organize the vote against the right-to-work initiative. Lewiston was the stronghold of Mr. Tom Boise, who had a vested interest in the achievement of open casino-type gambling on a statewide basis because he owned properties that would benefit from it. It was pretty difficult to fight his political organization on its own ground. For that reason, I concentrated on Bannock County and Pocatello in an endeavor to cut the thrust of the anti-right-to-work organizers.

It was pretty well understood that I was personally opposed to the right-to-work initiative, and I had said openly that I would vote against it. I said this because I thought this was an issue on which the legislature should stand up and be counted.

In 1954, I had come very close to carrying Bannock County, so for that reason, I thought it might well be a target of opportunity. I shook hands with every worker in and out of the gates of the FMC plant and the J. R. Simplot plant in Pocatello, one of the largest fertilizer processing companies in the United States, at every shift change on at least two occasions. I had some political paraphernalia to hand out that was designed especially for that type of voter. The Pocatello labor movement had strong leadership in those days, although it was mostly Democratic in its political orientation. We had a pretty strong Republican organization in Bannock County, and the leaders of the labor movement left me alone to court the voters at the big places of employment. Our efforts were successful and we carried Bannock County by a very narrow margin. It was enough to offset Derr's need for votes statewide

Our famous Girl Scout tea of February 27, 1955. The Girl Scouts are, left to right, Beth Rodwell, Kip McCormick, June Thompson, Rebecca Hogg, Sue Holmes, and Kristin Artis.

and perhaps even furnished the margin of victory that finally showed us the way home.

Last, but not least, there were the votes we gleaned from the Girl Scout tea in February of 1955. There were about 3,000 young ladies at that tea, and that too may well have provided a margin. In the last analysis, it would seem to me that Mr. Derr's too late embracing of his potato plan, his soft-pedaling of his gambling issue, and his failure to take advantage of the anti-right-to-work organization that was going on were what permitted me to be the sole survivor of the Republican catastrophe.

The Derr campaign was the first major flirtation by the statewide Democratic Party with the gambling issue as a means of financing government. They would try it again four years later, and then with the same results. Their candidate would be the erstwhile Republican Vernon K. Smith, a Boise lawyer whom I came to characterize as "the man with the green eyeshade" because of his espousal of gambling as the balm for Idaho's financial ills.

CHAPTER NINE

THE SECOND GOVERNORSHIP—1959–63

IDAHO'S STATE GOVERNMENT was caught in political gridlock at the beginning of 1959. Being confronted with a situation in which every constitutional board and agency and all of the constitutional offices, except the one to which I had been elected, were held by members of the opposition party was a bleak political prospect and not one which gave much promise in the way of progress for programs of benefit to the people. There was little reason to believe that I was not, as Judge McNichols had said, held prisoner in my own statehouse.

In retrospect, I think the Democrats were as surprised by their victory in 1958 as the Republicans were. Most of the winners in the Democratic primary elections of 1958 had been from the wool-hat remnant of the party that still could remember that it didn't like Franklin Roosevelt or Harry Truman. Robert Doolittle, the Speaker of the House of Representatives, was from a little town in Bonner County called Priest River, which had a population of about 200 people and was not a center of forward-looking political doctrine. Lieutenant Governor Drevlow was a resident of Craigmont in Lewis County, one of Idaho's least populous areas, and was not possessed of any great political theory or skill. He did know how to attract voters to his banner, and that proved to be his principal worth to the Democratic party.

Senate President Pro Tem O. J. Buxton was from Driggs, the county seat of Teton County next to the Wyoming border and another very small Idaho county. The Democratic convention in 1958 had been dominated by its attention to Alfred Derr's plank on legalized casino gambling. Most of the wool-hat Democrats were opposed to the plan, but had no way of escaping from endorsing it. As a consequence, they faced the convening of the legislature in 1959 without any coherent program for the state, with the possible exception of a somewhat grudging devotion to money for education.

The newly elected secretary of state, Arnold Williams, had succeeded to the office of governor after Senator Gossett appointed himself to the Senate in November 1945 when Senator John Thomas died. He had been treated rather badly by Republican members of the state

I joined Joe Albertson in celebrating the opening of Albertson's expanded "flagship store" in Boise on July 15, 1958.

Senate when he was governor. As a result, he tried to organize a vendetta against me because he thought that was the way for the Democrats to get the office of governor back again. Fortunately, Ruth Moon and Joe Williams, who had been elected to be state treasurer and state auditor respectively, would have no part of a partisan vendetta.

There were some bright spots on the Democratic side in the legislative lineup. Senator Howard Hechtner from Nez Perce County (Lewiston) and James Monroe from that same county were in leadership positions, but their hands were pretty well tied with the local political necessity of bringing back an adequate appropriation for Lewis-Clark State College and, they hoped, for reinstating a four-year degree again at that reviving institution.

There were others in that Democratic front line who had political talent. There was Don Pieper from Idaho Falls (we called him the Peerless Pieper), and he tended to contribute a good deal of humor to the work of the legislature. Unfortunately, he chose not to realize his full potential. John Evans from Malad, who would later be governor, was another who offered considerable Democratic leadership, but he was then, as now, fairly and consistently ultra-partisan, and for that reason not the kind of anvil on which you could forge cooperative, bipartisan achievement.

I spent November and December of 1958 trying to evolve a plan of action that would permit us to cope successfully with this new Democratic majority, which could work its will with us if it wanted. I talked on the phone with Charles Halleck, a member of Congress from Indiana, who was then minority leader in the House of Representatives. He had been obliged to accommodate Purdue University in his constituency for the last twenty years and had shown talent for political accommodation. He said if he were in my position he would move to the center, try to take over all of the new ideas that the Democrats put forward, and give them a little work of his own that might result in passage into law. I also consulted with former Governors C. A. Robins and Charles Gossett, one a Republican and the other a Democrat. They both counseled patience and said that it was not really necessary to enact a whole program just to show progress. Dr. Robins suggested

I not only wrote but typed my own speeches. This is in the governor's office. ISHS 77-163.46.

picking out two items and using them as the vehicle for a Republican program. He suggested, as I would have decided anyway, that education was one item that could do with consistent improvement, and that a highway program to match President Eisenhower's Highway Act of 1956 was not only indicated, but required. I also scouted around the state with some of my county leaders and other former members of the legislature, but mostly they couldn't get away from what they thought were the unavoidable consequences of the election disaster and the projected resulting gridlock. They did not take into consideration the ineptness of the Democratic majority or its lack of a program. That ultimately was what saved us.

When the consultations were ended, the loneliness of power set in. We had to decide what we would tell the legislature in January and how we would do the job that we had laid out in our campaign. The education program would cost more money and the highway user taxes would have to be increased to support an increased highway program. Correctly analyzed, the election results had told us that the people did not want casino-type gambling legalized nor did they want increased taxes. We found ourselves between a rock and hard place. On these premises we set about trying to build a satisfactory budget and a message on the state of the state that would be appropriate and politically palatable.

Our first task was to construct a budget for the fiscal period of two years commencing on July 1, 1959. The departmental and institutional proposals for expenditures for that period were far in excess of what might reasonably be expected in the way of enhanced revenues. This made it necessary at the inception to consider what things we were going to have to do without.

This was not an easy chore. Then, as now, the major portion of the state budget was used to pay the costs of public school education, the universities, the various public assistance programs, and public health. Only the university and state college budgets were capable of being reduced, although some savings could be accomplished by trimming the sails of various public health programs. The public school estimates were set by a formula that was enacted into law by the legislature two years earlier, and that figure could not be reduced. The public assistance budget contained funds for old-age assistance and aid to dependent children. Those were so politically sensitive that reducing the sum total of expenditures was very difficult. While campaigning for reelection, I had stated that we would once again fulfill the complete requirements of the public school equalization formula and appropriate funds to meet those costs. I was determined to keep this promise and the commitment was set forth in the budget that we sent to the legislature.

I asked presidents Dr. Donald Theophilus at the University of Idaho and Dr. Carl McIntosh at Idaho State College to give me an estimate of the bare-bones budget they could live with for the next thirty months. I made it quite clear that I was not talking about what we would like to do, but what we would have to do and how much it would take to pay for that work. After considerable soul searching, both

Theophilus and McIntosh obliged me with numbers saying that they were inadequate and that their institutions would suffer. I said that I knew that, and we would try to make it up in the next budget.

Some very minimal savings were possible in the public health budgets, and we took advantage of them in order to make it quite clear that everyone was being treated austerely in the preparation of this budget. We were able to trim some fat out of the remaining portions of the budget, but this amounted to so little in the way of dollar totals that it was difficult to make much progress in reducing the total amount of the appropriated requests so that they would match anticipated revenues. Projecting revenues in 1959 was not the thing of smoke and mirrors that it has now become. The task was to outguess thirty months of economic history that had not yet occurred and to make provision for two and a half years of government out of what data were available.

By the time we were putting the budget together at the end of 1958, the so-called "liquor curve" that Mr. Charlton presided over at the dispensary had begun to turn around and people were buying better whiskey than at the end of 1957. This seemed to make it safe to assume that they felt a little bit more secure about their employment and their money, and these facts would be reflected in the income tax returns that would be coming in through the thirty-month period. The banking statistics were increasingly favorable, and the general attitude of the public toward the economy seemed to be improving. This I thought justified a little overconfidence in our estimates of revenue from income taxes and from the so-called nuisance taxes on cigarettes and liquor and other types of excises.

It is obvious that these were primitive horse-and-buggy, seat-of-the-pants methods of projecting revenue estimates, but strangely they seemed to work. I think history will record that we were closer to having budgets that balanced without deficits or surpluses over those twelve years than many of the budgets that have been taken to the legislature in the years since then. We were lucky in our projections of revenue, but I think history records that we were intelligently lucky.

Estimating revenue and projecting expenditures were easier when the process only occurred once every two years. I think annual budgeting is very wasteful and can't keep up with expenditures. It is no substitute for vigorous, tight executive control. If a governor can be trusted to use his veto power, then he can be trusted to call special sessions for limited purposes when and if that becomes necessary. There is really very little excuse for the legislature meeting annually except to make being a legislator a sort of semi-profession and one which does not provide as much in the way of public good as is widely supposed. I think we had more effective legislatures when they were paid less money and met less often.

We had trimmed the departmental and institutional estimates to comport with our ideas of what revenues would be available, and we closed the budget at $70.9 million of general fund expenditures. In those days, we called the big fund the general fund and not the general account, as is now the habit. We sent the budget book to the printers and set about contriving a message that would present a palatable program and keep the Democratic legislature busy for the next sixty days.

As I mentioned, the Democrats had been surprised by the magnitude of their electoral victory. I did not think in their wildest moments that they had thought they would control both houses of the legislature by a two-thirds majority and all of the offices in the statehouse except one. As a consequence, they had no program to put forward in opposition to whatever it was I might propose. I think this was the result of disarray in the Democratic primary of that year. Senator Frank Church had neglected to take command of the policy-making processes of the party, I think largely because he and his troops were dismayed that John Glasby had not been nominated for governor. They sought to distance themselves from the candidacy of Alfred Derr and his casino gambling proposals. Senator Derr had made a considerable number of speeches about more money for education and about reorganizing—in these days they would call it reinventing—government, but he was short on specific proposals. As is usually the case when confronted with a candidacy like Derr's, the individual legislators tended to run their own campaigns on their own platforms in their own way.

There were few political issues in that 1959 session that were purely partisan. It was also difficult to attempt to differentiate on issues between conservatives and so-called liberals. The conservatives generally tended, in both parties, to want to spend less money and the liberals wanted to spend more. Therefore, leadership and progress could be found primarily in the middle of that spectrum.

We developed a program of governmental reorganization that involved a bundle of ideas about what to do with our unwieldy constitutional government. It would have required a flock of constitutional amendments, and I had no real hope that the Democrats would ever give us the two-thirds majority that we needed to send these proposals to the ballot. I proposed abolition of the office of lieutenant governor and placing the secretary of state second in line for the governorship should the governor be unable to serve. I proposed abolishing the office of state mine inspector as an elective office and making it an appointive bureau in the Department of Public Lands. I proposed combining the state auditor and state treasurer's offices into one office of controller general and giving it the duties of the existing offices. I proposed making the state superintendent of Public Instruction an office appointed by the State Board of Education with the approval of the governor. The Board of Examiners and the State Board of Land Commissioners would have been reconstituted to conform with the new constitutional alignment.

As I had anticipated, it developed almost immediately that the Democrats would rather discuss reorganization than actually reorganize government.

Mindful that the recession of 1958 was still not ended and that unemployment figures were running higher than they should, I suggested an increase in unemployment compensation benefits and an extension of the period for which they were applicable. This met with opposition from the state Chamber of Commerce, but the big lumber companies and the mining companies backed the proposal. Speaker of the House Robert Doolittle commenced a long fight against the increase until it was pointed out to him that Bonner County, which he represented, received the most money in the way of unemployment compensation benefits of any Idaho county and that all the towns in

Bonner County received the largest amount of benefits. This tended to bend his thinking in the direction of passage of the proposal.

I suggested an increase in the highway-user revenues in order to be able to get on with building a statewide network of state highways and commencing work on the interstate highway system that had been authorized by the 1956 Highway Act, which had been enacted by

Nelson Rockefeller, on a 1959 campaign swing, greets two youngsters at the Boise airport. At right is his wife Mary.

Congress at the instance of President Eisenhower. The legislature responded with an increase in the gasoline tax.

Meeting the requirements of the public school equalization formula required only a modest increase in appropriations. As I had predicted, the Democrats in the legislature found it necessary to restudy and reevaluate the formula in order to permit the expenditure under the formula of additional funds. I indicated to their leadership that I would have no objection to this if they provided the funds with which to pay the bill.

After wrestling at some length with the various types of taxation that might close the gap their expenditures had created, the legislature finally came up with a tax which they euphemistically termed "the income tax license fee" of ten dollars per return. We did a bit of quick arithmetic and arrived at the conclusion that this fee would indeed close the gap between the expenditures and revenues that the education bill created, and I signed the bill and sent the legislature home in varying degrees of unhappiness.

The Republicans quickly began referring to the ten dollar license tax as a "head tax," which was reminiscent of the old discredited poll taxes that had been collected in the southern states for many years. We routinely requested that the tax be repealed, but we did so with tongue in cheek, and it is curious that the ten dollar tax is still on the books some forty years later. It is the best example I know of the fact that a tax once enacted never goes away. You can find it on the second page of your income tax return—a mandatory ten dollars printed in. When the need for it in the general revenues had disappeared, we managed to slide the ten dollar tax over into the public permanent building fund, and that provided a basis for building funds for various state institutions. To my knowledge no one has ever seriously considered repealing it. I referred to the "license fee" in the 1960 campaign as "that grisly thing." I was being grossly unfair, but 1960 was a political year, as we found out later with the victory of John Kennedy.

Upon adjournment of the legislature, the Republicans initiated plans to retake control of at least one house of the legislature and perhaps two. The first step in the execution of this plan was to secure candidates who would vigorously contest every seat in the legislature. This involved offending some old Democratic allies, such as Howard Hechtner and James Monroe, who had been staunch friends. Seats like Hechtner's and Monroe's could not really be successfully contested, but it kept them busy if they had opposition.

We also organized a so-called campaign school with a faculty that could be taken on the road and which held meetings with legislative candidates in seven different locations around the state. This gave us an opportunity to indoctrinate new candidates and to update those who were running for reelection or who had previously served, and it provided an opportunity for us to get to know some of the players who would be of importance in the 1960 elections. It also provided a means of acquainting sources for financial support with these legislators so that when a need for funds for their campaigns arose, we would have someone we could turn to. This was probably the first state central committee intervention in local legislative races in the history of the Idaho legislature where both academic and financial support were made available. The effort was much more successful than we had hoped. Our goal was to recapture control of the House of Representatives, but we were fortunate in ending up with a thirty to twenty-nine margin in the House and a twenty-three to twenty-one margin in the Senate in the elections in 1960.

There is an ironic footnote to this highly successful endeavor to recapture control of the Idaho legislature. In searching for a candidate to oppose an incumbent state senator in Bonner County, we discovered a drill-tool salesman named Don Samuelson who was willing to undertake the race. I encouraged him to enter the campaign and arranged some financing for him, and also campaigned around Bonner County one day on his behalf. He was elected. It was the same Don Samuelson who would cost me the governorship in 1966. Samuelson was a far-right conservative and was chosen by that wing of the party to seek revenge against me for my progressive style of government.

Although we won a famous victory in the 1960 election, it was not the kind of victory that was productive of legislative progress. The Democrats insisted on tinkering with the election laws on the theory that somehow their primary was always invaded and they were denied the opportunity to nominate a candidate who could win. This really was not the case. What was wrong with the Democratic party in those days was that it refused to quit toying with the idea that casino gambling would provide a means of meeting all the financial problems of the state.

The principal accomplishment of the 1961 session was the establishment of the Permanent Building Fund and the Permanent Building Fund Advisory Council, which provided a method of meeting, ultimately, the needs of the state. It was not adequately financed, but it wouldn't be until some new source of revenue, i.e., the sales tax, was enacted to fill the gap.

We did increase support for public schools and for our public health programs, but we turned our attention now to the possibility of running for a third term in order to be able to accept Senator Dworshak's challenge to run for his seat in the Senate in 1966.

CHAPTER TEN

INTERNATIONAL TRAVELS—RUSSIA, ARGENTINA, BRAZIL, JAPAN, AND MEXICO

MY LOYAL OPPOSITION tried valiantly during my first term to make political capital out of the fact that I was out of the state for many days. Most of these trips did not cost the state anything and were made for political purposes in response to invitations arranged by Republican National Chairman Leonard Hall of New York. I think the Democrats had difficulty understanding why the governor of Idaho was invited to speak in places like Los Angeles, San Francisco, Salt Lake City, New York, Toledo, and Des Moines. I do not think it had ever happened before, and thus it introduced a new dimension to the governorship of Idaho.

Little did the opposition know that they had seen just the beginning. My second term was to take me on travels that led to four continents and five independent nations. The first of these, and the most exciting, was Russia.

In mid-March of 1959, I was designated by the Governors' Conference of the United States as one of six governors who would receive an invitation to make a five-week visit to the Union of Soviet Socialist Republics. I called Lieutenant Governor William Drevlow and informed him about the invitation. I asked if it would be offensive to him if I left the state for nearly six weeks. Drevlow told me that it was no problem and that there would be no partisan, political high-jinks while I was gone. I accepted the invitation and began reading up on Russian history and geography, a daunting assignment and one that could not be completed in two or three weeks. I brushed past most of the history and tried to concentrate on gaining insight into modern Soviet Communist ideology.

The trip began in Washington with a visit to the White House and a conference with President Eisenhower. We were extensively briefed by the State Department, by the FBI, and by the CIA with helpful hints about what not to do. No one ever told us whether we had a mission or not, although it was generally understood that this would be a forerunner for a presidential visit to the Union of Soviet Socialist Republics. Chairman Nikita S. Krushchev had visited the United States the year before, and a return trip by President Eisenhower was cooking on the back burner. These were the first of the so-called Summit Conferences.

We departed New York the next day in time to arrive in Paris for lunch on the Eiffel Tower and then departed Paris for Moscow. We were met by staff members of the Ministry of Foreign Affairs who dutifully collected our passports and disappeared. We proceeded in surprisingly fancy limousines to the hotel, which was called Sovietskaya. It was a guest house for very important visitors and was elegant and modern, although decorated in a heavy Russian style. We were told that we would have very little need for money but we could exchange dollars at the hotel at the rate of a dollar for ten rubles for small items we might wish to buy.

The next day we met with some of the ministers of the Russian Republic. We had filed a proposed itinerary with the Russian Embassy in Washington, but the ministers in Moscow claimed never to have heard of it. They suggested that we take a trip to Leningrad and then come back and see them again. It was curious that Leningrad was the first stop that we had put on our proposed itinerary.

The Russians were excessively proud of their high-speed train between Leningrad and Moscow, which they called The Red Star. The train departed from Leningrad and Moscow at midnight for arrival in the other city at eight o'clock in the morning. This was late in June, and it would be daylight almost all of the twenty-four-hour span of the clock. We left Moscow at midnight and by 1:30 in the morning it was still almost full daylight, so we had a daylight trip to Leningrad. Leningrad, formerly St. Petersburg and now St. Petersburg again, was the imperial capital of the Romanov dynasty from the time of Peter the Great until the fall of the Romanovs in 1917.

Our arrival there was a little more gracious. We were met at the station by Ivan Ivanovich Smirnoff, chairman of the Leningrad City Central Soviet, a position roughly equivalent to that of the mayor of Chicago. Smirnoff asked us to have lunch with him and his council of ministers at the Hall of Ministers in downtown Leningrad, and we

The Associated Press photographed five of us governors strolling through Red Square on June 25, 1959. From left: Cecil Underwood of West Virginia, Robert Meyner of New Jersey, myself, Leroy Collins of Florida, and Luther Evans of North Carolina.

accepted and went to the Hotel Astoria first to spruce up. At lunch, Smirnoff invited us to be his guests at the Kirov ballet performance of *Spartacus* that evening.

The next two days were devoted to a whirlwind tour of the historic sights of old Leningrad, including the Winter Palace (now the Hermitage Museum), Smolny Institute and the Summer Palace at Petrodvorets, the Fortress of Peter and Paul, the Coronation Cathedral, the Admiralty Buildings, the Port of Leningrad, and the great equestrian statue of Peter the Great. We toured an impressive machine-tool factory where a turbine was being manufactured for one of the power plants on the Volga River. I was told that it was the largest turbine that had ever been crafted for service in a hydroelectric plant.

The two days ended with a dinner party given in our honor by Smirnoff and his ministers in the boathouse of Catherine the Great on the Neva River. It was a night filled with music, good fellowship, excellent food, and copious amounts of vodka. The Russians took us to the train station and saw us off for Moscow while singing rollicking Russian folk songs. Leningrad was reputed to be the most European of Russian cities, and the questions which the ministers asked were pretty much a confirmation of that fact. They inquired about families and houses and schools and institutes, which was their word for community college. I told Smirnoff that I had two sons, and he asked their ages. He remembered them when he came to Boise on a return visit a year later and brought the boys a toy bear that danced and talked.

Upon our return to Moscow, we commenced negotiations again about our itinerary. Meanwhile the Russian hosts had set up a trip to their laboratory at Dubna and visits to the Moscow Circus, to the theater, and, as a special treat, to the Bolshoi Theater to see Ulanova dance the lead in the ballet *Swan Lake*.

In our negotiations about the itinerary, we had renewed our request for a conference or audience with Russian leaders at the highest levels. We were told that this was unlikely, but that it would be presented for decision. At the end of two days, they handed us an itinerary that would take us all around Russia, and, strangely enough, it was identical to the itinerary which we had submitted to them before we left Washington, D.C.

We were scheduled to leave Moscow for Kiev in the Ukraine that evening. Our Russian hosts tendered us a stand-up reception at Aragvi, the Republic of Georgia restaurant in the Russian capital. It was a splendid affair and the food was excellent. The Russians, as was their wont, were prodigious partakers of vodka. I suppose if we had stayed much longer that afternoon, it would have become a fairly inebriated affair.

Before leaving Moscow, I had sent a wire to Lucille in Boise asking her to call me at four A.M. Kiev time, which was roughly three P.M. in Boise. The telephone lines were open then to the transatlantic operator in London. I had asked her to assemble members of the government who might want to talk with me so we could dispatch any business that needed to be done quickly. Promptly at four A.M. Ukraine time, the telephone jangled with my call from stateside. Lu and I had a brief visit, I spoke with the two boys, and then I talked with members of the government in what amounted to a cabinet meeting via long-distance telephone halfway around the world.

Kiev was a city which had been reduced almost to rubble in World War II when the Germans and Russians fought back and forth across it four times before finally surrendering it to the Russians and to history on the fifth assault. By 1959 it had been almost completely restored and was a beautiful city of broad boulevards and ten- and twelve-story apartment buildings adorned with balconies that were covered with geranium plants and other greenery.

The only Ukrainian government official whom we met with was the minister of agriculture, who took us to an agricultural affair that was impressive. We toured the city and visited somewhat freely with citizens up and down the street. There were soldiers in Kiev who looked like garrison troops; that was the first time we had seen a military presence anywhere in Russia.

From Kiev we went on to Sochi, a Black Sea resort almost next door to fabled Yalta. These resorts were the winter playground of the

Russian hierarchy, and a dacha at either Sochi or Yalta was viewed as a tremendous asset. Our stay on the shores of the Black Sea was only five or six hours long, and we flew on from there to Tbilisi, the capital of the Republic of Georgia.

Our hotel in Tbilisi was located on the Avenue Rostonveli, which is said to be one of the oldest streets in the world. It was the highway along which Alexander marched his Macedonian troops when they were en route to the conquest of India, and one could see the remains of the bridges they built across the river upstream from the city of Tbilisi if you looked closely and knew where they were to be found.

We arrived in Tbilisi on July 3, and our Georgian hosts insisted that they entertain us at dinner in a restaurant 2,000 feet above the city. You reached the restaurant by way of a cogged railroad that ran from the Avenue Rostonveli to the restaurant's front door. When we boarded the railroad car, we did not know how abruptly steep the ascent to the restaurant would be, but by that time it was too late to worry.

The next day we went to a collective farm outside of the city and were entertained at a picnic in an apple orchard with food, music, and dance. The music and the dancing had a great resemblance to the music and dances performed by our own Basque people, and it made one wonder if deep in the recesses of history the Basque had passed through the Georgian valley. That evening we received a message that "persons at the highest level of the government of the USSR" wanted to have an audience with us, setting the time for this occasion at three P.M. Moscow time the next day. The message obviously meant that Mr. Krushchev was going to receive us. We took the early plane from Tbilisi to Moscow the next morning, went to the hotel to clean up, and prepared to go to the Kremlin to meet the Russian leader.

Limousines had been furnished, and we drove up Leninskaya Prospekt to Red Square, past St. Basil's Church, through the Moscow River entrance to the Kremlin wall, and up to the building in which our appointment was to take place. We went up a flight of stairs and entered a hall that appeared to be about sixty feet long by thirty feet wide. I was told later that it was the hall where the meetings of the Council of Ministers of the USSR took place. This would make it very similar to the Cabinet Room in the White House. There was a long table in the center of the room that was about six feet across with an array of soft drinks on it. Over against the wall in a sort of receiving line was Chairman Krushchev surrounded by our interpreter from the U.S. Embassy and his interpreter and a fourth person whom I took to be a security person.

To my great surprise, I knew the interpreter for Chairman Krushchev. He was Oleg Troyanovski, the son of the first ambassador from the USSR to the United States, who accompanied his father to Washington in the early years of the second Roosevelt administration. Oleg had attended George Washington University when I was in law school there. We used to meet at a restaurant on Connecticut Avenue called the Deauville, and I formed a fairly close student friendship with him. I did not think that I would ever see him interpreting for Krushchev back home in Russia, but there he was. We had a chance to chat later in the day for a few moments, and he said he got to the United States about once every two or three years to hone his linguistic skills. As an official interpreter for the Kremlin, he operated at extremely high levels in the government of the Soviet Union.

As chairman of the Central Committee of the Soviet Party of the USSR, Nikita Krushchev was the most important political leader in all of Russia. He was not a physically impressive person. He was short and fat, and although he was inclined to be jovial, he had a hard, mean look about him that would have told almost anyone to beware. During the conference, it became very apparent to me that he had a good staff and he knew how to use them. He had done his homework. For instance, he was well aware of the fact that the Idaho State Police had stopped and detained two trucks containing a shipment of Russian shrimp in Sandpoint, Idaho. The truckers had dropped down into the United States in northern Idaho in order to detour around a break in the trans-Canadian highway. He reminded me of the incident almost as soon as we met, and I was very greatly surprised that a matter of such minute importance would have come to the attention of the chairman of the Soviet Union.

The conference took a total of about three and a half hours, although the useful portion of the conference would have to be reduced by at least two-thirds if time hadn't been taken up by translation and interpretation. Krushchev did not give us any startling information, although in response to questions he said there would always be two Germanies and there would always be two Chinas. Forty years later, he turns out to have been half right, which is not a bad batting average for someone engaged in trying to outguess a half-century of history. He asked intelligent questions about our several states. He knew, for instance, about Idaho potatoes and said jokingly that their potatoes were not very good by comparison. I would have to say that I agreed with him.

When the conference concluded, he presented each one of us with a small box containing a replica of Sputnik, about which he had engaged in considerable braggadocio. The replica was a small music box which, when you wound it up, played the "International," the Soviet national anthem, which is known to us by the title "Arise Ye Prisoners of Starvation." We cordially invited Chairman Krushchev or his representatives to come and visit us in our states and then took our leave.

I did not think then, nor do I think now, that anything very important was accomplished by the visit with Krushchev, but it was an exciting adventure for a young governor from Idaho and I am pleased that I was able to undertake the trip.

We left Moscow the next morning and journeyed to Tashkent, the capital of Uzbekistan deep in the Moslem country of Central Asia. This was agricultural land, and I was particularly interested in their irrigation systems because many of them had been designed under the direction of Mr. Lyman Wilbur of Boise, who was a Morrison Knudsen engineer in those days.

I had expressed a desire to go to Samarkand, where a great restoration project was under way, and it developed that we could take a side trip there. Samarkand was the ancient capital of Tamerlane, a descendant of Genghis Khan, who was another of the great Mongol conquerors. The restoration project in Samarkand was so interesting that it would be a joy to go back and take a second look at it. The Mosque of Bebekhanum was being restored with little tiles exactly like the ones that had adorned it originally, and the other buildings in the compound of "Timur the Lame" were also being rebuilt. We had lunch at a collective farm, and, after an afternoon of sightseeing, returned to Tashkent and departed for Alma-Ata.

Alma-Ata was the capital of the Kazak Republic, the easternmost territory of great Russia, and was only ninety-five miles from the Chinese border. As nearly as I could determine, there were no border crossings or travel across the border allowed. The border must have been heavily armed because there was evidence of Russian troops in and around Alma-Ata. Alma-Ata had been one of Joseph Stalin's favorite resorts. He was said to have come there regularly simply to rest. There were no hotels in Alma-Ata of consequence, so we stayed in a dacha a short distance out of town. It may well have been one of those used by Stalin. Halfway up the hill across a ravine from our dacha was a little stone house that was the neighborhood sauna. It was here that I had my first experience with coeducational saunas where dress was optional. The sauna was attended by an old babushka who came and yelled at you to turn around and then beat your back with willow switches. This was said to be good for you and to encourage circulation. The sauna was for the general use of the dwellers in the suburb and belonged to nobody in particular. I guess it was just proof that it takes a neighborhood to make a village.

The countryside around Alma-Ata was agricultural and looked a good deal like the Finnish country in the Long Valley north of Boise. There were a lot of birch trees and conifers and what probably was an Asiatic equivalent of the quaking aspen, with which we are familiar. We arrived at the height of the growing season, and the country vegetables were excellent. We had lunch at a collective farm on the outskirts of Alma-Ata and enjoyed it very much. The next morning we boarded an airplane that would take us nonstop to Moscow, a flight of about four hours. When you saw the airport at Alma-Ata, you knew that you were on the borders of Russia. It was very heavily militarized and many military planes were in evidence.

When we arrived in Moscow we went to the hotel to pack for the trip home. That night I went with three or four other members of our party to a restaurant in the center of Moscow which was reputed to be one of the best. It turns out that its reputation was not overstated, and we had an excellent meal and said goodbye to some of the resident newspaper people from the United States who had been introduced to us by Henry Shapiro. Shapiro had been a resident correspondent in Moscow for seventeen years for United Press. He tried very hard to be friendly and helpful, but I always thought that his long residence there made him suspect to anybody who was not part of the Soviet apparatus.

Next morning I got somebody to take me down to Red Square to GUM, the department store, to buy a record of the song called "Moscow Evenings," which had been a part of the great celebration on the evening we left Leningrad. I found it without difficulty and took a look around the store. The Russian people were busily grabbing up wrist watches and phonograph records and cameras and other consumer goods that they had been without for many years. It was obvious that Chairman Krushchev's experiment in furnishing goods to the consumers was in full swing and was very much appreciated by the public. About noon we left for the airport and went through the process of getting our luggage through Russian customs. This, it turned out, was a major effort. I started trying to clear customs at about one o'clock, and at five I was still at the airport waiting to get aboard the Scandinavian Air Systems plane for Stockholm. Finally everybody in our party had boarded except myself, and I was seated in the airport lounge with two *apparatchiks* of the Ministry of Foreign Affairs who said they wished to visit with me. They wanted to know if I thought the governors really meant it when they invited the Russians to send a delegation (they liked that word) to visit our states. I assured them that everybody was sincere, and that they could send a delegation with every hope that it would be well received. They told me that it was the view of the Russian government that more cultural exchanges should take place, and I said I would carry that message to our president. With this they handed me my passport and my clearance from the airport, shook hands, and said goodbye. I walked out to the airplane and got on SAS Flight 1401 for Stockholm. Very shortly we were taxiing for takeoff and had our wheels up for the flight up the Gulf of Finland and out over the Baltic Sea to the estuary that led to Stockholm. I do not know whether it was the air conditioning on the Swedish plane which made things seem so different, but even the air smelled clean for a change.

I do not know whether the Russians knew at the time we were leaving Moscow that Gary Powers was down with his U-2 flight that had been carrying out reconnaissance over the Russian heartland, which occurred on May 1, 1960. In retrospect, it is obvious that they knew all about the U-2 flights, but whether or not they had managed to stop one remains a secret.

One can only speculate about whether a trip like this was worthwhile or necessary or if it served a useful purpose. The White House apparently thought so because they called us all back to Washington to give the president a report on what we had observed, and we did this willingly. The appetite of Idaho people for information about Russia was pretty intense, and I was invited to make upwards of 150 speeches in the state that were devoted in one way or another to distributing information about Russia. I also made about 25 speeches outside the state.

The governments of Argentina and Brazil subsequently invited a group of fifteen American governors to visit those two countries in November 1960. Mrs. Smylie and I were among those included. The trip was to be undertaken solely at the expense of the governments of Argentina and Brazil and at no cost to the American governors. This was an offer too good to be turned down.

Mrs. Smylie had spent some time as a secretary in the United States Embassy to Brazil during the war years 1942 and 1943. She came home at the end of 1943 traveling shipside on Pan American clippers to meet me in New York and we were married. As a part of the consideration, I promised to take her back to Rio sometime in the future. The future had now arrived.

This was essentially a "show me" trip to give the American governors more information about Brazil and Argentina. It had no visible connection to the task that I had undertaken to govern Idaho, yet, to my great surprise, my loyal opposition had no objection at all to our journey to South America, although they did seem to have great objection to my traveling to Los Angeles and San Francisco when I went there at no expense to the state to make a political speech. I finally decided that objections to my interstate travel were simply examples of political, partisan chauvinism.

Our arrival in Buenos Aires was celebrated as if we were visiting heads of state. This might well have been due to a misconception on the part of the Argentine planners because there was no comparable office to governor in their country. There were two bands, an honor guard of military personnel to be reviewed, speeches of welcome by the minister of Foreign Affairs and the minister of Commerce and Industry, and return speeches by a designated member of our party. We set off for the city and our hotels in a caravan that was met by citizens lined up along the highway waving flags and shouting greetings. That afternoon we traveled to the Casa Rosada, the presidential palace and office, where we were introduced to President Arturo Frondizi and officials of his government. He had not been in office long and would not survive the next election.

Argentina was just emerging from the long, dark winter of economic smoke and mirrors that had dominated the regime of Juan Domingo Perón and his wife Evita. The Perón dynasty has been characterized by a devotion to easy money and with no really hard decisions being made for the working class. Inflation finally brought Perón down. Frondizi was an advocate of hard money, and he fostered economic programs that were difficult to impose on the people. We heard a surprising number of adverse comments on these policies openly made and often openly agreed with. There was a reception at the Ministry of Foreign Affairs, a luncheon at the Argentine U.S. Chamber of Commerce, a reception in our honor at the U.S. Embassy which was attended by President Frondizi, a trip to the race track, and a boat ride on the canals that pass as streets in parts of Buenos Aires.

On Sunday morning, we were invited to Olivos, the residence of the president of Argentina, which was set in a twelve-acre park. We were greeted at the door by President Frondizi and went in to breakfast, which took about two hours. It was an all-male affair. The conversation was very interesting and probative of Argentina's problems and securing support for the Frondizi regime from the U.S. government. The Argentines were extremely curious about our president-elect, John F. Kennedy, and his plans for the Alliance for Progress. We tried to enlighten them, but President Kennedy had not yet taken office, and his policies were still in the formative stage, although most of us were pretty sure that the governor of North Carolina, Luther Hodges, would become the new Secretary of Commerce.

Our hosts were gracious, and they left us time to view their beautiful capital city. Buenos Aires was adorned with all of the finery of late spring in the southern hemisphere. The mimosa trees were in bloom, as were the dogwoods and redbuds, which had obviously been imported. The central city resembles Paris and is as impressive as Washington, D.C., the Champs Elysées, and some of the main thoroughfares of Madrid. The culture, of course, is a combination of all of those. I hope that the troubles that have beset Argentina in the period since I saw it have not served to diminish the grandeur and beauty of the capital city.

We left Buenos Aires and journeyed on to Mar del Plata, the summer playground of the capital. Mar del Plata is located at the mouth of the Rio Plata and is to Buenos Aires what the Jersey coast is to Philadelphia and New York. We traveled to Estancia, where we watched the *gauchos* playing polo, and they did some fancy rope tricks for us that were very entertaining. We had lunch there and traveled on to the cattle and wheat country of central Argentina.

We left central Argentina and traveled as far south as we were going on this trip to San Carlos de Bariloche, the town and airport closest to southern Argentina's great ski resort at Joa Joa. There was still snow on the slopes and some very small amounts of it on the valley floor. They took us for a ride in motorboats on a lake called Nequen that stretched across the international border between Argentina and Chile. The lake is famous as a fishery for brown trout, and the boatmen had a very in-house joke about the international brown trout who lived in the lake of Nequen, but ran up the rivers in Chile to spawn. There was a great deal of laughter about whether one could tell an international trout from a plain brown trout. They gave us a dinner that evening at one of the hotels in San Carlos, and Argentine style, it was not over until 2:30 A.M. We rose early and took a plane to Mendoza high up on the slopes of the Andes west of Buenos Aires. We had dinner that evening at the Club Andino at a proceeding as formal as anything I have ever attended. I felt quite underdressed because I did not have white tie and tails with me.

From Mendoza we traveled on to Cordova, the city to which Henry Kaiser had moved his automobile plant when it gave up the ghost in Detroit. The plant was then manufacturing a vehicle known as the Caballo. I understand that the plant has since given up the ghost in Cordova as well, but the city was very historic, and we enjoyed our visit there immensely. We left Cordova for an overnight stay in Buenos Aires and then took off, after a goodbye to our hosts, for Rio and our visit to Brazil.

Our airplane landed in Rio de Janeiro just as the sun was setting. The lights that illuminate the statue of Christ the Redeemer on Corcovado Mountain had come on, and, as was intended, the statue dominated the city. We were greeted at the airport terminal by our host and then driven to our accommodations at the Copacabana Hotel on the beach of that name at the end of the Avenida Rio Branco. Our designated host in Rio was a professor at the university and he was most gracious. The capital of Brazil had been moved officially to Brasilia far up in the central highlands. We would be greeted officially when we arrived there.

Our hotel on Copacabana Beach was an elegant establishment, except for the fact that the tap water was said to be unfit to drink or use. The beach across the avenue was not a nudist beach, but it might as well have been. String bikinis were the order of the day. The next suburb on the coast of Guanabara Bay was the village of Ipanema where Lucille had lived when she was a secretary in the U.S. Embassy.

There was little in the way of official business in Rio, except a reception in the local hall of government by some ministers of the state. A trip to a local steel mill was offered, as was a trip to a construction project for a dam on the Santa Catarina River, which was being built by Morrison Knudsen Company for the Brazilian government. I decided, on the advice of our host, to play hooky and to enjoy Rio for the brief time that we were there.

We were entertained at a reception at the U.S. Embassy by the ambassador and his wife and attended a soccer game in a stadium that I was told had 125,000 seats. Our professional football teams of today would be envious. The local vice president of Morrison Knudsen took us to lunch, and Lucille spent an afternoon on Christmas Street finding the old stone cutter who had cut her aquamarine ring and mounted it twenty years earlier. She was gratified that he remembered her and the ring, and he offered to buy it back from her, although she was stoutly of the opinion that it was not for sale. Our Brazilian hosts were amazed that she could remember where the shop had been and more amazed that it was still there. We entertained our hosts at dinner and then returned to the hotel prepared to take off the next morning for Brasilia.

Brazil's new capital is situated about 600 miles northwest of Rio. We were taken on a tour of the legislative assembly halls of the two houses of the Brazilian parliament and through some office buildings which were still not in use, but would house government departments. The architecture was exceedingly avant-garde and did not appeal to me, but was thought by some to be the wave of the future. At about noon we arrived at the presidential residence for a reception and luncheon in our honor. We were received in full regalia by Juscelino Kubitschek de Oliveira, who was dressed in white tie and tails and was wearing his presidential sash. It was a mark of great honor, and I for one was very glad that I had saved my sincere blue suit for this very morning. We dined and there were the usual addresses of welcome, felicity, friendship, and a response from one of the governors. We were back in the business of double translation, so things progressed slowly. We left the presidential palace and went to our appointment with the American Embassy people who had set up a ceremony called "the planting of the trees." We had each arranged to send a tree ahead of us from our home state to plant along the avenue that led up to the embassy. I had sent a ponderosa pine, believing it to be the sturdiest of our native trees, and hoped it would survive in the Brazilian highlands.

After the tree planting was completed, we went to a hotel—the only one in Brasilia—to rest a little and clean up. In the late afternoon we took off from Brasilia for São Paulo, the second largest city in Brazil and our next port of call.

We were running behind schedule and our arrival in São Paulo was delayed until extremely late in the evening. The host committee abandoned plans for an airport welcome and hustled us off to our hotels.

We were rolling along in a Volkswagen sedan when a sand and gravel truck threw up a rock and shattered the windshield. The driver managed to keep control, although he was unable to see, and pulled over to the side. The highway patrol did not know what had happened, and they came storming up to our driver. I think it likely that they would have put him in irons and hauled him off to jail if it had not been for Lucille's intervention. She thought she had forgotten her Portuguese, but when the police threatened the driver, she came to his rescue. The police decided that Ricardo was not to blame and let him take us on in to our hotel in São Paulo. It was obvious that he believed he would be in jail if it had not been for Lucille's timely intervention, and he became her slave for the rest of our visit to the city.

The schedule of events in São Paulo was mostly social, and we had been assigned to be hosted by a couple from Cleveland, Ohio, Gus and Betsy Schrader, who ran a machine-tool factory in the city. They knew all the good restaurants and the really interesting things to see. We broke away from the official schedule to spend most of our time with them.

We journeyed down to Santos on the coast to visit one of the real wonders of São Paulo. Santos is located below an escarpment where the Brazilian highlands make an almost sheer drop 2,000 feet to the seacoast. A river downstream from São Paulo had been dammed to make a huge lake that backed up against the continental escarpment. There on the cliffside were approximately twenty penstocks that dropped water down 2,000 feet through a series of generators to produce almost endless amounts of electrical power. This was the energy that fueled the industry of São Paulo. Santos was also a seaport where coffee was collected and shipped to other places for roasting and grinding. We got a chance to see how that industry worked. That was entirely appropriate because all my life I have been one of the principal supporters of the Brazilian coffee industry. We had a late afternoon lunch in Santos and then drove back to São Paulo, where we prepared, after dinner with the Schraders, to take off for New Orleans and home.

Argentina and Brazil in 1960 had great potential, and they still do. The question is whether they can develop the governmental self-discipline necessary to right their economies, get their industries cranked on to a workable schedule, and begin to furnish an adequately postured government for the working people in order to ultimately develop the strong middle class that is essential to a free democracy.

Presidents Frondizi and Kubitschek have both disappeared into the mists of history. The period between 1960 and now has been unfortunate for both nations. One hopes that sooner or later someone will arrive with the sure-handedness that is necessary to guide these two great nations into the sunshine of a free democracy.

"The emperor will grant your group of governors an audience at 3:30 P.M. this afternoon," were the words spoken by the attaché from the U.S. Embassy when we were privileged to travel to Japan in 1963 as part of a group of ten governors and their wives. We were visiting under the auspices of the Council of State Governments at the request of the Japanese government, and I believe the expenses for the enterprise were underwritten by the Ford Foundation.

Limousines, with Japanese drivers, picked us up at the Imperial Hotel and drove us directly to the Ginza Gate at the palace grounds. The grounds were ancient and were surrounded by first a moat and then a thick wall through which a tunneled gate had been driven. The palace gardens are located in the center of Tokyo, and I have no idea how large they are, although I got the impression that they were very extensive.

We were not introduced individually, but the court chamberlain approached the emperor and apparently asked permission for us to enter the hall. We were ushered to little tables at one side of the room facing the emperor and his party, who were arranged, apparently in order of importance, along the other wall of the room. The court chamberlain then introduced each of us individually to the emperor, coming to pick us up at our tables and assisting us in approaching the emperor. This was the formal presentation, and it occurred in Japanese and English.

After the formal presentations concluded, we were presented to the empress as well, and Emperor Hirohito began to mingle. The emperor used the English language with great facility. Hirohito seemed to me a very impressive person. He was dressed in a beautifully tailored banker's grey flannel suit and white shirt and a figured blue tie. He was slight, but he did not seem to be slight. I have to admit that I was a pretty awed young man when faced with this person who was not only the imperial emperor, but a deity to about ninety-five percent of the Japanese population. Hirohito had an aura about him that was unlike anything I had ever seen before.

I heard him ask one of the other governors for the governor of Idaho, and when I was pointed out, he came over to say hello. He was interested in kokanee salmon and the lake trout that were found in Pend Oreille and Priest Lakes. I did not know he was an ichthyologist of note and that kokanee salmon was one of his specialties. I wished then that I had been listening a little more closely when our Fish and Game representatives were describing the "blueback" salmon of Lake Pend Oreille. He chatted briefly with each of us and our wives. When the audience was concluded, the court chamberlain announced that it was very pleasant that we were able to come to call on the emperor, and Hirohito and his court disappeared behind the screen. We were ushered out of the hall and back to our limousines.

Our trip had been organized at the request of a group of Japanese prefectural governors who thought an organization resembling our Governors' Conference might be useful in the conduct of affairs in Japan. I think we were able during our visit to explain to our Japanese counterparts something about what our Governors' Conference attempted to accomplish. The prefectures in Japan are roughly comparable to our state governments. We did not see much of the national government of Japan on this trip, but devoted ourselves mainly to conversations with the local units of government in the various places where we visited. I am told that as a result of our visit, the Japanese governors organized a conference which is still in existence and which has served them fairly well in their dealings with the national government.

We visited first in Tokyo and Yokohama and were shown the usual tourist sights in those locations. We then took the bullet train to Osaka, where we stayed overnight with a family in their residence in one of the suburbs of the city and were introduced to the wonders of the ceremonial greeting, bath, and tea ceremony. We spent the late afternoon and evening in kimonos, a new experience. From Osaka we went to Kyoto, to Nara, and to Isushima. We rode the hydroplane service from Isushima to Nagoya and were met at the dock by the government officials of that city. We drove into Nagoya along broad, tree-lined boulevards, and, without thinking, I remarked everything

Representatives of the Japanese prefectures we had visited came to the United States in 1964.

seemed so new and that it was indeed a beautiful city. The government official with whom I was riding rather wryly observed that it was pretty much all new, but that they had had a good deal of assistance with urban renewal a few years back when we had come to call with our airplanes. We had fire bombed Nagoya in 1945 and almost totally destroyed the city.

From Nagoya we traveled by plane over the mountain range that forms the spinal ridge of Honshu Island and stopped at one of the seaport cities on the north coast of Japan. We went to a town up in the mountains and were entertained at an authentic geisha party. We traveled through a twenty-five-mile tunnel housing a great hydroelectric project that dropped water from high up in the mountains down to Matsumoto City, where it went through turbines to generate electricity. Lucille and I had been entertained at lunch by Mr. Kajima of the Kajima Construction Company, who occasionally did joint ventures in Southeast Asia with Morrison Knudsen. Mr. Morrison had asked Mr. Kajima to accord us hospitality, and he did.

After a brief visit to Matsumoto City, we returned to Tokyo and spent a couple of days being entertained and seeing the sights and shopping. Our Japanese host thought we might like to go to a night club and took us to a place where, he said, "kimono strip was performed." He was as good as his word. The lights were not very good, the music was delightful, and the lady did take it all off, although you had to be able to see with the speed of light if you were going to catch anything outrageous. We went to a kabuki theater and shopped in the big department stores in the Ginza.

We had invited the Japanese governors to come and visit us in the United States, and, with their promises to do so, we flew out of Tokyo for Anchorage and Seattle and home.

The Japanese governors were as good as their word and ten of them came to visit me in Idaho. We were able to entertain in grand style with the cooperation of civic groups in Boise and the Japanese-American community. We showed them the sights, sounds, and civilization in Treasure Valley.

In November 1965, Lucille and I were invited, along with six other

American governors, to tour the newly established tourist accommodations in central Mexico. The invitation came from Miguel Alemán, a former president of Mexico, who had taken on the task of being director of Tourist Affairs and was engaged in attempting to reestablish Acapulco as a resort and to establish a tourist attraction in central Mexico, where much of the history of the early republic had occurred. We undertook the trip at the expense of the Republic of Mexico, and I was designated by our group to make a speech in response to the governor's speech in the city of Guanajuato on the occasion of the 150th anniversary of the first Mexican Revolution. Lucille and I started our trip in Mexico City and proceeded from there to Cuernavaca, thence to Taxco, and on to Acapulco, where we were greeted by Alemán and given quarters for our stay in that city at Las Brisas, a hotel on the south coast of Acapulco Bay.

We were entertained at a state reception hosted by Alemán and the president of Mexico, Gustavo Diaz Ordaz, and then proceeded to see the sights of Acapulco, including the high divers that are still an attraction in that city. From Acapulco, we flew to Guadalajara. When we left Guadalajara, we traveled to León and from there to Guanajuato, where we spent the next two nights. On our first night in Guanajuato, we were entertained at a brilliant reception and dinner in a hall that they called the Hall of the Bats. It had a tall, vaulted ceiling and actually was inhabited by bats when they were permitted to stay there, which was very seldom. I was told that if they were left undisturbed, they would return in great numbers. We were entertained by a 100-piece string orchestra from the University of Guanajuato that played Mexican music of haunting beauty.

The next evening was the great celebration of the Independence of Mexico, and there was a formal presentation in the Hall of the Indian Hero. The hall was named for an Indian who had tied himself to a flat rock and swung it against the door to the viceroy's palace, letting the crowd in to carry on the revolution. It was largely a symbolic show, but much was made of the rock and the rope and the viceroy's door. We were welcomed by the governor of Guanajuato and then it was my turn to respond. I had memorized enough of the speech in Spanish to go for about three minutes and took that route. Everybody was very pleased that I knew Spanish which, of course, I didn't, but it made a good impression. I was glad that I had gone to the trouble of having the speech prepared and memorizing it. After the ceremonies had been completed, the town was alive with fireworks the like of which I had never seen before. It seemed to me that it was immensely dangerous they were used so profusely.

When we left Guanajuato, we went to San Miguel de Allende. This little town has a place in history as the site of the incarceration of Maxmillian and Carlotta, the Hapsburg prince and princess who had been sent to reign over Mexico in 1865. We traveled on from San Miguel to Queretaro, where we had lunch and listened once again to a large string orchestra playing Mexican music. After a long, lazy afternoon lunch, we boarded a bus for Mexico City to spend the next few days. We were entertained in Mexico City at the American Embassy and stayed in one of the hotels on the Avenida de la Reforma, which runs through the center of the city. We were taken on a tour of the Museum of Natural History—one of the finest museums of this world—and to an excavation at the ancient Aztec capital of Tenochtitlán outside the city. That evening, we went to see the Ballet Folklorico. The next morning we departed Mexico City for Dallas, Texas, and home.

I do not know whether former President Alemán accomplished what he had set out to do with our trip through Mexico, but I do know that it was of sufficient interest to me that it brought me back two more times to see Cuernavaca and Mexico City.

When the Russians returned our visit in 1960, it was an interesting experience. I knew that if we did not have interpretive capabilities the visit would be a disaster because nobody would be able to communicate without running the risk of being misunderstood. We tried contacting people in the Boise vicinity who could speak Russian, and, to our very great surprise, we found about fifty people who were, if not fluent, at least capable of doing interpretations of English and Russian on double track. So all the Russians had an interpreter standing beside them who was able to discuss what the Americans were trying to say.

I thought it very remarkable that there were that many people between Weiser and Gooding who could speak Russian well enough to be useful.

My little notebook of important people kept growing. It started with Senator William E. Borah, at whose casket I stood as an honor guard when he lay in state in the Senate Chamber in Washington. As a uniformed Capitol Policeman in 1939, I was assigned to stand at the foot of the steps of the Capitol's east front when the king and queen of England came to pay their respects to Congress in the Rotunda of the Capitol. I had met every president since Herbert Hoover and shaken hands with all but one of them.

Now I could add to that list the names of Chairman Krushchev of the Union of Soviet Socialist Republics, President Frondizi of Argentina, President Kubitschek of Brazil, his Imperial Majesty Hirohito of Japan, and the President of Mexico. Idaho was becoming recognized as more than a small western state and was being noticed at an international level. In that regard, we had grown together and stepped into the international political realm of the second half of the twentieth century.

CHAPTER ELEVEN

A MUSEUM, A JUDGE, AND A COMMISSION

THE IDAHO STATE Historical Society is almost as old as the state. It had grown from a group of pioneers who organized themselves in 1881 to a state agency managed by John Hailey, a pioneer himself, in 1907. The collections of the Society were jammed into a room in the basement of the Capitol and into storage areas. During World War II the Society came under the care of Margaret Roberts, whose father, George H. R. Roberts, was the state's first attorney general. Miss Roberts, whom I knew in her last years, was a remarkably energetic person who had brought the state traveling library into existence, and through most of the first forty years was a supervisor or an employee of the traveling library.

The impact of the library was greater perhaps than that of the museum in the early years. It provided a means of bringing culture to the crossroads, villages, and small towns of rural Idaho. Like the museum, the library was housed in the basement of the Capitol. There was no professionalism involved in the operation of the museum. It was simply an accumulation of things thought by Miss Roberts and her predecessors to be historic.

A decision was made that the museum and the library should have a permanent home, and a site was given to the state by the City of Boise in the northwest corner of Julia Davis Park. A WPA project was initiated by Governor C. Ben Ross and the congressman from the Second District, D. Worth Clark. A foundation was poured, but after December 7, 1941, the concrete footings for the proposed museum building lay unused and weed covered through the war years.

Governor C. A. Robins managed to eke out a small appropriation in 1949 that would provide for completion of a building on the old foundations, and work began on the first wing of the Idaho Historical Museum. Miss Roberts and her associates insisted that the library have space in the new building too, so the basement rooms were in large part allotted to the library.

The museum began to acquire some storage space at Gowen Field and a somewhat modern looking museum began to emerge, although many thought it still inadequate. Among them was J. R. Simplot, who encountered me one evening in 1956 at a cocktail party in Boise. He asked me pointedly why we didn't have a decent museum. I replied that we were trying, but that the problem was one of money. I said we needed to recruit an expert in museum management and that we would have to offer that person a salary, which the legislature had neglected to appropriate. Mr. Simplot said that he would be good for a gift of $10,000 to establish the museum on a sound footing if I thought that I could hire somebody who could stay long enough to do the job. I said I was willing to undertake the search for a museum director, but that I would need to have the money in hand to be serious about it. He said he would attend to that.

Two days later his check arrived in the mail. We began the search for a museum director, and the trail led through the Council of State Governments and some of the agencies of the United States who dealt in such matters. We located a young man named Holman Jerome Swinney, who had worked briefly in museums in Sturbridge, Massachusetts, and with the Remington Arms Company. Jerry Swinney was just what we were looking for, if we could afford him. I made him an offer with what money we had, and told him that he would have a free hand in building our museum into a laudable educational institution. He made a trip to Boise, and we closed the deal. The future of our infant museum was in Jerry Swinney's hands. They turned out to be extremely capable.

At our first conference, I told Swinney that he would have to organize a cheering section statewide so that when the legislature met he would have some friends who would plead his cause. I said that if we could not get the legislature to buy the idea by the time the next session rolled around, we might as well give up on having a good museum. He began organizing a group of people into what they named the Friends of the Museum and achieved close to a statewide coverage for the organization and its work. The major work of the Friends of the Museum was to convince the legislature to appropriate more money. I gave Swinney a modest hand up in this endeavor by appointing Bud Alford of Lewiston to be a trustee of the Society. He was the publisher of the *Lewiston Tribune*, the leading Democratic voice, editorially, in Idaho, and the most important newspaper in the ten northern counties. This almost at one blow guaranteed the cooperation of the Democrats in the legislature on the issue of appropriating money for the new museum.

When the legislature came into session, Swinney charmed them with his knowledge of history and his obvious dedication to building the museum into an educational asset. They responded by appropriating everything that he asked them for, which was modest but adequate.

The museum building has now been enlarged and is a real asset to the work of the educational institutions of the state. The historical library, located in the Capitol Mall, has left the original building in Julia Davis Park for use as a display area for the museum's collection of Idaho artifacts. The Society publishes an excellent journal, *Idaho Yesterdays*, which is a source of information about Idaho that is easy to access and a pleasure to use.

Idaho has many reasons to be grateful to J. R. Simplot. His philanthropy is legendary, but I think one of the most laudable things he ever did was to jump-start the rebirth of the state museum with a $25,000 gift. It was superb planning and superb philanthropy, and I deem it one of the major accomplishments of my administration that we were able to get the new museum on track for greater service to our

With Secretary of State Jim Young, state historian and archivist Merle Wells, and Jerry Swinney, director of the Idaho State Historical Society, in attendance I signed a proclamation declaring December 2, 1957, "William E. Borah Day" in honor of the fiftieth anniversary of the senator's beginning his work in Congress. ISHS 3359.

---

people. However, it was not the most important event during my administration with which I was intimately involved.

When Judge William Healey decided to retire from the United States Circuit Court in San Francisco, he left a vacancy in what has come to be known as the "Idaho seat" on that bench. The scramble for appointment to the vacancy was intense. For a time, I aspired to perhaps be appointed and consulted with U.S. Senator Henry Dworshak about it, who gave me his blessing. I talked with Senator Thruston Morton of Kentucky, who was Republican national chairman, and he, too, approved of my aspirations, although he deplored the fact that my departure from the governorship would lead to a Democratic takeover of the Idaho statehouse. I then asked Fred Seaton, who was Secretary of the Interior, to inquire on my behalf of President Eisenhower whether my aspirations could possibly be successful. Seaton came back and told me that President Eisenhower had said that they had an old Kansas proverb—if you pulled the wagon, you couldn't ride in it—and he thought I should go on being governor because it would be a shame to let the Democrats take over the Idaho statehouse. With that mild presidential rebuff, I put my judicial aspirations behind me (and my liking for retirement benefits as well) and went back to work as governor.

This left Senator Dworshak with the task of providing a recommendation to the White House for someone to be appointed to that position. The American Bar Association had busied itself, as it usually does, with investigations of availabilities and was prepared at no time that I know of to ever make a recommendation. Over the Labor Day weekend in 1959, the senator called me and said he didn't want to recommend anyone who was on the State Supreme Court or anyone who practiced law in Boise, which pretty well ruled out almost all of the aspirants to the appointment. He asked me if I had any suggestions. I could think of nobody else at the moment except Judge M. Oliver Koelsch, who was a judge on the Third Judicial District Bench in Ada County. He had a good record and his character was impeccable, although he was relatively slow in reaching decisions. The senator called me the next day and said he was going to recommend Judge Koelsch to the president and would keep me advised. He called back a day later and said that the White House had advised him that on the next Monday they were going to send Judge Koelsch's appointment up to the Senate for confirmation. At that point in time, everybody was inside the loop of information except Judge Koelsch, and I felt it my duty to get in touch with him and inform him of the events that were quickly to follow. As my memory serves, the appointment went up to the Hill on Monday and hearings were scheduled on Wednesday, so Judge Koelsch did not have much time to prepare. The hearings were relatively perfunctory, as they often are, and Judge Koelsch was confirmed without difficulty.

When news that the appointment had been submitted to the Senate for confirmation was made public, it came over the wires to Boise and that was the first public notice that Judge Koelsch was being considered. I was having lunch in the Hotel Boise when Richard Charnock of the United Press came roaring into the restaurant and asked if I knew that Judge Koelsch's name had been submitted to the Senate for appointment to be Circuit Judge in San Francisco. I said, "Yes, Richard, I have known that for three days, now hand me that bar towel so I can cry."

I do not know whether I would have liked the splendid isolation of the federal judiciary or not. I am sure I would have enjoyed the retirement benefits, which are copious, but it was probably just as well that I was not appointed. Perhaps if I had been, Idaho would still be without a sales tax and without adequate finances to meet its obligations. I can say that I enjoyed governing, and apparently did a good job, for I came to the attention of national figures as a result of my effectiveness.

In 1958 and 1959 I served with Secretary of the Treasury Robert Anderson as cochair of a joint President's Cabinet/Governors' Conference Committee on intergovernmental relations. This ultimately resulted in the creation of an independent agency of the federal government known as the Advisory Commission on Intergovernmental Relations. I was appointed by President Eisenhower as one of the first members of that commission and was subsequently appointed to it by President John F. Kennedy and President Lyndon B. Johnson. I served as a member of the Advisory Commission until I left office in 1967.

The work of the commission was very interesting, but it was not particularly press-worthy and so attracted very little attention in Washington, or, for that matter, in the states. It produced about fifty volumes of very worthwhile research, and by the time it came to celebrate its twenty-fifth anniversary, it had become a very useful adjunct of both the White House and the Congress in dealing with the affairs of the states. I was invited to the dinner which marked the anniversary of the twenty-fifth year and was presented with a plaque, which is now in the archives of Albertson College. I found the work of the commission most satisfying. Although it did very little for me in terms of political advantage in Idaho, it was something of which I had justifiable reason to be proud.

When I left office I resigned the position with the commission. In 1969, President Richard Nixon was scouting around for someone to be chairman of the Advisory Commission. I told the White House and the national committee that I was available, and, as it turned out, I was one of two serious candidates. Following the usual procedure, I secured the endorsement of all of the Idaho congressional delegation who were Republicans and the party officers of the Idaho State Central Committee. I was asked by the White House to call on Vice President Agnew and be interviewed, and I was told that it would be necessary for me to receive the endorsement of the incumbent governor, Don Samuelson. He wanted me to visit him in his office to explain to him why he should endorse my aspirations. Reluctantly, I finally wrote him a letter saying that I would like to call on him to discuss the matter. As I expected, he asked me at the inception of our conference to tell him why I thought he should endorse me as a candidate for the post of chairman of the Advisory Commission.

I told him, "Governor, I can understand your reticence, but find it very difficult, because I have the endorsement of the entire party hierarchy in Idaho. Secondly, I believe I am fully qualified to fulfill the position of chairman of the Commission. Finally, and perhaps most relevant to your question, I suspect that you desire to be reelected. I think for that to happen it would be advisable for you to endorse my aspirations." Samuelson said he would think the matter over and let me know. I never heard from him again.

I learned later that Vice President Spiro Agnew had given Samuelson his word that he would not recommend my appointment without approval from Samuelson, and this, in essence, gave Samuelson veto power. When I learned this, I withdrew my name from consideration. I think it was mean-spirited of Governor Samuelson to prevent me from receiving a fourth presidential appointment to the Advisory Commission, and I would dearly have liked to serve through the Nixon years and perhaps even the Ford years in that position, which was the history of the person who received the appointment instead of myself.

I am told that Governor Samuelson does not understand why I seem to dislike him. I hope this recitation of the facts, as they developed, will assist him, and the public generally, in understanding those events of almost thirty years ago.

CHAPTER TWELVE

THE 1962 CAMPAIGN

THE 1962 CAMPAIGN for the governorship really began the moment the Thirty-sixth Legislature convened in January 1961. I had already served longer as governor than anyone in the state's history, and the big question was what I might do again two years hence.

The Republicans in the legislature, who were in the forefront of the fight for what they called "tax reform" (spell that sales tax), were already pressing hard for an announcement of my intentions. The Democrats were still bemused with their search for a revenue source that would permit big spending with painless revenue impositions.

I had not made up my mind at that time, but I had already determined that I would keep my intentions to myself in order to permit maximum mobility in dealing with the Thirty-sixth Legislature. The Republicans had a very narrow margin in the House of Representatives and a two-vote margin in the state Senate. It was an abrupt turnabout, almost as striking as the Republican victory in the Congress in 1994. The 1961 legislature was not spectacular, but it did a quite acceptable job. By the time they adjourned, its members had made appreciable progress toward the long-term goals of my administration.

The state's economy had been steadily improving since its low point in the 1958-59 recession. Agricultural prices were up and building permits were increasingly sought for new housing. Our old reliable indicator of economic well-being—the sale of red whiskey in the state dispensary—was also improving. For that reason, I told the legislature that I did not believe it possible to undertake new departures in revenue sources in this session, and that the best time for a new tax was when it would be politically acceptable and could no longer be avoided.

Nevertheless, some ambitious legislators from the more populous counties introduced a sales tax measure in the House of Representatives and were able, with a good deal of arm-twisting and horse trading, to secure its passage in the lower house. It went over to the Senate where, I am told, it never attracted more than seven or eight votes. The House of Representatives was as usual more in tune with public sentiment about expenditures and was already feeling the lash of

Some of Idaho's 1962 Republican candidates with Dwight Eisenhower. From left, Orval Hansen, running in the Second Congressional District; Jack Hawley, running for Senate; myself; Eisenhower; Carl Burt, running for secretary of state; and Senator Len Jordan. Only Jordan and I were elected.

inadequate revenues to fund the public schools. After the Senate was put to the sales-tax test and failed, we began to piece together a program that would be acceptable to the people.

My financial advisors had told me that we might anticipate adequate revenues from the existing structure, which would permit modest increases in the budget, especially in the field of public school education. The legislature was able to significantly increase the appropriations for public school education, although it was not enough to please the professional educators. Once again it was necessary to neglect appropriations to the Teachers' Retirement System Endowment Fund.

Significant advances in funding the statewide highway system were made which would sooner or later bring every county in the state into almost direct communication with the capital in Boise. We did not spend our money on President Eisenhower's new interstate highway system because I believed, and I think the legislature agreed, that a road system that served the small, outlying counties and communities was preferable to one that ultimately would be mainly a highway for the trucking industry.

The legislature enacted a permanent building program to be operated by a Permanent Building Fund Board of Directors and which was independently funded from tax sources designated in the enabling act. A hallmark of the Democratic revenue structure enacted in 1959 had been the so-called head tax, the ten dollar license fee imposed on filing an income tax return. In the 1960 elections, the Republicans had taken what I think was unfair advantage of the Democrats and used this tax to defeat several incumbent legislators. In what I freely admit was one of my more cynical moments, I changed the name of the head tax to the Permanent Building Fund Fee and made it one of the keystones in the funding structure of the Permanent Building Fund program. No subsequent legislature has ever adequately funded the Permanent Building Fund, but if they ever do, it will provide an ongoing source of construction funds for our institutions of higher education, our hospitals, and our other public institutions.

Merchandise trading stamps had been legal in Idaho for a considerable period of time, but in the late fifties, the use of Green Stamps and competing Gold Strike Stamps had gotten out of hand as far as the mainstream merchants were concerned. Offering trading stamps was not particularly good mass merchandising, but it was a way that a small mom-and-pop grocery store could compete with larger enterprises. Gluttony had led the large merchants to offer double and triple green stamps to entice customers, and ultimately their profit margins were disappearing in clouds of trading stamps. The big merchants came to the legislature asking to be rescued from the consequences of their own folly.

Idaho's legislature, which traditionally makes great speeches against government regulation in favor of free market economics, promptly complied with the wishes of the main street merchants and passed a law outlawing the use of Green Stamps, Gold Strike Stamps, and other trading stamps. The legislature passed this anti-competitive legislation almost unanimously, and it came to my desk after they had adjourned and left town. I vetoed the bill and was widely condemned for having done so, but I believed in free enterprise economics and thought we should practice what we preached. I also thought that the issue was a good one to carry to the people in the 1962 elections, and it turned out I was right.

We had been at work transforming the old Farragut Naval Station on Lake Pend Oreille, north of Coeur d'Alene, into a state park by using National Guard and Army Reserve engineering training funds and had yet to ask the legislature for any appropriations to complete the task. Secretary of Commerce Louise Shadduck and Mrs. Warren Brown of McCall had invited the National Council of the Girl Scouts of America to hold their 1963 roundup at Farragut State Park, and it was necessary to put completion of the task into high gear. We asked the legislature for an appropriation of about $700,000, and with those funds completed the park so that it could be used as the site of the roundup, which would host about 5,000 people for a ten-day period.

Farragut State Park is probably the greatest bargain the Idaho legislature ever funded and one of the greatest bargains in the history of western park building. It lies on 5,000 acres of beautiful country in northern Idaho. The site originally was a tangled mess of concrete foundations left there by the U.S. Navy after World War II. I think we paid the United States somewhere in the neighborhood of $35,000 for the entire project. The president of the Richfield Oil Company had been distributing wildflower seeds in little seed packets as a promotional device for his gasoline stations. I thought it likely that there might be some of that left over, and I called him up and asked. We received a gift of 50,000 pounds of wildflower seed which were put into a slurry and distributed by helicopter over the 5,000 acres so that it would be virtually a carpet of blossoms in the spring. I suspect that some of the descendants of that seed are still blooming.

It was necessary to build an amphitheater and various permanent facilities for the Girl Scouts according to their specifications, but most of the buildings could be used later as part of a public park. We built a swimming beach on Buttonhook Bay. In 1964, the Girl Scouts formally accepted our invitation, and we completed the work of developing Farragut State Park.

The Girl Scout Roundup demonstrated to the legislature that there was considerable economic merit in the State Park System, and they were much more sympathetic to the idea of developing that system. The Girl Scouts were followed by the Boy Scouts in 1967 and again in 1969 with a National Jamboree, with 15,000 attending, followed by a World Jamboree. By 1970, Farragut had already paid its way. It is now one of the most used parks in our whole state system. I had conceived it as the northern anchor of a park system that would extend in a chain all the way down the Snake River and around the southern end of the state to be anchored by Harriman State Park when it came on line. In 1961, we completed the negotiations on and preparation of a contract for the acquisition of Harriman State Park. The park would be on the old Railroad Ranch properties belonging to Roland and Averell Harriman, which they proposed to give to the state of Idaho as a gift. It is difficult to estimate what would have been an appropriate value to place on that splendid property, but it is a magnificent wildlife refuge and the anchor for the Idaho State Park System in the southeastern corner of the state. It ranged across a 25,000-acre spread that encompassed the nesting grounds for trumpeter swans, a magnificent array of four-footed wildlife, and some of the finest trout fishing waters in all of North America.

A few words seem in order about the origination of the idea for a state park at the Railroad Ranch. Harley Markham and I had entertained Senator Thruston Morton of Kentucky at Mr. Markham's fishing lodge located near Alma Kunz's resort on the Teton River. This was the place where Herbert Hoover used to come to fish and it was for that reason quite famous in the local lore of the Teton Valley. That Sunday afternoon, E. Roland Harriman called from his house at the Railroad Ranch to ask if he might come to see me. I had been acquainted with Mr. Harriman for some time.

Harriman drove over from the Railroad Ranch at Ashton and we sat down to visit in the front yard of Mr. Markham's fishing lodge. Harriman had been impressed with the manner in which our Department of Fish and Game had cleaned up the Henry's Fork of the Snake River and restored that fishery to its original magnificence. He said that he did not want the Railroad Ranch, once he was gone, to be cut up into a commercial development and he would like to preserve the area in one piece as a wildlife refuge. He inquired whether or not I thought the state would be willing to accept it as a gift for the purpose of establishing either a state park or a wildlife refuge or both. Harriman wanted to be sure that once the area was a state park, it would be under professional career management and that it would be preserved for the uses that he intended in his original gift. I told him that I would think it necessary to secure ratification of such a proposal by the legislature because it would require ongoing expenditures, and he agreed to that suggestion. We agreed to study the proposal further and to get back together again later in the fall in New York City. It is now history that in 1977, the park became a part of the Parks Department of the state of Idaho and has been an adornment of that agency ever since. The contract provided that the park had to be administered by the state pursuant to a system of professional career employees, which in essence meant a civil-service type administration, and that the contract could not be carried into effect unless and until it had been ratified by the legislature. When the contract was presented to the legislature in 1963, they ratified it. With that ratification, the decision was made for a professional career park management that would be used in all of the parks in the state system. We had already set aside the property for Veterans' State Park in the heart of downtown Boise, and that pretty much guaranteed a statewide constituency for parks and their services. The provisions in the Harriman Park contract, which were my idea, pretty much acted as the catalyst which made it necessary for the legislature to adopt professional career management for its parks.

That year of 1961 was also a big year for Lucille Smylie. Sometime earlier, with the assistance of the Idaho Food Commission, she and their home economists developed a recipe for Plum Prune Chutney. The recipe was excellent and produced a splendid product. It was used in some of the promotional material by the Prune Commission and by

---

Lucille, in a portrait by Stan Burns.

the Idaho Sheep Commission to help sell lamb. Sometime later a columnist for one of the national weekly Sunday supplement magazines named Clementine Paddleford picked up the recipe and publicized it. This produced an almost unprecedented flood of mail. We had to hire an extra secretary in order to respond to all the requests for an autographed copy of the recipe.

By now, we were veteran members of the Lowell School Parent-Teacher Association and were about to become members of the same group at North Junior High School. It was obvious that time was pressing on toward a decision about what I would do with my life after the completion of my second term. The 1961 legislature had tinkered with the election laws and contrived an idea that somehow forty percent of the primary vote was sacred—if you got that many votes, it meant that you were a popular choice. This was meant to keep candidates like Senator Derr and Vernon K. Smith, who won their nomination in 1962, from being the Democratic candidates. It was the politics of exclusion, and it did not work. This same election law tinkering led to a change in the date of the primary from August to early June. The campaign season was shortened and my decision was therefore made more pressing as we entered the fall of 1961.

I do not recall that anybody really urged me to run for a third term with one exception. By the same token, I do not recall that anybody really urged me not to run. Anyone who has been a governor knows that it is one of the most intriguing jobs that one can ever hold, and to say that I was fond of being governor is a majestic piece of understatement. I enjoyed the job and liked living in the old residence, although Lucille didn't like the house. Also I would have to decide what to do if I didn't run for reelection. The circumstances finally led to a decision almost by default. Sometime late in 1961, we began to lay plans to formalize my third candidacy.

In August of 1961, Lucille and I commenced building the little cottage that we called the Mountain House in a pasture west and a little north of Donnelly. We had a contractor who built the frame and got it turnkeyed in eighteen days. Then Lucille and I and the boys began spending our weekends there finishing off the inside and otherwise completing the work of building a second home. The Mountain House would have little significance in this discussion of my third candidacy, but because Vernon K. Smith had an inquisitorial mind and didn't follow through on his details, it had a significant effect in the campaign of 1962.

It was already apparent that we would have opposition in the Republican primary, although it was unclear then as to who the opposition might be and how many candidates would be fielded. The major opposition turned out to be my old friend George Crookham, Jr., who was the mayor of Caldwell at one time and who had served in the legislature as an ardent proponent of the sales tax. He was joined at a later date by the mayor of Blackfoot, Elvon Lindquist, who was the husband of the state committeewoman from that county.

The major difference between this campaign and those that had gone before was that we were able to finance it in advance and to lay plans in January for what we wanted to do in June. This is a luxury not afforded to many in contested elections. There was nothing like the ineffectual, silly sunshine law on the books in those days, and we were able to receive money with impunity. I am happy to report here that most of our contributions in 1962 came from inside the state, with the exception of a couple of donations from people who hoped someday to be president of the United States, named Richard Nixon and Nelson Rockefeller. E. Roland Harriman, who considered himself to be at least a part-time Idahoan, was also an exception to that general statement. Another contribution came from Thomas McCabe, president of Cummings Engine Company. None of these contributions exceeded $5,000.

Because we were able to plan in advance, we put together a budget that was both realistic and workable. I think we planned to spend $175,000 for the primary and general election, and we came in, as memory serves, well under budget.

Toward the end of November in 1961, we began to pass the word to our committee people in the counties that it was likely that I would be a candidate for a third term. This was sort of a test run to see how much falling away there had been from the strength of our initial campaign machinery. It turned out that the erosion had been negligible, and that our committee strength was about the same as it had been earlier in the administration. I would have to say that I was not at all surprised to find some lack of enthusiasm for a third-term candidacy, especially with committee people who had close ties to the industrial establishment. I had to tell Roland Wilbur of Lewiston, a Republican state committeeman from Nez Perce County who worked for Potlatch Forest Industries, that I would not accept the nomination if I got less than forty percent in the first election. That sobered him up substantially, and he was pretty well behaved for the rest of that year.

Wilbur and his associates were people who mainly wanted unimpeded access to the governor's office. I had been a trifle too self-reliant for their purposes, and they thought that it would be better if they had somebody else. The trouble with their program was that there wasn't anybody else with even a modest show of force. George Crookham and El Lindquist would have been as unacceptable to Roland Wilbur and his cabal of powerbrokers as I was. George Crookham, in addition to having been mayor of Caldwell, had been an independent Canyon County legislator. Even though El Lindquist was the presiding mayor of Blackfoot, Idaho, at the time, he would not have been a strong candidate. Neither of them had any statewide election campaign experience. We did, however, view George Crookham as extremely dangerous because he came from Canyon County, which we counted as one of our own power bases. Both Crookham and Lindquist would have governed independently and not been subject to outside influences because they were strong-willed, intelligent, and effective leaders.

Crookham based almost his entire campaign on a perceived need for a sales tax to provide adequate revenue to do the tasks that the government was increasingly called upon to perform in the fields of education and highways. He was right, but he was just a little before his time. We all owe George Crookham a debt of gratitude because he laid the foundation for what would become a successful drive to enact a sales tax three years later.

Economic data were becoming much more accurate than they had been in our early years in office, and it was apparent that the revenue structure at that time would produce enough money so that the legislature would be very reluctant to consider a radical new source of revenue. In the 1962 campaign, I took the position that no new tax was necessary until it could no longer be avoided and that 1962 was not that time. I did not take a "never-ever" position against the sales tax. I simply waffled on the subject for the purposes of the 1962 campaign.

Mr. Lindquist took approximately the same position that I did, although he was a little stronger in his opposition to a sales tax as a source of revenue. Lindquist had been late getting into the campaign, and, as a consequence, his vote totals did not seem to me to indicate a true measure of how a sales tax would do on a referendum basis. Nevertheless, the sales tax became the principal issue of the Republican primary election in 1962.

Contrary to conventional wisdom, I was fairly pleased to have opposition in the 1962 primary election. Contested nominating procedures served a useful purpose for a candidate who is in office. They provide a basis for identifying pockets of dissension and opposition within the party that might otherwise remain undiscovered until it is too late in the general election campaign. A contested primary also provides a basis for identifying issues and measuring their support among the voting populace. For instance, 1962 proved fairly early that the sales tax was not going to be viable in the next legislature. Another case in point was Senator Frank Church's failure in 1982 to recognize the opposition in Idaho to his attitudes toward the intelligence agencies of the United States following Senate committee hearings he chaired investigating those organizations. There was a fairly deep and bitter resentment toward his opposition to those agencies, and I think if his Senate seat had been contested in the primary, he might have been able to identify the antagonism. It was, in the last analysis, probably this issue that drove him out of the United States Senate.

We began the primary campaign after the first of the year in 1962 by setting up a series of town meetings in each of the county seats in all of the forty-four counties, and we hoped before June to be able to reach them all. I think we finally did get to all but four of them. This provided an opportunity to organize a meeting on our own without reference to the plans of the local central committee, and it made it possible for us to set our own schedule rather than be obliged to fit one around other events. It worked well, and our meetings in the various county seats were well attended. They were not as productive of issue conversation as I might have liked, but there was a good deal of give and take on local projects and local problems. This was useful in preparing for a general election campaign. On a couple of occasions our paths crossed with the opposing candidates, and it was possible to set up joint meetings that were both spirited and informative to the public and to me.

Even though I had already informed Mr. Wilbur and some others that I would not be inclined to pursue the nomination unless I received forty percent of the vote in the first election, Wilbur complained bitterly that I was holding the party hostage to my renomination. He was quite correct. I did not feel inclined to go through a runoff election for a third nomination and felt that it would be useless to undertake it if all that was accomplished was a nomination to lose in November. This was no idle threat. Our polling indicated that we were close to the winning side on the forty percent figure and that the threat would not have to be carried out. The remainder of the primary campaign was relatively uneventful, and, in the first week in June, the people went to the polls, and I was renominated by about forty-six percent of the vote.

On the Democratic side, the party had nominated an advocate of casino gambling as a means of resolving the revenue problem—Vernon K. Smith. Smith got about forty-seven percent of the vote, much to the dismay of some of the organization Democrats and especially those in the legislature who would be running for reelection on the same party ticket. The stage was now set for another trial heat regarding the question of whether the people of Idaho wanted to embrace casino gambling in the Nevada style, or whether they wished to make the hard decisions to finance an adequate, mature government by more legitimate means. I was personally confident that they would reject casino gambling, but the forty-seven percent vote that Mr. Smith received in the Democratic primary election gave us cause to be concerned. There was apparently a stronger public sentiment in favor of gambling than there had been four years earlier.

Mr. Smith was a flamboyant Boise lawyer who had an extensive practice in criminal law. He represented some of the least respectable people in the area and had not been active in politics before he sought the Democratic nomination for governor. His nomination could not be explained on any other basis. Clearly there were that many Democratic voters who preferred casino gambling as a way out of the revenue crisis.

For a while we thought that Senator Frank Church might reject Smith's candidacy as unfitting to his style of democracy. Church was running for reelection, and the Smith nomination put him between a rock and a hard place. He managed to ignore Smith until sometime late in October when he made a speech in St. Anthony, fifty miles from any newspaper or television station, in which he endorsed Smith's candidacy. He must have been convinced that his tacit rejection of Smith was costing him votes.

It was clear from day one that we had our work cut out for us, and we began running a vigorous campaign. Taped television commercials and materials for distribution to the counties for use in our campaign were prepared. Robert Hodge, who by now had become a first-class schedule maker, began putting plans together that would take us almost everywhere in the state before November, and by July 1, 1962, he had worked out a schedule which utilized all the time available between then and October 15. We had recorded radio spots and roughed out the newspaper advertising. This was very different from later years when to run for governor meant having to spend upwards of $750,000 and maybe as much as $1 million. I think it was better then, but after all, I am one of the older fellows.

The most amusing event in the 1962 campaign may well appear in the Democratic files as the Great Smiley Creek Fiasco of 1962. They thought they had discovered me with my hand deep in the cookie jar and were planning to make the most of it in an endeavor to win the election. It turned out there was no scandal, no cookie jar, and no hand.

As mentioned earlier, in 1961 Lucille and I had built a little cabin on the North Fork of the Payette River on some land which we had purchased from Doris and Jim Cruzen near a town called Norwood. Meanwhile the Department of Aeronautics had constructed an airstrip in the Stanley Basin about halfway between Sun Valley and the town of Stanley. The planners of the Aeronautics Department thought there should be a strip in the area where a small plane could be set down if it was too mucky over Galena Summit and weather made flying dangerous. They found land where Smiley Creek flows into the Salmon River and built a very primitive airstrip suitable for single-engine planes. I am told that Smiley Creek was named after an old lady who had a store to serve cattle ranchers and others at that location in the early days. Her nickname was Smiley.

Vernon Smith heard about these two items of interest—our cabin and the airstrip—and immediately assumed that the cabin was located somewhere on Smiley Creek and that the airstrip had been built to be of use to us exclusively. He set the whole Democratic machinery to work attempting to make the connection and find out how much the airstrip cost and where our cabin was. It developed that our cabin was 150 miles northwest of Smiley Creek across some of the roughest terrain in the Sawtooth Range. Smith told me later that they spent about $25,000 trying to find a basis for using the strip at Smiley Creek to prove that I was some kind of a crook, but that he had to give it up.

In this campaign we planned a quick-response television series that I think were the first call-in, talk-back television shows used politically in Idaho. We called the show "Ask Your Governor" and serviced it with a toll-free number that could be used to call us in the studio where the show was being produced. We planned six weeks of "Ask Your Governor" programs—one on each of the major stations in the state—in Idaho Falls, Twin Falls, and Boise. We had no idea how the format would be received by the voting populace, but by the time we had done two of the shows we knew we had a winner. It was a kind of television exposure ready made for an incumbent because we had access to all of the information, and, if we didn't have it when we got a call on Tuesday, we could come back with the answer on Thursday's show.

This exercise in voter education and participation was a magnificent success. After the first program, we enlarged the phone bank in order to handle more questions. Over the entire series of programs, we averaged about 210 phone calls per thirty-minute program. We couldn't answer all of them on camera, but if we had an address an answer was sent in writing over my signature within five days of the program. The television program was a forerunner of the much heralded candidate debates that are part of elections now. From the standpoint of issues, this format of voter questions and candidate answers lifted the campaign above political harangue regarding whether or not the state should have casino gambling. This infuriated Mr. Smith, but I believe it served the people well.

By midsummer of 1962, it had become obvious that Vernon Smith was deadly serious about opening the state to all types of casino gambling and perhaps other promiscuous endeavors. He was no practitioner of family values, and I think one had to take his proposals seriously. I first called him "the man with the green eyeshade" at a picnic in Municipal Park sponsored by the Ada County Republican Women's Club. It was a biennial event and always attracted a good crowd. The phrase sort of slipped out without my really intending to use it that night, but the moment it did, Pandora's box had been opened and the phrase resonated with the crowd. In retrospect, I am not proud that I hung that epithet around Mr. Smith's neck. It was my own little contribution to what the media gurus now term negative campaigning, but it worked.

Idaho politics has a modest record in the realm of bad campaign tactics. I am told that Governor James H. Hawley back in 1912 and 1914 was a master of political insult and vitriol. Former Senator D. Worth Clark and Herman Welker used a book called the "Red Record of Glen Taylor" in order to defeat Senator Taylor for the Democratic nomination in 1950. Once again, there was third party participation at the time. I am told that James Brown, publisher of the *Statesman*, and W. Lloyd Adams, a Rexburg lawyer, were co-authors of the tract. In 1960, Ralph Harding used slander about attendance at Mormon Sunday School in his successful endeavor to defeat incumbent congressman Hamer Budge. Up until very recent elections, our record of negative campaigning has been pretty slight, but we are getting better at the art form. I suspect we will see a good deal more of it before it is over.

Robert Hodge and I were returning from a campaign swing through the upper Snake River Valley counties when we received word that Senator Dworshak had died. Dwight Jensen had reported the fact on the nine o'clock news from Radio KBOI in Boise. We had just passed Glenns Ferry and we stopped at a telephone booth in Hammett so I could call Lucille. She said she was besieged by reporters. I told her to send them home, that there would be no news tonight, and we got in the car and continued toward Boise.

Down the road, Hodge inquired of me, "Will you appoint yourself to the Senate?" Without giving the matter much thought, I replied, "I don't believe I could do that." Hodge indicated that he did not know why I could not do that, but I had no immediate answer for him. I brooded over the pros and cons of the question the rest of the way to Boise.

When I reached home, all the newspaper boys had retired with the exception of Richard Charnock of United Press, who insisted that he had to have an answer. I told him he was not going to get an answer to any questions that evening and that he was being a journalistic scalawag. He was a tenacious reporter and did not give up easily, but finally he departed.

I poured a drink for Lu and myself. We discussed for a time the decision which we were facing. We were not possessed of the financial means that would permit an easy transition, and that was a cloud on any consideration I might have of attempting to go to the Senate. Some time after midnight, we retired for a night that was not sleepless, but was certainly restless. Sometime during that tossed and tumbled night I reached the conclusion that there must be some way one could have his cake and eat it too. I began thinking about the possibilities of interim appointments and other devices that would preserve both the governorship and the vacancy for me. These were admittedly not unselfish considerations. However, they did serve the purpose of preserving some degree of peace and good order in a party that was already growing fractious over the Dworshak succession.

Next morning the reporters were waiting outside the office door when I arrived at the Capitol. They demanded to know what I was going to do, and I told them I was going to do nothing at the moment. I declared that it would be inappropriate to discuss the Senator's succession until his funeral had been conducted. We did not know whether the family wanted to bring the Senator home to Idaho or have him lie in state in the Rotunda of the Capitol.

Some time that morning I called Lieutenant Governor William Drevlow at his home in Craigmont and asked him to stand by. He told me that he hoped I would not have to leave the state because he was already feeling pressure from the young Democrats in the Senate class of 1959 who aspired to be appointed to fill the vacancy if perchance I should leave. Drevlow said that he thought action like that would violate the terms of his commitment to me to be lieutenant governor and not governor and that he did not wish to be subjected to that kind of pressure. I told Mr. Drevlow that I was going to talk with the Dworshak family about their plans, and that I would be in touch with him later on.

Next I called the senator's widow, Mrs. Georgia Dworshak, and expressed my condolences personally and those of the people of Idaho in whose service Senator Henry Dworshak had performed with distinction for nearly twenty years. I offered to arrange a lying-in-state in the Rotunda of the Capitol and burial in Morris Hill Cemetery in Boise, but Mrs. Dworshak said that the family had already determined that the senator should rest in Arlington Cemetery, where he was entitled to be buried in recognition of his military service in World War I. This was understandable because Senator Dworshak had been an active member of the American Legion and had served as its state commander for one term. I informed Mrs. Dworshak that it might be difficult for me to arrange to attend the funeral in Washington, D.C., and she said that the family would thoroughly understand that my duties as governor came first.

I called Lieutenant Governor Drevlow and informed him of my

decision not to attend the funeral and said that his presence in Boise would, for that reason, not be needed. He was then able to return to the wheat harvest, which was in full swing on the Camas Prairie. The decision not to attend Senator Dworshak's funeral gave me a little time to examine the legal precedents and to consider the alternatives that were available for selecting candidates for his succession.

From the outset there were four possible candidates to succeed Senator Dworshak. They were Harley Markham, Republican National Committeeman from Pocatello; Judge Hamer Budge of Boise; former Governor Len Jordan, who was residing in Boise at that time; and myself.

In my deliberations about the appointment I did not consult very many of the party leaders, and, strangely, very few came forward to offer advice. There was one person who rather loudly insisted that I should appoint myself, but he was careful not to do this publicly. There didn't seem to be any massive enthusiasm for any one of the four possibilities. As is the case with so many decisions in the governor's office, this one finally came down to a decision which had to be made by one man alone and that person was me.

It was already obvious that the Democratic party was going to unite behind Congresswoman Gracie Pfost of Nampa, who would be a formidable candidate. She would attract large contributions from eastern sources because she had been widely applauded as an opponent of private development of the Hells Canyon Dam. Mrs. Pfost was also a talented, veteran campaigner who had won about sixteen elections in a row at the county and congressional district levels. Her campaign team would be headed by George Greenfield of Boise, who was my old friend and antagonist and who had been Democratic state chairman in 1954 when I was first elected governor.

My first consideration in these somewhat clandestine deliberations was what to do about myself. We had collected a large sum of money that was designed to insure my reelection as governor. It seemed improper to spend it running for another office without consulting the donors. To spend that money running for the Senate would have been something akin to embezzlement, although there was nothing illegal about it. Our campaign paraphernalia had been accumulated and paid for, and we would have to dispose of it. The television commercials that we had put on tape would have to be abandoned and redone at very considerable cost. However, the major reason for abandoning any idea of appointing myself to the Senate was strictly personal. The Smylies had never been wealthy and were not then even modestly well off. I would have had to borrow money to move the family to Washington and would have had to go into debt to accomplish the transition from being governor to being senator. The governor's residence of those days made the governorship affordable, and similar accommodations would not be available in Washington, D.C. I was not at all certain that the Republican central committee would voluntarily nominate me for the Senate, even if I asked them to do so. They had nominated me for governor by about half of the total vote, and that was not at all reassuring. A sturdy, well-financed campaign for reelection as governor was one thing, but a start-from-scratch race for the Senate was quite another. I concluded I should stay in the governorship and make other arrangements for a later attempt on the Senate seat. The date for that attempt to gain a seat in the Senate was already tentatively targeted in my mind. It was the 1966 general election when the six-year term for the Senate seat would be available for contest.

The Idaho election laws made no provision for the situation which confronted us in 1962. The death of an incumbent senator after the primary election and before the general election posed a unique problem and one for which there was no statutory direction. Some argued that an appointment made in the interim would be valid until the next general election two years hence. There were no precedents to support that argument either. It seemed to me to be a little shady and perhaps guilty of partisan shenanigans. I rejected that argument and proposed a solution of my own. I asked the two state chairmen to call meetings of their respective central committees and to nominate somebody to represent their parties in the general election in November. I announced the fact that I would be a candidate for governor and was not a candidate for the Senate nomination at the same time that I released copies of the letters to the Democratic and Republican state chairmen to the press.

The Democrats had no problem. They quickly convened a central committee meeting and nominated Congresswoman Gracie Pfost of Nampa as their candidate for the Senate. I was told by the state Democratic chairman that had I been the candidate, Mrs. Pfost would not have run.

The Republican nomination was a different story. The central committee meeting would occur in about ten days, and there were three viable candidates.

Once again I was urged to appoint somebody before the central committee met which would, of course, have circumvented any free and open discussion and decision by the central committee since they would almost certainly have had to nominate whoever had been appointed. Had I attempted an appointment before the central committee meeting, I am quite confident it would have had a detrimental effect both on my candidacy for the governorship and on the individual I appointed to the Senate seat. I concluded that the most defensible course of action, and the one that was really preferable to the people, was to let the convention central committee make its own decision.

Of the three leading candidates none had considerable strength among the delegates who would make the decision. Harley Markham of Pocatello was the Republican national committeeman, but he had never held public office on an elective basis and that was a mark against him. Judge Hamer Budge of the Third Judicial District was serving as judge pursuant to my appointment and had been a ten-year member of Congress who had been defeated in 1960. Budge had a reputation as a lackadaisical campaigner. The third candidate was former Governor Len Jordan, who was then a stockbroker in Boise. As might have been expected, I inquired of each one of them about their intentions for reelection in 1966 and was assured by all three that they would not be candidates. That meant the road would be clear for me to seek the Senate seat that I was foregoing in 1962. Markham and Budge both called on the phone to suggest that they would be pleased to give me a commitment that they would not be candidates in 1966. These two calls were voluntary and the idea of asking for a promise not to run in 1966 had not occurred to me. It did, however, seem reasonable, and I called Governor Jordan and asked him to make the same commitment, which he voluntarily did. I did not ask for a written commitment from any of the three, feeling that such a request would be politically dangerous to them and to me. Members of the press corps were already making pointed observations with respect to whether or not such a commitment would be asked for or given. Had there been a piece of paper that they could have seized on or found out about, they would have had a big story and it would have been very destructive.

The committee convention met in Pocatello on a Saturday, and, after concluding its organizational business in the morning, adjourned until two to nominate a candidate for the Senate. Judge Budge and Mr. Markham had withdrawn as candidates in any active sense and another candidate had taken their place. He was State Senator A. W. "Tony" Naegle of Idaho Falls, who had been president pro tem of the last legislative session and who had just recently been defeated as a candidate for lieutenant governor in the Republican nominating primary. When the committee reconvened, there was no clear indication whether Jordan or Naegle had a majority. After the roll was called, Jordan had the majority by, I believe, two votes by virtue of a fast gavel on the rostrum in the hands of Speaker of the House William Eberle, who was presiding officer.

We returned to Boise that evening in order to resume as rapidly as possible our campaign for reelection as governor of Idaho. I was greeted in the Sunday paper the next day by an interview given by Vernon K. Smith, who alleged to be very happy that I was going to stay in Idaho and not "run away" from the terrors of a campaign against an ardent disciple of casino gambling. Governor Jordan asked me to give assistance for raising some funds for his campaign, and I said I would do what I could, mindful of the fact that I might still have to raise some additional money myself. I was also aware of the fact that our campaign for reelection was already pretty well financed. I received contributions for Jordan from Nelson Rockefeller, from the Scranton people in Pennsylvania, from E. Roland Harriman, and from Thomas McCabe. I think the total amount of money I raised for Governor Jordan was somewhere in the range of $27,000. All of that was raised in cash and without any paper trail that would embarrass the donors, Governor Jordan, or myself.

We were now about ten weeks from the general election and our television time was all booked and paid for. Our billboards were going up all over the state. Our radio spots were beginning to beat a tattoo that would reach a crescendo in the last week of the campaign, and our newspaper ads would begin to appear sometime in the next three weeks. We planned and executed caravan trips to the Upper Snake River Valley, to Twin Falls County, Ada County, and Canyon County in the old tradition of campaigns in those days. I never really knew how many votes those caravan trips garnered, but it was a splendid way to meet a lot of school children.

The big event of October was the last visit to Boise by former president Dwight Eisenhower. The general had planned to make and did make six campaign speeches in 1962, and he made the selection of where he would make those speeches himself. He said he would like to come out and help old Smylie. Bryce Harlow, his secretary, called to ask me if we could fit him into our schedule which, of course, was absurd. We could fit him into any schedule. General Eisenhower did not want to make speeches, but he thought that by making appearances he could be of assistance. He certainly was.

When the day of his appearance in Boise arrived, it was one of those clear, blue, beautiful October days that seem somehow to be made for southwest Idaho. I think I have seen at least 900 of them, and they are all wonderful. Harlow called from San Francisco, where the general had stayed overnight, and asked me if there was anything special I wanted the general to do. I said just get off the airplane and throw his arms in the air and give us the big victory smile, then if he might pat me on the back a couple of times as we rode down the avenue, I would appreciate it. He did that and more. He told the crowd assembled in the legislative chambers that I "was one of the great governors of the United States," and that he wished he had the opportunity to vote for me. We had set up photo opportunities for all of the candidates in the Governor's office so that everybody had at least one picture with the general, and I have a picture of my two boys, then aged seven and eleven, with the general and myself in the old office before it was remodeled. We prevailed on President Eisenhower to make a brief appearance on the front steps of the Capitol where he had commenced his campaign for election in 1952. He was greeted, once again, by a great throng of people.

Former president Eisenhower with the Smylie men, 1962.

With Senator Barry Goldwater at Sun Valley in 1962. ISHS 77-163.68.

We returned the general and his party to the airplane and said goodbye for the last time. It had been a brilliant campaigning afternoon, and I am sure that it garnered a large number of surplus votes for our campaign.

Vernon K. Smith continued to moan and whine because I would not debate him on the issue of casino gambling. I did not believe in debates to start with, and by then we had about a four-point lead. I decided it was useless to squander it on an opportunity to make mistakes that could obviously come up in any debate contest. We continued to use the "Ask Your Governor" programs and to do ad-lib television appearances when the opportunity presented itself and it seemed profitable to do so.

On election day night, we had a count by at least ten o'clock in the evening that clearly indicated that I had been elected to a third term as governor. This was extremely gratifying because it would now provide an opportunity to bring all of the loose ends of my twelve-year program together and perhaps even allow me to accomplish that elusive program known as tax reform.

The election results in 1962 indicated once again that the Idaho electorate is not very partisan in its choices. It elected Frank Church and Len Jordan on opposite sides of the ticket, myself and Lieutenant Governor Drevlow on opposite sides of the ticket, and two congressmen who were of opposite party persuasion. We had made many of our plans in 1962 based on concern over Vernon K. Smith and Gracie Pfost. It is one of the ironies of history that both of them were dead within the year.

My margin of victory in 1962 was the largest plurality I had ever received. This gave me leverage with the party and with the Democrats that I had not possessed before. This would be very different from the beginning of my second term, when the Democrats controlled both houses of the legislature.

Lu and I took a two-week vacation and went to the Mountain House at Norwood. I rested and received visits from some of the cabinet members who were planning the program for 1963.

At the end of two weeks, I emerged from Long Valley full of vim and vigor and returned to the political hustings. Once again, this was the biennial meeting of the North Idaho Chamber of Commerce, and I took great pleasure in telling them that the Crown Prince had emerged from his captivity in the statehouse, that the Democrats' Prince of Foxes had been driven from the land, and that I would proceed to govern in a proper fashion with a legislature quite to my liking.

CHAPTER THIRTEEN

THE THIRD GOVERNORSHIP—1963–67

GOVERNOR WILLIAM HENSON Wallace arrived at Lewiston Landing in 1863. He was the first territorial governor of Idaho. He had been sent there by President Abraham Lincoln to organize a government in what had been designated as Idaho Territory. The territory then consisted of the Dakotas, west of Bismarck, and all of Wyoming and Montana and Idaho. The southwest border of Idaho, with Nevada, Oregon, and Utah, was still undefined and unsurveyed. The reason for territorial designation had been the discovery of gold along the Clearwater River upstream from Lewiston Landing. The miners in the Clearwater diggings were primarily Confederate soldiers whose term of service had expired and who had come west to find their fortune. I am told they laughed at Governor Wallace, calling him Mr. Lincoln's governor, and promptly elected him territorial delegate to the Congress of the United States so that he would return to Washington.

They did not improve their lot a great deal by driving Wallace back to the Congress. Instead, they ended up with Caleb Lyon of Lyonsdale, New York, who promptly infuriated the people of Lewiston by "stealing" the seal of the territory and making off with it to Boise, where a greater and more productive gold field had been discovered in the Boise Basin.

By that time, Montana had been organized as a territory, the Dakotas had become a territory of their own, and Wyoming had become a territory. This left Idaho in the shape in which it now exists and it would make its way in that condition into the history books.

The centennial year, 1963, marked the celebration of the first 100 years of organized government in Idaho territory. It also was a seminal year. By 1963 Idaho had achieved a vigorous, almost independent maturity that we could build on in bringing our state into its second century of history.

A distressing out-migration of population had pretty well ceased by the end of the fifties, and by 1963 more people were moving into Idaho than were moving out. Work-force opportunities were improving. The food processing industry was beginning to be a force in the economy, led by frozen french-fries and Tater Tots. Our three statewide banking organizations were beginning to be financially strong enough to attend to the needs of our industrial development without having to rely on the old captivity to the East Coast and California. Although railroad passenger traffic had pretty well disappeared, we were served by the best airline system of intrastate transportation that the state has ever known. There was still much to be done, but by 1963 we had a foundation on which the future could be established.

Our government agencies and the personnel who directed them had been in place for nearly ten years and were performing at peak efficiency. The legislature had steadily improved its performance and was poised for the great accomplishments that were not far down the road.

The only cloud on the horizon was the lack of an adequate, productive tax structure that would meet the needs of the future. The possibilities of improving that tax system were beginning to be more politically apparent, and it looked as though we might be able to address those tax and revenue problems with some degree of success in the next four years.

The 1960 legislative elections and those in 1962 were kind to the Republican party. In 1960, we recaptured control of both houses of the

Idaho legislature. In 1962, we increased our majorities modestly so that we had a very workable team in place as we faced up to the problems of 1963.

I think historians will get a much more accurate picture of the last six years of my administration if they consider the achievements of the Thirty-sixth, Thirty-seventh, and Thirty-eighth Legislatures within the context of being the last legislative sessions before reapportionment was fastened on the state by the Supreme Court's *Baker v. Carr* decision. It is my opinion, and I think the record will bear me out, that the legislatures before reapportionment were much more capable of producing sound legislation than those since reapportionment was literally forced upon the state—almost against its will. Theoretically reapportionment was supposed to produce a more representative, and thus more liberal, legislature. Actually, exactly the opposite has occurred. There has been less opportunity for the exercise of real political acumen and courage since reapportionment than there was before. Somehow we have not produced legislators like the late Thomas Heath, Tony Naegle, K. C. Barlow, and others like them. There can be no turning back, of course, along the path that led us to reapportionment, but I think it will illustrate, if studied appropriately, that the Thirty-seventh and Thirty-eighth Legislatures achieved their very real accomplishments largely because they represented broader bases than was possible under a one-vote, one-person arrangement.

When the legislature met in 1963, we had made progress toward our long-term goal of achieving a fifty percent state contribution to the cost of public school education. That objective was then thought to be an ideal apportionment of the financial responsibility for education between local interests and those of the state at large.

We had progressed in the construction of a road system that would serve the entire state. There was still a very great deal of work to be done on the North-South Highway (U.S. 95 and State Highway 55), as traffic and terrain continued to remind us in storm-ridden winters and flood-damaging springs.

We built the 1963 budget on the existing revenue structure and did not recommend any substantial increases in taxation. This was widely criticized as lack of leadership on my part, and it may well have been. I then believed, and still believe, that what was possible in 1965 was not possible in 1963. I thought we only had one shot at enacting a sales tax and that failure to do so before it would be able to achieve victory and a referendum would probably set the possibilities of a new revenue structure back at least thirty years and perhaps forever. Oregon provides an apt and difficult example of what can happen in such circumstances as it routinely places sales tax measures on the ballot and sees them defeated year after year.

In a real sense the 1963 session of the legislature cleared the way for the achievements of the Thirty-eighth Legislature in 1965. The session moved in on lots of unfinished business that needed to be resolved for

Lucille and me at the Territorial Centennial Ball at the Bollinger Hotel in Lewiston in 1963.

Idaho to have a modern state government. The Thirty-seventh Legislature in 1963 finally accepted the notion that we needed an independent department of Parks and Recreation that would have as its sole mission the maintenance and operation and, for that matter, the origination of a park system for this luxuriantly endowed state of ours. The action came about as a result of the ratification of the contract which I had signed with the Harriman brothers, E. Roland and Averell, which promised to convey to the state at the appropriate time the Railroad Ranch. The legislature could summon the resolution to ratify the contract, but it was not yet ready to go the whole road and establish the independent park system that was necessary before the Harriman gift of the Railroad Ranch could fully vest as property of the people of the state of Idaho. The Democratic minority in the Senate had always opposed the organization of an independent parks department, and I asked them again in 1965 to take such action. The partisan logjam was broken by Mr. Darrell Manning, a legislator from Bannock County, who put together a bill which I could accept and which the legislature would adopt under his sponsorship. With that the Department of Parks and Recreation was officially born.

I count it as one of the great positive, long-term achievements of my twelve-year administration. The twenty-eight parks and recreation areas which the Department of Parks and Recreation administers are not only a very successful attempt to preserve a part of what Idaho was for what Idaho will be, it also constitutes a tremendous commercial advantage to the tourist trade of the state and is an economic asset of great value.

It is obvious that the Harriman contract had pushed us into the position of establishing a State Parks Agency. For that reason, it seems appropriate to say that the principal players in the negotiation of that contract, who I believe should get major credit for the gift to the people of Idaho, were Gladys and E. Roland Harriman. Their brother Averell was a willing participant, but the major thrust behind the idea of the creation of the Harriman State Park of Idaho belonged to Gladys and E. Roland Harriman.

Legislative ratification of the Harriman State Park Contract led inexorably to the organization of a state government-wide merit system of personnel administration. We already had five different merit systems of personnel administration covering five different departments where that sort of personnel handling was required as a condition of the receipt of federal funds. The Harriman contract made it obvious that a sixth personnel system would have to be devised. The legislature enacted a Merit System of Personnel Administration which covered all state employment, with a few exceptions. It was patterned after the federal merit systems we had been living with in the years since World War II and which had served us reasonably well.

With enactment of the merit system for personnel, it became necessary to consider the creation of a public employees' retirement system. Here again, the federally funded agencies had been marching ahead of the agencies of state government. I appointed a cabinet committee to devise a plan which could be considered by the legislature, and they came up with a system that is essentially the one now in existence. This committee was headed by Mr. H. Fred Garrett, one of the finest public servants the state ever had. Mr. Garrett was in charge of the Employment Security Agency for many years and was the principal author of the Public Employees' Retirement System Act. We had given the legislature a tentative look at this proposal earlier, and they had been remarkably unenthusiastic. We then devised a plan for covering the part-time boards and agencies, and, under that definition, were able to include legislative membership. This changed the legislative attitude toward the retirement system, and it was adopted in 1963, although we were unable to fund it for prior service until additional revenues were achieved through the sales tax. There were many people who had worked up to twenty years continuously in state service, and the prior-service benefit was designed to permit them to participate in retirement based on their total service.

There is nothing in these later years of my lifetime that is quite as gratifying to me as to have someone who worked in state service encounter me on the street and say thank you for helping bring into being the retirement system that provides retirees with a dignified and decently funded old age. It makes the retirement system almost the best thing we ever did.

Sometime in the early sixties, the Metropolitan Water Board of Los Angeles County, California, released a report designed as a guideline for furnishing adequate water supplies to the golf courses and green lawns of the desert Southwest. One of the principal sources of additional water which the Metropolitan Board thought they might use involved tapping into what they called the unappropriated waters of the Snake River at Hagerman, Idaho, and pumping the water all the way to Los Angeles through a great conduit that would have been something like the conduits that bring the Owens Valley water into the Los Angeles Basin. The Los Angeles plan was an imminent threat to our water resources and a threat to the entire future of the state of Idaho. I recognized that this was going to require immediate action. One could not take the position that it would be years before the California threat was a reality—the stakes were too high.

I devised a plan for the creation of a constitutional agency which would have jurisdiction over the waters of the state, both as to quantity and quality. This required a constitutional amendment, a special session of the legislature, and passage of the amendment by two-thirds majorities in both houses. I unveiled my plans in a speech at Idaho State University in Pocatello and began a series of public addresses designed to illustrate the need for action.

I consulted with the legislature and its leadership. There did not seem to be any great opposition to the proposed constitutional amendment, and so I called a special session in 1964 to enact a constitutional amendment proposal that could be placed on the 1964 general election ballot. The legislature met, adopted the proposed amendment in one afternoon session, adjourned, and went home. This action provided a spectacular example of the proper use of the gubernatorial call for a special session of the legislature to consider extraordinary items and should have made it unnecessary to ever consider the adoption of the plan for annual sessions of the legislature, which, in my judgment, has been a mistake and one which we already have learned to regret. There is not enough legitimate legislative business to require the legislature to meet more than every two years. Annual meetings provide an opportunity for lobbyists to do their work twice as often and thus to cause expenditures to mount faster than would be necessary or possible if they only had an opportunity to work on the legislature every two years.

There was little organized opposition to adoption of the constitutional amendment, and the people approved it by a substantial majority in the 1964 general election. The Idaho government had never formally taken advantage of the opportunity to organize the use and protection of its water resources until 1964. It is a curious omission in the history of the state probably explained by the fact that we thought we had all the water we would ever want. It turns out that we did not have that much water.

In 1965, the Thirty-eighth Legislature enacted a statute which created a Department of Water Resources and empowered it to do most of the things that the constitutional amendment had forecast. There was a modest additional expenditure, but it was quite obvious that down the road this new department would cost us a good deal of money.

At almost every turn in the road, we found ourselves wanting and reaching for new government activities that were going to be costly. In 1963, we created the Idaho State Capitol Mall in the eight blocks bounded on the west by Eighth Street and St. Michael's Cathedral and the State Capitol and on the east by Third Street and what is now the Idaho State Library and Archives. In between a splendid series of buildings would be constructed that would be an asset to the state and provide an adequate home for its agencies. All this cost money too.

Boise Junior College was undergoing a metamorphosis to Boise College to Boise State College to Boise State University and the campus that now houses 17,000 students. I believe it fair to say that we have spent more money on Boise State University than we did on all institutions of higher education prior to 1946, but the important consideration is that in 1965 one could foresee the ultimate cost of our university on the river would require a state sales tax.

We were also beginning to put together our response to the interstate highway system, and even though only eight percent of the cost of that construction was borne by the state, it was a substantial sum, and we were also constructing our statewide highway network.

It was apparent when the legislature went home in 1963 that we were going to have to forego some of the things we wanted to accomplish or that we would have to find new revenue sources, and we began to consider the possibility of enacting a sales tax. With adequate money, we could fund the public retirement system, move public school education support to fifty percent of the cost of education, complete the highway system, and develop the Capitol Mall. For the next year and a half we began a search for revenues to support our maturing appetite for public expenditure.

CHAPTER FOURTEEN

THE SALES TAX OF 1965

ENACTMENT OF THE 1965 sales tax was undoubtedly the most important legislative act of Idaho's 100 years. Its passage marked a defining moment in the state's struggle toward political and economic maturity. The new tax permitted building a balanced tax and revenue structure and provided funds so we could begin to really do the things we wanted to do, needed to do, and which would keep us from being condemned to mediocrity. The Thirty-eighth Legislature that met in 1965 was composed of a star-studded group of statesmen brilliantly led on both sides of the aisle, and they were willing to make the decisions that were bold enough to be great and great enough to last. It seems desirable to lay out with some clarity and precision the story of the sales tax of 1965 by placing it within the context of Idaho's tax history.

For the first forty-one years of statehood, Idaho had relied primarily on a system of license fees and excise taxes of various sorts and a biennial levy of a property tax for the use of the state government, which was collected by the county treasurers and transmitted to the state treasurer. The Supreme Court had held that the state's levy was entitled to come off the top of the money collected in the counties, and this proved to be a reasonably reliable source of modest revenues.

In 1931 when C. Ben Ross became governor, the Great Depression was tightening its grip on the state and the collection of the property tax at the county level was insufficient to permit the state's revenues to be collected and forwarded intact. This literally forced the 1931 session of the legislature to enact what was euphemistically referred to as the Property Tax Relief Act of 1931, which was in reality a graduated income tax. It applied to both persons and corporations. The corporate inclusion was designed by the Democrats to make the tax politically palatable. From the beginning the tax was apparently regarded largely as optional. There was little effort on the part of the state to collect the new tax, and, as it became apparent that payment was not obligatory and could be disregarded with impunity, the revenues began to shrink.

The principal call on state funds in 1935 was to defray the cost of various public assistance programs and other programs designed to ease the burden of the increasingly tighter Depression. Through the first four years of his administration, Governor Ross had been a genius at exacting money for these purposes from the United States. I am told that finally he was informed by Mr. Harry Hopkins, President Roosevelt's chief of staff, that push had come to shove and that the state would need to enact new revenue measures if it was going to hope to participate in the various federal relief programs that were planned and were being implemented in Congress. With extreme reluctance, Governor Ross asked for and received from the legislature a bill imposing a sales tax. It was a reasonably primitive type of impost, but it did raise the money that was required for participation in the federal recovery programs. There was no particular hue and cry immediately against the sales tax, and one would have thought it was safely and permanently ensconced as part of the state's revenue structure. The business community, however, apparently decided that a sales tax would have a ruinous effect on their ability to do business and began securing the signatures necessary to hold a referendum on the new tax in the 1936 election.

Opposition to the sales tax was led by the late Mr. C. C. Anderson, who owned department stores that ultimately became known today as the Bon Marché. Opposition to the tax used the slogan "Pennies for Bennie" (Bennie was Governor C. Ben Ross) and it was probably this slogan that brought the tax down. I have always thought it curious that the business community in Idaho opposed a sales tax in that early enactment simply because they were so strongly in favor of one in 1965. The business communities in other states that enacted sales taxes were equally in favor of that type of revenue raising rather than placing extreme reliance on an income tax or other similar impost.

Sometime in 1935, Governor C. Ben Ross decided to challenge the late William Edgar Borah for his seat in the United States Senate. Mr. Anderson had always served as Borah's finance chairman, and this perhaps explains why Anderson found it necessary to conduct a vendetta against the 1935 sales tax. In any event, it was soundly defeated in November of 1936, and that rejection kept it from being seriously considered for another thirty years.

Nothing much occurred in the way of revenue legislation until the first Bottolfsen administration in 1939. The automobile license plate fee was reduced to a flat five dollars in that year leaving no revenues left over for building the needed highways. The state put up with the five dollar license plate fee until 1955, when it was finally raised to fifteen dollars.

In 1945 the legislature placed the first tax on cigarettes, which were selling for about twelve cents a package at the time. The legislative history of that first cigarette tax indicates that there was more in the way of moral legislation involved in its enactment than revenue raising. In 1947, the state commenced a brief flirtation with slot machine revenues and liquor-by-the-drink licensing fees as a means of solving our revenue problems. It was apparent by 1950 that this wasn't going to work either. In 1953, Governor Jordan insisted on reducing the income and property taxes by twenty-five percent, much to the dismay of many, including myself. The tax cut was no vote getter, and, as a matter of fact, it probably had an adverse effect upon Jordan's fortunes. In any event, it left my new administration in a very severe financial bind when we met to consider the future in 1955.

Governor Len Jordan's budget director left a bundle of departmental and institutional requests for appropriations on my desk totalling about $55 million. The revenue structure which was then in place after the ill-conceived tax cuts of 1953 was estimated by my people to produce $40.5 million. This would have meant a $15 million shortfall or almost thirty percent of the total cost projected for the next two years for state government. When the administration changed hands, we were $600,000 in the red ink and would have to make that sum up in the six months remaining in the fiscal year.

We managed to bring the budget request down to about $50 million and still had to find $10 million in revenues in order to balance revenues and expenditures for the period 1955 to 1957. Representative Ralph Wickberg and his Revenue and Taxation Committee in the House of Representatives put together a package of what we termed patch-and-scratch taxes composed of excises of one kind or another, but mostly focusing on cigarettes and booze. The legislature trimmed my appropriation request by about $1 million (for which I was deeply grateful), and with Wickberg's revenue improvisations, we were able to close the books with a budget in very close to technical balance. It was already clear to everyone that the existing revenue sources could not be stretched much farther and that ultimately a new revenue source was going to be required. The question was not whether, but when.

Toward the end of the 1955 legislative session, and while we were still wrestling with our financial problems, Mr. Les Randall, the chief executive officer of Hecla Mining Company, came to call and suggested that a statewide commission to study the revenue structure would be a good way to start the discussion of what we should do. Like any successful businessman, Randall knew all the answers to governmental problems. He had no way of knowing that there were not more than a dozen votes in either house for a sales tax in this session, and that it might be three or four sessions before a workable majority could be put together behind such a proposal. Nevertheless, his idea of a study group of some kind had a good deal of merit as a vehicle for educating and molding public sentiment. Mr. Wickberg fashioned a plan for an interim committee to study our revenue structure and make a recommendation to the Thirty-fourth Legislature. It was quickly adopted, and with that action, most of the work of the session was ended and adjournment was accomplished.

The media gave the session general approval, and it was well received on the main streets of Idaho, but not everybody was happy. The universities thought they had been shortchanged, and they had. Nearly every operating budget in the state departments had been trimmed to the bone, and we still had not appropriated any funding for the Teacher's Retirement System. This left about $15 million of unfunded obligations that would have to be met sooner or later. The shape of things to come was now visible.

The interim tax study committee met, held hearings, conducted studies, and finally wrote a report which reached the public in the months before the 1956 elections. As expected, the tax report recommended the enactment of a sales tax and the use of some of its revenue to replace other taxes thought to be more onerous. Which tax you desired to have replaced depended on your situation. There was not any great public outcry about the Wickberg report, but when the votes were counted in the legislative elections that year, it was obvious that disapproval was the order of the day. Wickberg was defeated in his own stronghold and one of the civilian members of the commission, Mr. Perry Swisher of Bannock County, was defeated in a try for the legislature. This would have left a sales tax without its principal proponents to guide it through the legislature. It would have been hopeless to try and enact a sales tax in 1957; as a consequence, I waffled in my presentation of the budget with a lot of pious language about when and how a new tax might possibly be achieved. Once again, the legislature was obliged to "skinny-up" the appropriations and make do with some more patch-and-scratch additions to the income tax.

The Democrats assailed my failure to embrace the sales tax as the savior that they thought it would be, and they called my failure to do so lack of leadership. It was in a sense just exactly that, but it would have been useless to have made the legislative wheels grind on each other. There just were not enough votes to get the job done in 1957.

After the elections in 1958, the year of the "Great Republican Disaster," it seemed relatively useless to suggest a sales tax as a remedy for fiscal woes as long as I would have to depend on a Republican minority and a few Democratic votes to attempt to try and pass it. This was impossible, although I did offer to cooperate with the Democratic majority in achieving a solution to our fiscal problems if they desired to join hands and jump over the cliff together with me. The Democratic majority quickly rejected this offer and came up with their head tax as a solution to meeting the needs of the budget in 1959.

In 1961, the House of Representatives could pass a sales tax bill, but the Senate would have no part of it, and it would have failed there by perhaps as many as ten votes.

George Crookham, former mayor of Caldwell and a member of the legislature from Canyon County, had been a principal supporter of the sales tax. In 1962 he decided to force the issue by filing as a candidate against me in the Republican primary. Crookham's announcement of his sales tax plan polarized the issue and made it necessary from a political point of view for me to say that it was not yet time for a sales tax. With that sort of waffling on the issue, I was able to blunt the thrust of his support for a new revenue structure.

Meanwhile, Vernon K. Smith had announced his candidacy for the Democratic nomination on a platform which would have legalized casino gambling in all of its parts. The Democrats did not take Smith seriously at first, but he finally ended up as their candidate and with forty-six percent of the primary vote. Crookham's aggressive sales tax campaign achieved a twenty-six percent share of the primary vote, and perhaps was an accurate measurement of the then-existing strength of sentiment for a sales tax in the body politic generally.

A few weeks before the general election in 1962, the Cuban Missile Crisis occurred. We were advised by the White House to hunker down and keep in close communication with our headquarters at all times. I think the Cuban Missile Crisis reinforced the campaigns of all incumbents simply because the American public tends in times of crisis not to want to change things too much. In any event, incumbents seemed to be greatly favored by the electorate in the election of 1962. Of course, I was an incumbent.

While we were preparing the budget and the accompanying messages for the 1963 legislature, we did not think a new departure in revenue and taxation was possible in light of the international situation. As a consequence, we stretched the revenue projections as far as we safely could, and, even though the legislature outspent those estimates, we felt secure in closing the books on the Thirty-seventh Legislature. The Thirty-seventh Legislature had passed the retirement system and various other bills which would provide an ongoing increase in the cost of government. It was necessary for us to take that into consideration as we began to plan for 1965.

When the budget office had received the informal request of the institutions and agencies and other activities of government, the sum, added to the total cost of funding the retirement system, reached an astounding $145 million. We were looking at this proposed expenditure with a revenue structure that could not be relied on to produce a nickel more than $110 million. It was the largest revenue shortfall in the history of the state and push had finally come to shove in the Idaho statehouse.

The Thirty-eighth Session of the Idaho Legislature, which would convene in January, was to prove that experience was an excellent ingredient in legislative management. It was probably the most brilliant assembly of legislative talent in the history of the state. In the governor's office, we began to count votes almost as soon as the legislature was elected. It was apparent that a sales tax bill could pass the House of Representatives and that a vote in the Senate would likely be very close to twenty-two ayes and twenty-two nays. That was not enough with Lieutenant Governor Drevlow in the position to cast the deciding vote. It did begin to seem worthwhile to give serious consideration to strong endorsement of a new revenue and taxation policy that would put us in condition to face the future with confidence for the next twenty years. In the governor's office, we prepared two informal budget projections. One budget was based on the assumption that we would be able to enjoy the revenues derived from a new sales and use tax. The other budget was a bare-bones proposal that would be dictated by necessity if we had to go forward with the existing revenue structure of $110 million. The question of which road to take from this crossroads was of sufficient practical and political consequence that it seemed to me to require that I take the party leadership and the legislature into my confidence and give them some idea of what might lie ahead.

I asked President Pro Tem of the Senate Jack Murphy to have a breakfast meeting at his home in Shoshone and to invite Speaker of the House Pete Cenarrusa, Senator George Blick from Twin Falls, who was Senate majority leader, and William Lanting from Hollister in Twin Falls County, who was majority leader in the House of Representatives. I flew down from Boise with two staff people who could furnish budget information if it was needed. Cleora Murphy cooked a beautiful breakfast. After we had finished eating, we got down to the serious business of deciding what we were going to do. None of the legislators had the slightest idea of what I had in mind.

I told them that I was seriously considering a request of the Thirty-eighth Legislature to enact a three percent sales and use tax, and I wanted them to know the reason why. I asked them to keep what I just said and what I would say in secrecy and hold it in confidence solely between themselves until I had reached a conclusion as to what we were going to do. All four of them agreed to these conditions and we proceeded.

I told them that the asking price on the upcoming budget was in the neighborhood of $150 million, and that it could probably be trimmed to $145 million without doing substantial damage to the existing programs or those that had been authorized by the 1963 session. I said that a three percent sales and use tax would probably provide adequate funds for a budget of that size and would also provide enough latitude for substantial tax reform and tax relief in the property tax sector. I showed them the other budget, which would have proposed spending $110 million, and it was apparent that this would be a disastrous course of action for the institutions and agencies involved—especially the universities.

None of the four legislators seemed entirely dismayed by the proposed sales tax. As a matter of fact, one of them said he thought we could no longer afford to do without it. I said I was almost persuaded that the consequences of not doing some of the things that people wanted done would be politically more disastrous than the imposition of the proposed new tax. It was at this meeting that I heard the first word spoken about the possibility of a college in Twin Falls. This has since come about and it now has a student body of about 4,000 students.

As I remember, our discussions lasted about four hours. I had assured them that as soon as I decided on the course of action I would pursue at the opening session of the legislature I would let them know.

I did not finally make up my mind until New Year's Day of 1965. We were spending the New Year's holiday at the Mountain House deep in the snow of Long Valley. After breakfast everybody left except myself and went to McCall to visit friends. I spent the afternoon pondering the decision about whether or not Idaho should have a sales tax. Sometime about mid-afternoon I decided to try some language on for size on the typewriter. The message on the state of the state had already been written, but the new, alternate conclusion could present the sales tax. The decision now had to be faced. I spent a few brief paragraphs explaining the alternatives that might be before us in the way of service to our people, and then came down to the paragraph which reads in the message, "The budget, when it reaches you, will be based upon and will strongly recommend the enactment of a three percent sales and use tax." That language seemed to ring a bell for me. We returned to Boise the next day, and I spent the week polishing the state of the state and the budget message.

Just before the weekend, I unveiled the state of the state message to the press. When I delivered it to the legislature and got to the part about the three percent sales and use tax, I received a surprise. For the only time in twelve years as governor, I was interrupted by applause when I finished the sentence. It seemed an excellent harbinger of things to come.

The budget message would come five days later and would spell out in detail the proposals for tax reform and tax redistribution. Once this was accomplished, the legislature could set about preparing implementation of the message. George Crookham had a draft of a sales and use tax proposal, which provided a pretty good launching pad for the efforts of the Revenue and Taxation Committee. The House authorized the committee to retain staff, and they sent for Philip Petersen from the University of Idaho to assist them in drafting a proposed piece of legislation. After a proposal is in legislative chambers and is beginning to move through the processes of legislative enactment, there is very little that a governor can do to influence bits and pieces of the legislation. As nearly as we could ascertain, the committee was staying fairly close to the measure that I had outlined in the concluding paragraphs of the budget message. About thirty days into the session, a bill was introduced in the House by the Revenue and Taxation Committee and moved through the usual channels fairly quickly and was enacted by that body by a reasonably substantial margin.

Now that the bill was in the Senate, we were going to be hard put to secure the necessary majority. Senator Murphy and some of the others had an idea that we should enact the bill subject to a referendum by the people that would be held before the legislation was in effect. I was pretty sure that popular reaction to the new tax would rest almost entirely on what people saw in it that was good for them. The most important item was the fact that we were increasing state support of public school education to the fifty-percent-of-total-cost figure that had been an elusive goal for almost a generation. This would afford the opportunity for some substantial property tax relief from the maintenance and operation levies in the local school districts. The municipalities would get assistance out of revenues from the liquor dispensary, and the universities would be accorded almost exactly the funds they had been asking for. There was some modest tax relief in the income tax law which provided further attraction for approval of the new tax. If the tax were enacted and these "goodies" were in place, they would tend to secure approval of the new revenue structure. Murphy and a couple of other senators came down to try and convince me that the referendum should come first before the tax went into effect. I told them that there was no way I could approve such a proposal, and, if they persisted in that activity, I would feel obliged to veto the public school educational equalization bill and call them back in special session.

When the bill was placed upon final passage in the Senate, it failed by a vote of twenty ayes and twenty-four nays. Notice of reconsideration of that vote was filed in due course, and the legislative leadership began to repair some of the defects that the first vote had revealed. Legislative grease in terms of increased appropriations for this, that, or the other item was applied where necessary. When the vote was taken on reconsideration, the bill passed twenty-four ayes and twenty nays. On July 1, 1965, Idaho would have a new sales tax and a new tax structure that was modern enough to last for the next twenty years without substantial change or substantial addition to the revenue structure. With that vote, the work of the great Thirty-eighth Legislature was almost complete.

I probably think this legislature was great because they did almost everything I asked them to do. When they concluded, they had brought the state into full scale maturity—both economically and politically. The legislature adjourned and went home, I think with very considerable trepidation, but it is important to note as a matter of history that twenty years later they met for dinner in the Hotel Boise's Crystal Ballroom to celebrate the excellence of what they had done. They invited me to the party, although I was the only one who had failed to survive politically.

Twenty years later one could safely claim that the sales tax of 1965 did indeed have a thousand fathers, but in 1965 there were a lot fewer heroes who were willing to take a position on the edge of the cliff and lead the charge into the future.

In the House of Representatives, where the bill was drafted, the margin of victory was fairly comfortable, and the work progressed without much difficulty under brilliant floor management by William Lanting, the majority leader from Twin Falls County, and Speaker Pete Cenarrusa from Blaine County. My memory serves that Ernest Allen from Canyon County was a strong backer of the bill and effective in the floor work that secured its passage.

In the Senate the margin, of course, was going to be razor thin. It was absolutely necessary to avoid mistakes. George Blick, the majority leader, helped immensely and managed to keep President Pro Tem Jack

Murphy working in harness. Senator Perry Swisher of Bannock County, who had long been a proponent of the sales tax, managed the bill on the floor of the Senate. He was possessed of extremely competent legislative skills, and his leadership was crucial, especially in the days between the first vote on the bill and the vote on reconsideration.

Outside the legislature, considerable credit goes to George Crookham, who had forced the issue on a sales tax in the 1962 gubernatorial primary. He probably did more than any other person to shape public opinion in the early days of the discussion. W. Lloyd Adams of Rexburg, a lobbyist who told me that with respect to the sales tax he was unemployed, did a very good job of helping Swisher negotiate with the Democrats, and he also managed to keep the business community from doing anything silly in its endeavors to satisfy its appetites for tax advantages. There were many others who contributed to the achievement of victory, but these names stand out as persons who made a very great contribution. I think I am entitled to claim that the sales tax of 1965 would not have been enacted without my strong leadership, and I am grateful for the opportunity to have been a part of the movement that led Idaho and its government into substantial political maturity.

The tax bill became effective on July 1, 1965, and the revenues began to be available within the next quarter. The referendum petitions secured sufficient signatures and the approval or disapproval of the new revenue structure would be on the ballot in 1966. The business community, who took the position that there could have been improvements in the bill, rather sat on its hands during the first six or seven months that the new tax was in effect. Everyone seemed to take approval of the new revenue structure for granted, until my defeat in the primary by an opponent of the sales tax. This woke everybody up, and the business community immediately began a campaign which they denominated, "Save our Schools." This was really not their motivation, but it was good enough to provide a vehicle that would secure approval of the tax in a popular referendum. I took to the hustings myself in a rigorous effort to carry the message that the sales tax was inevitable and failure to approve it would be a disaster.

As early as the 1965 school year, the public could begin to see the effect of the infusion of this new money into their public schools. When the tax bills were being computed, they could see the effect on their income tax liability. As the state moved along toward the 1966 general election, the approval of the sales tax seemed to become more apparent, and it was finally approved by a very adequate majority in the general election of 1966. We had thus avoided the fate of Governor C. Ben Ross's endeavor to enact a sales tax thirty years earlier.

CHAPTER FIFTEEN

NATIONAL RECOGNITION, DEFEAT, AND THE "DESCENT FROM GLORY"

When I took the office to commence a third four-year term, I became the senior governor in the fifty states of the Republic. At the end of the term, I would have served twelve years, and that record had only been equalled by three other governors before me. One was Jonathan Trumbull, a colonial governor of Connecticut. The second was Thomas E. Dewey of New York, and the third was Theodore McKeldin of Maryland. The fact that I was now senior to all the rest of the members of the Governors Conference was enough to attract some attention from the national press.

In 1954, not even the weekly news magazines carried any notice of my election as governor of Idaho. We did a little better in 1958, but I have a notion they were more interested in the right-to-work initiative, which went down to defeat in that election, than they were in who was going to be governor of the state of Idaho. As a consequence, news of my narrow, lonesome victory rode piggyback on the right-to-work story. After 1959 I began to be invited to appear on weekly talk shows like *Meet the Press* and *Face the Nation*, and occasionally a touring correspondent for one of the big national print media would drop by Boise and come to call.

After the 1958 elections, there were only thirteen Republican governors in the nation, and we fared not much better in 1960 when we managed to increase that number by one. In 1963, we decided that maybe direct action was what was needed to correct the disparity in gubernatorial incumbencies. We were only fourteen Republican governors, but it was a pretty select group. There was George Romney of Michigan, Nelson Rockefeller of New York, William Scranton of Pennsylvania, John Volpe of Massachusetts, Mark Hatfield of Oregon, and John Love of Colorado. At a meeting of all fourteen governors, we decided to form an organization called the Republican Governors' Association. Its purpose would be to increase our voice in the development of political objectives on a national level and to increase our numbers in order to have more effective representation in the electoral college when the next president was nominated and elected. I think largely because I was senior, I was elected chairman of the association and was assigned to organize an office for its operations. There was no time to raise funds, and the 1964 presidential election was fast approaching. We deemed it appropriate to postpone action until after the 1964 election year.

We encouraged incumbent governors to recruit candidates for the governorship in surrounding states where that seemed appropriate and politically acceptable. We also laid plans for a series of campaign conferences, as we then called them, where we could be of assistance to gubernatorial candidates in various states who might want to have some suggestions about how to conduct a campaign. There are no textbooks on this arcane business, and so it seemed appropriate for those of us who had won to attempt to be helpful to neophytes.

In the late summer of 1963, what polling existed indicated that President Kennedy was no sure bet for reelection. The president and his semi-imperial entourage had begun to move about the country in a campaign mode which took them in November to Dallas and the unfortunate assassination of John F. Kennedy.

The late president was buried in Arlington Cemetery with great pomp and ceremony and in the presence of many world leaders. President Johnson insisted that all of the governors come to Washington for the ceremony and for a conference with him. Lyndon Johnson was deeply concerned that there might indeed be some plot afoot to bring him down and with him the government of the United States. He thought it important to demonstrate the solidarity of our union to the world. The absence of Prime Minister Krushchev of the Union of Soviet Socialist Republics was a notable cause for concern.

I traveled to Washington with Governor George Clyde of Utah and Governor Tim Babcock of Montana in a plane belonging to the Utah National Guard. We arrived late Sunday afternoon and went up to the Capitol to pay our respects where the late president was lying in state in the Rotunda. That evening at dinner, talk turned to what one might expect would be the number one topic in Washington, D.C.—who would be a candidate for president against Lyndon Johnson, who it was anticipated would certainly run for the office. It was the consensus among the governors that Lyndon Johnson would be more difficult to defeat than John F. Kennedy would have been. Johnson's landslide victory in November of 1964 seemed to bear out this contemporaneous estimate of his political strength.

The funeral occupied most of the next day, and we were preparing to depart for our various capitals when we received a summons to attend a meeting in the old Indian Treaty Room in the Executive Office Building across West Executive Avenue from the White House. We met there until nearly midnight with the president and most of his cabinet and then returned to Andrews Air Force Base for the flight back to Salt Lake City, where I connected with a plane to Boise.

I do not recall very much about the conference with the president and his cabinet on that occasion, but I do recall that the emphasis was on developing a posture of extreme political solidarity in order to demonstrate the strength of our government in the face of a crisis. It was a very solemn gathering and one which portrayed a picture of unity to the foreign leaders who were our nation's guests.

The period of mourning for President Kennedy extended well into the Christmas season and early 1964, an election year. It was apparent that the Democrats would nominate President Johnson to succeed himself. The only question for their convention was who might be the vice-presidential nominee.

At the beginning of 1964, there were two principal candidates being talked about for the Republican nomination for president. They were Senator Barry Goldwater of Arizona, who was the pride of the conservative wing of the party, and Governor Nelson Rockefeller of New York, who was regarded by some as a moderate and others as a liberal, but by none as a conservative. Governor Rockefeller had been divorced by his first wife in 1963 and had remarried, and would become a father in June. The governor's marital difficulties were made much of by the press, which I think concentrated on Governor Rockefeller's difficulties largely out of a sense of shame for not having reported President Kennedy's peccadilloes. Even so, Governor Rockefeller had a very substantial lead going into the primary season in 1964, but as the year wore on, the race between Goldwater and Rockefeller became closer. It seemed as though a decision would go down to the wire at the California primary in June. Our neighboring state of Oregon held its primary early in May, and largely, I think, because he thought he could not win there, Senator Goldwater did not conduct a campaign. Governor Rockefeller won handily in what was then regarded as a liberal stronghold. After Oregon, it was quite apparent that whoever won in California would be nominated for president at the Republican's San Francisco convention.

In the week after the Oregon primary, I received a telephone call from George Hinman, who was Republican national committeeman from the state of New York and who was widely regarded in political circles as Nelson Rockefeller's roving ambassador-at-large. He asked if he and his wife might come to see Lucille and me. I said we would probably be at the Mountain House at Norwood. My trusted lieutenant, Robert McCall, met the Hinmans at the Boise airport and drove them up to Donnelly and Norwood, where we spent a pleasant afternoon, and, for me, in retrospect, a very exciting one. Hinman knew that Idaho's delegates were already pledged to Senator Goldwater, and that there was not much that could be done about that, so that was not the reason for his visit.

Hinman said that everything now depended on California, and that they would make no real plans until that race had been decided.

The polls indicated that the result was a toss-up. Hinman then turned to a discussion of some of my colleagues in the Republican Governors' Association in terms of who might possibly be considered as members of a government headed by Governor Rockefeller. Finally, he quietly inquired about whether I knew of any reason in my background why I should not be considered as one of the people about whom they were conducting inquiries. I said no without really realizing what it was he had been talking about. After a time, he said that Governor Rockefeller thought extremely well of me, and that he had been instructed to inquire if I would be interested in being considered as a candidate for vice president and/or Secretary of the Interior. I told him I would be pleased to be considered, and with that our conversation about political affairs ended and we sat for a time enjoying the spring afternoon by the North Fork of the Payette River looking at the mountain across the way, which is called No Business. About four o'clock in the afternoon,

The house at Norwood from the back. In the distance, across the North Fork of the Payette, is No Business Mountain.

after a three-hour visit, the Hinmans were driven back to Boise by Robert McCall.

Sitting there on the deck of the Mountain House at Norwood I had no way of knowing how many people Hinman had made that same speech to, but I learned later that there were at least three or four. It was nonetheless flattering and very heady conversation for the governor of a small western state. In any event, it would all come to naught because Nelson Rockefeller would fail to win the crucial California delegation by a very narrow margin and would withdraw his name from consideration. This left Senator Goldwater an open road to the nomination, although he was perfunctorily opposed by Governor Scranton of Pennsylvania, who jumped into the race very late in the game. Goldwater was nominated in San Francisco and went on to conduct a campaign which almost looked as though it was trying to find a place where it was respectable to lose. In any event, he was defeated by President Johnson in a landslide of the same proportions as that by which President Roosevelt had defeated Governor Landon of Kansas in 1936. In the meantime, Senator Goldwater's Arizona confederates had taken over the national framework of the party and were proceeding to administer it for their own use and benefit. The Arizona group was led by a gentleman named Dean Burch, who was Senator Goldwater's handpicked national chairman.

On election night when the dimensions of President Johnson's landslide victory began to be apparent, I did some telephoning around the country to talk with my colleagues in the governors' offices. There was almost unanimous opinion that we needed a new national chairman and that we needed that change almost immediately. I had no intention of going public with this idea until I was called by Earl Mazo, political editor of the *New York Times*, who was an old and trusted friend and who asked what we were going to do about the condition in which we found the party after Goldwater's disastrous defeat. At that point, I mentioned our intention to replace Dean Burch. We had planned a meeting of the Republican Governors' Association in Denver in early December, and it seemed desirable to go forward with our campaign to get a new national chairman at that Denver meeting. The meeting was held on December 3 and 4, 1964, and convened in the Brown Palace Hotel and in the residence of Governor John Love of Colorado. After nearly fourteen hours of nonstop deliberation of one kind or another, we issued a unanimously approved declaration of policy which came to be known as the Denver Declaration. The declaration did not call for the removal of Mr. Burch as national chairman, but called for a leadership of the party that could achieve national unity. We asked for a policy organization which could adopt policy statements for the party during the interim between presidential elections and concluded with a call for a party that was all encompassing and permitted representation from every shade of political belief—moderate, conservative, and liberal.

While we were meeting in the Brown Palace Hotel, the national committee was conducting an informal meeting in the Cosmopolitan Hotel across the street. How the national press corps, which was there en masse, managed to miss this development, I do not know, but they never did report it. By the time we left Denver, we had pretty well decided that our candidate for national chairman was the honorable Ray Bliss, state chairman of Ohio, who was a magnificent political tactician and one who was almost, but not quite, acceptable to all of the political spectrum.

In mid-December, Mr. Burch and Senator Goldwater made a vain attempt to get General Eisenhower to intercede with the national committee on Burch's behalf. They were unsuccessful. It was fairly apparent that Burch had counted the votes and knew he was going to come up short. He announced that he would resign as national chairman in January and leave office on the first of March. Immediate departure would have been preferable as far as the governors were concerned, but what had been negotiated by the national committee was acceptable and we could undertake to move forward with the committee and the members of Congress who needed to be consulted. Upon taking office, Mr. Bliss created what he called a Republican Coordinating Committee composed of members of Congress, governors, members of the national committee, and former candidates for President of the United States. It was the task of the committee to prepare position papers on issues of current importance to the party and to publish them in lieu of platform documents so that the party would have an ongoing and updated statement of principles with which to react to initiatives of President Lyndon Johnson. This was essentially the kind of organization that the Denver Declaration had suggested, and so the governors were quite pleased. I was named to be a member of the Republican Coordinating Committee and served as a member for as long as I was governor of Idaho.

Meanwhile, we had laid plans to open an office for the association in Washington in the same building as the one where the national committee was located. Some funds had become available through donations from interested citizens of the United States, and we were able to place a skeleton staff in the Washington office when it opened, with Chairman Bliss's blessing, in mid-May of 1965. This completed the items specified in the governors' Denver Declaration of December 1964.

In that springtime of 1965, almost everything seemed to be coming up roses. The Thirty-eighth Legislature had completed its historic work. The sales tax was about to go into effect. Our schools could open in the fall with the prospect of adequate funds to satisfy their needs. Editorial approval of the administration was almost unanimous. On a national level, the Republican Governors' Association was up and running, and our plans for the 1966 elections were being put together. The only cloud on the horizon was the fact that nobody seemed to be speaking out in favor of retaining the sales tax against the coming referendum vote. For that reason I began making speeches at various service clubs around the state pointing out the inevitability of having to find a new source of revenue should the referendum repeal the sales tax measure. Although I did not realize it at the time, I think those speeches and my strong support of the sales tax began to polarize public opinion against me. It is entirely possible that by giving the public some person to be against, we had saved the sales tax for the future of the state. It was curious that none of the educational associations nor the business community seemed to care to openly support the new tax, although they were the principal beneficiaries of its enactment. The members of the legislature who had supported the tax and who would be hailed by history as heroes because of its enactment also were hunkered down in their local districts and were not heard to strongly support the tax, with a few exceptions.

Much to my surprise, and without consultation, Senator Jordan announced that he was a candidate for reelection to the Senate. I could have chosen to oppose Jordan in a primary campaign, but I thought that would be utterly destructive of party unity and would also jeopardize the sales tax when it came to be tested in the referendum. After some agonizing, I decided I almost had a duty to run for reelection for a fourth term.

Senator Don Samuelson of Bonner County announced his candidacy against me for the Republican nomination for governor. I think almost everybody was as surprised as I was, and I have to confess now that I did not take Samuelson seriously and was guilty of tremendous overconfidence. This was a gross miscalculation on my part.

The primary election was in August that year, and about three weeks out from election day, I began to be concerned that I might be defeated. We had planned our campaign to take the Democrats head-on on the sales tax issue in the general election. As a consequence, we did not pursue Senator Samuelson with the vigor that, it turns out, was required.

The results were not long in coming on the night of the primary election in August of 1966. It was not a defeat, it was devastation. Without checking, I believe I carried only four counties, and those by narrow margins. Curiously, nobody else who had supported the sales tax was defeated in that election.

It would be useless speculation to attempt to divine the reasons for my defeat. In retrospect I know I was overconfident. I suspect I was a little arrogant about the necessity of preserving the sales tax and managed to wrap the mantle of righteousness on that issue around me a little too tightly. In any defeat as devastating as mine was in 1966, it is fruitless to attempt to assign any one reason. There were probably no less than a hundred. I remember people walking up to me on the street for weeks after that election and telling me that they had voted against me, that they were sorry, and that they didn't know why they had done

On November 22, 1966, Senator Art Manley of Coeur d'Alene—president of the Idaho Wildlife Association—presented me with an award as Conservationist of the Year.

so. The defeat in that election might well be viewed as a judgment by the people that I had accomplished as much for them as they wished for me to accomplish.

Some of my associates who were present at most of the events of 1966 have urged me to be a little less kind to Senator Samuelson. They would prefer that I be a little bit more definitive about his behavior. I think this would be a fruitless endeavor and not one which would be helpful to historians in assessing the worth of my years in office.

I am perfectly willing to submit my twelve years in the governor's office to the verdict of history confident that when the historians have evaluated those years with their balanced budgets, their steady progress, and their lack of any hint of scandal they will reward my endeavors with gracious praise.

CHAPTER SIXTEEN

THIRTY YEARS UNWINDING IN THE AFTERGLOW—1967–97

THE MORNING AFTER the primary election disaster, I went down to the office and met with the press. They had very few questions and very little to contribute in the way of additional information that might make the result easier to understand. It was, however, quite obvious that with the election defeat, the erosion of power had already set in. It would rapidly develop a momentum of its own.

We left that afternoon for Norwood for the remainder of the month of August. Bob McCall brought mail up that he thought needed attention, and from time to time other people came to visit. Generally speaking we had the Mountain House to ourselves and were not bothered much with official traffic.

Shortly after Labor Day, we returned to Boise and I began the task of closing out my twelve-year administration. Lucille began looking for a place in Boise where we could set up housekeeping, and our sons returned to school.

I dispatched a message to Senator Samuelson offering to be of assistance during the transition in the office of governor. We specifically offered assistance in the way of secretarial help and in the preparation of a skeleton budget for his perusal. Also office space was offered where he could conduct his pre-gubernatorial business. He did make use of the space on the third floor of the building, but there was no further response to any of our offers of assistance. I instructed the budget staff to prepare a budget for his perusal and for his approval or disapproval. This document was delivered to Senator Samuelson in mid-December of 1966, and to my knowledge was the only budget that was prepared for the 1967–68 biennium.

Lucille found a home on Locust Street, in Boise's East End, and at a reasonable price. We moved there in mid-December of 1966 so the governor's residence was available to the Samuelsons if they wanted it. By this time the office had been pretty well wound down and was ready for transfer. My personal papers had been moved to Locust Street, and all that remained was my duty to introduce Senator Samuelson to the House and Senate as the new governor. This I did on the day of his inauguration.

On February 20, 1986, Lucille and I visited the White House.

My next task was to provide a living for the family. The two boys still had to finish school, and we had some living to do. Nobody had prepared a soft landing for me when I left the governorship. No one offered me a job and there were no board memberships with high-pay salaries that were being dangled about. I finally rented a small office from my old friend Bill Langroise in what was then known as the Simplot Building at the corner of Eighth and Idaho and began finding some way to occupy my time and utilize my talents.

I had spent the last twenty years working for the State of Idaho, and the highest salary that I ever received was $15,000 a year. I think I had a net worth of somewhere near $40,000. That would not be much cushion if I didn't quickly begin generating an income. To my great surprise, I found that making money wasn't as difficult as it had been portrayed.

In the next eighteen months, I earned more money from my endeavors as a legal consultant than the State of Idaho had paid me in all the twenty years that I had served in the attorney general's office and as governor. That first year out of office helped my self-esteem, and I was able to face the task of raising the family and maintaining a presence in Boise.

Harold Geneen, who was chairman and chief executive officer of ITT, asked me to consult with regard to the acquisition of the American Broadcasting Company by ITT. There ensued a series of hearings before the Federal Communications Commission. This work led to some other engagements in the field of acquisitions and mergers. My work for ITT took me to Europe and visits to Copenhagen, Brussels, and London. In 1967 ITT decided that it wanted to acquire a wood products company, and I was asked to set up a meeting between the officers of Potlatch Forest Industries and ITT in San Francisco. I arranged a meeting with Benton Cancell, the chief executive officer of Potlatch, and Mr. Geneen and Mr. Hart Perry, treasurer of ITT, and Felix Rohatyn, a financial consultant. Mr. Geneen made a firm offer to acquire Potlatch Forests, but Mr. George Weyerhauser, who was a principal stockholder, declined to participate and that brought the discussions to an end. I had more than a little interest in the Potlatch acquisition because, had it gone through, Roland Wilbur would have had to secure different employment. He was my old enemy, and I did remember. When it became clear that Potlatch was not available to be acquired, Mr. Geneen turned his attention to the acquisition of Rayonier, another western forest products company. Harold Geneen was the conglomerate builder of the sixties. He was a fascinating character, and it was exciting and interesting to be associated with him.

I did some consulting work with El Paso Natural Gas in connection with their vain effort to secure a congressional reversal of the antitrust decision which denied them the opportunity to acquire Northwest Pipeline Company. I represented Pacific Power and Light Company in their various endeavors in the state of Idaho. The law firm also represented the Idaho First National Bank (later West One Bank and now U.S. Bank), and we were privileged to participate in the defense of the bank's acquisition of Fidelity National Bank of Twin Falls in an anti-trust action brought by the United States. We defeated the United States' attorneys very handsomely, and the acquisition of Fidelity by Idaho First was permitted to go forward. It was a big step in the advancement of the banking business in Idaho.

Practicing law was not as exciting as twelve years in the governor's office, but the travels that were associated with my consulting work were far more interesting than an office in a building in Boise. The boys were growing up rapidly and were about to go off to college. It seemed appropriate for Lu and me to begin to do some traveling. Bill, our older son, finished his work at Boise State and enlisted in the U.S. Army and joined the Berlin Brigade in the days before the wall came down. We went to Europe to visit him and to take a trip through Denmark and Holland, up the Rhine River to Cologne, and then along the romantic road from Rothenburg and Salzburg and Innsbruck and down the Danube to Vienna. Steve went off to college, graduated, and began a career teaching in the junior high schools of the Boise School System. He teaches history at West Junior High School, and it is a source of satisfaction to me that he is following in the footsteps of my father, who was a schoolmaster for fifty-five years.

These last years have been blessed by the addition to our family of two lovely and charming granddaughters. Anna is a student at the University of Idaho. Lisa is a high school senior. They have been a real joy to Lucille and me.

We went back again to London and to a place in Sussex called Wilton Park, a sort of European think tank operated by the British Foreign Office for the furtherance of its ideas in what had once been Central Europe. William Hall, the third president of the College of Idaho and my old friend, had secured a fellowship for me at Wilton Park at one of their convocations. I was invited to be a principal speaker and to deliver a lecture on some of our labor practices in the United States. Our travels took us to New Zealand, to Australia, to Hawaii, and to Alaska. We enjoyed a Caribbean trip through the canal and a lovely cruise down the St. Lawrence River in the full glory of a northeast American autumn.

All through this period of time, I had been writing a weekly column for *The Idaho Statesman*. Writing those columns and reflecting on

---

A family dinner at the Top of the Hoff in Boise. From left, son Bill, Steve's wife, Marsha and daughter Lisa; myself; Lucille; Steve's daughter Anna and son Steve. Photo courtesy Steve Smylie.

them afterward was a rich and rewarding experience. It was no way to make a living, but it served to make the absence of political concerns from my life a little easier to endure.

Political affairs became a small part of the Smylie agenda in the years after 1967. In 1968, I helped out occasionally in the financial efforts of the Nixon campaign in their New York headquarters, and I assume as a consequence was rewarded with an appointment to be a member of the inaugural committee when Mr. Nixon was sworn in as President in 1969. Before that President Lyndon Johnson had temporarily and tentatively dangled before me the possibility of an appointment in the Office of Budget and Management. After some consideration, I wisely and respectfully declined to be considered.

In 1972 I made the mistake of thinking that the people might be willing to send me to the United States Senate after all. I made an ill-advised and costly attempt to secure the Republican nomination for the United States Senate when Len Jordan stepped down. I learned the hard way that the people had meant what they said in 1966. It was, however, not a futile exercise. It was an answer to a question that I had to ask. Now I knew that my political career was ended.

In 1975 Governor Cecil Andrus asked me to defend him in a case involving the length of time which a governor might take considering legislation before he was either obliged to veto it or let it become law without his signature. I represented the governor against the attorney general and happily was able to prevail on behalf of Governor Andrus. It was an interesting exercise in the practice of appellate law and one of three times that I appeared before the Supreme Court of Idaho after I left the governorship.

In the mid-eighties Governor John Evans offered to appoint me to the Northwest Power Policy Planning Commission, and I was deeply honored that he would think me capable of being of service. However, I decided that I didn't know enough about salmon and steelhead and downriver navigation to be able to make much of a contribution to the work of the commission and declined.

Governor Evans also appointed me to be a member of the Idaho Centennial Commission, which was designed to produce a plan for celebrating the 100th anniversary of statehood. This was one of the highlights of my post-gubernatorial service. The commission asked me to write a mission statement in order to produce a celebration for all of Idaho and its people. The Idaho Centennial Commission was able to achieve that goal through observances in every one of the forty-four counties and a tremendous centennial celebration on statehood day in Boise. The Union Pacific Railroad sent an elegant old passenger train for the festivities, and there was a ride to remember from Nampa to Boise along the route of the old Portland Rose. The state measured up in every way to its new maturity, and residents had a reason to be proud that they were Idahoans.

I made modest contributions to both of Governor Batt's campaigns for the governorship and helped out with the campaigns of Larry Craig and Butch Otter. My principal interest was in attempting to stem the continual drift of the Republican Party toward the councils of the radical right. The ineffectiveness of those endeavors is apparent in the domination of that wing of the party in the legislative affairs of the state today.

I shall always be glad that I recruited Lydia Justice Edwards to be a candidate for state treasurer when that office became vacant some years back. Mrs. Edwards had been a good legislator from Valley County, and it seemed a waste of her talents to continue in the House of Representatives. She ran successfully against the candidate who was supported by the Republican party organization for the nomination for state treasurer and was elected and has been reelected two times since. Her tour of duty as state treasurer has been very successful, and I am gratified to have been able to be a part of making that career possible.

My "Days of Wine and Roses" finally came to an end. I had always been enthusiastic about whiskey and vodka, and for that matter almost anything alcoholic, and had partaken reasonably freely of the stuff. In 1981 my enthusiasm was beginning to turn into an addiction, and my thirst was becoming an outrage. I decided to do something about it and went down to the Care Unit at Mercy Medical Center in Nampa and became a friend of Bill W. This, of course, is a euphemism for being a member of a support group called Alcoholics Anonymous. When I left the care center, I was about ready for the twelfth step and happily have been able to keep on the straight and narrow every since. I have now enjoyed almost fourteen years of continuous sobriety. Alcoholism is a disease of denial, and for that reason confession is good for treatment of the disease. Shortly thereafter, I decided that having smoked for fifty years was quite enough, and I put my pack of cigarettes down. It still occupies the same place on the shelf in the house in Norwood, and I have not smoked since.

I suspect that having knocked off smoking and drinking has made it possible for me to successfully complete open heart surgery two or three years ago and to prolong my life long enough to finally finish this book.

My story and this book are inextricably intertwined with the history of the College of Idaho. I came to the campus in Caldwell in 1934 and enrolled as a freshman. It was there that I marked the completion of my undergraduate education by receiving a Bachelor of Arts Degree in 1938.

For two of those college years I had a job sweeping out the old field house where the athletic teams dressed for games that were played on Hayman Field. Getting the job had more to do with my willingness to play football than it did with any excellence I was able to establish as a "sweeper outer" of the field house. It was on this campus in 1956 that I received the college's honorary degree of Doctor of Laws in recognition of my election as governor of Idaho. In 1967 I was asked to become a trustee of the college and accepted. In 1972 I was elected by the board to be chairman of the trustees. In 1974 I served as acting president of the college, and it fell my lot to confer the 5,000th baccalaureate degree on a young student from Richfield, Idaho, by the name of John T. Lezamiz. In 1983 I was asked to teach a course in state and local government and to accept appointment as an adjunct professor in the Department of Political Science. I taught the course for four years and greatly enjoyed the challenge of trying to keep ahead of the bright young minds of the students who go to school these days on that campus. In 1994 the trustees elected me to be a lifetime member of the board, a recognition which I accepted with great pleasure.

The college has now named its archives after me, and the archives have become the repository of my personal papers from my years as governor together with various memorabilia which have some historic value concerning those years of service to the state. The collection is appropriately housed on the second floor of Sterry Hall, and I am proud to have had a part in bringing about a permanent home for the books and records of the history of the college. The college is now in its second century of service to the people of Idaho, and as the years roll along, it is appropriate to make recognition of the fact that I am eternally indebted to the professors who taught on the campus when I was enjoying my studies there in the 1930s. Not many of them had doctoral degrees, but they were great teachers and great leaders and something that they imparted made those graduating classes very special.

I am extremely grateful that "my" college has continued to recognize the excellence of its faculty as its most important task, and the faculty remains a glittering academic assembly of great talent and scholarship, as it always has been.

I am pleased to be able to be of service to the college and to recognize with gratitude and honor my debt to all those great people who have gone before.

Old men like to sit in the sun or around the coffee table at the Interlude Bar and Grill on Eighth Street and offer advice to the new generation now in charge of rectifying the problems that the old men were unable to correct in their own time. It seems to me appropriate to offer my few little kernels of advice about what should be done about a few recurring difficulties.

Annual sessions of the legislature were the major mistake of the last half of this century. If the members of the legislature had the courage, they would go back to biennial sessions and in doing so save themselves a magnificent number of headaches and a great deal of money.

The wicked winter weather of 1996 and 1997 should convince us that we can no longer delay building a modern highway to north Idaho. This will be one of the most imposing highway construction tasks of the next century, but it should begin without delay. For too long the north-south "goat trail" has delayed progress, both economically and socially. The project will take a bond issue of immense proportions, but we should be about it before it costs us a great deal more money in the future than it will now.

History and political connivance have given us three universities, and the time has come when we should quit quarreling about what university should do what and let them compete freely in the marketplace of ideas for the student customers who will ultimately make one or all three of them great. We should grow great universities and not middle-class athletic training camps.

The legislature should forget some of its tax legends, such as the fact that our property tax is too high, and be about raising the money that it will take to jump-start us into the twenty-first century. We will need more than a bridge—we will need a broad new highway, and it will have to be paid for from revenues on taxes that have yet to be enacted.

Throughout all of our history, our legislatures have been far too parsimonious in their expenditures on those items that are important to the building of a state. We have not spent enough on education, and we have had a bias against higher education. We have delayed making expenditures until the cost of doing the job was almost impossible. The library at the University of Idaho, which would have cost $25,000 in 1927, ended up costing $1.7 million in 1955.

The legislature would be well-advised to commence practicing the "openness" it insists on in the affairs of other state agencies. I have a notion the public would be outraged if they really knew the price of all the perquisites with which we have rewarded our public servants, past and present.

Once upon a time a sixty-day session was regarded as extremely virtuous legislative behavior. The virtue of sixty-day sessions might well be reexamined. The great Thirty-eighth Session enacted the sales tax and finished up its work and adjourned on the sixty-fifth day.

Our legislature works more productively when we keep its membership close to an even division between our two major parties. We should return to the two-party system. This might end the odious practice of legislating in closed party caucuses.

One final suggestion. The legislature should prepare and keep a legislative record that would contain a verbatim report of every word spoken on the floor of both the House and Senate. Then they could abolish those illegitimate and meaningless "statements of legislative intent" attached to legislation in the form of letters, memoranda, and even verbal indications of what the legislature intends to accomplish.

Lastly, they might stop calling the governor by the snide label they devised in the seventies. "The Gentleman on the Second Floor" is the duly elected governor, and that is what they should call him. Anything less lacks civility and constitutional correctness.

Some of these ideas will be assailed as dangerously liberal and financially unsound, but I would submit that we'd better start getting on with the task of building Idaho into the state that it deserves to be or it will sooner or later be far too late.

Now that the years are dwindling down to "a precious few," I sit by my window in the Warm Springs Meadow and let memory carry me back down the years to where it all began in 1934 at the college in Caldwell, Idaho. People like to inquire of persons like me, "What did you do that you would have done differently?" I really have no answer. All I know is that all of the years have been good years, some better than others, some less exciting than others, but none of them have been dull. Thank God!

ROBERT E. SMYLIE
March 5, 1997

INDEX

Ada County Young Republicans, 59, 65
Adams, Sherman, 59–61, 94
Adams, W. Lloyd, 52–53, 77–78, 172, 203
Agnew, Spiro, 156
aid to dependent children, 119
Ailshie, Robert, 36, 46, 48–49, 59
Albertson College of Idaho, xi, xv, 106, 156, 222–23. *See also* College of Idaho
Albertson, Joe, *116*
Alemán, Miguel, 147–48
Alford, Bud, 152
Anderson, C. C., 103, 193–94
Anderson, Robert, 155
Andrus, Cecil, 220
annual versus biennial legislatures, 120–21, 189–90, 223
Argentina, 137–40, 143, 149
Artis, Kristin, *114*
Aschenbrenner, Ed, 50–51
assistant attorney general, xi, 36, 46, 48–49, 63
attorney general, 18, 49–62, *50*, *52*, 83, 104, 217
Ayres, Estella, 48, 61
Babcock, Tim, 101, 207
Baker v. Carr, 185
Barlow, K. C., 185
Basler, Loren, 15, 19, 20, 106
Basque, 132
Batt, Phil, 221
Benson, Carville, 36
Benson, Frank, 109
Bergey, Joe, 34
Blick, George, 199, 202
Bliss, Ray, 211–12
Boise College, 190
Boise Junior College, 190
Boise State University, 190
Boise, Tom, 91–92, 113
Bon Marché, 103, 194
Boone, William Judson, 23–24
Booth, John, 85
Borah, William Edgar, 15, 32, 34, 35, 39, 149, 153, 194
Borlaug, Norman, 6
Brandriff, Alice, 3
Brazil, 137, 140–43, 149
tree planting ceremony, 141–42
Breshears, Ralph, 49

Brown, James R., 76, 83, 109, 172
Brown, Robert, 70
Budge, Hamer, 97, 173, 175, 177–78
budget, balancing, 77, 84–89, 95, 97–100, 119–21, 185, 194–201, 215–16
Burch, Dean, xii, 210–11
Burns, W. C., 68, 70, 105
Burroughs, Ham and Bunny, 61
Burt, Carl, *159*
Burton, Earl, 33
Bush, George, 105–06
Butler, Carl. *See* Butler-Miller Hardware Company
Butler-Miller Hardware Company, 21–22, 27, 29–30
Buxton, O. J., 116

Caldwell, Idaho, 13–14
Callsen, Bernice, xv, 80–81
campaign tools
- airplanes, 66, 73, 207
- billboards, 68, 72, 73, 94, 179
- negative ads, 94–95, 172–73
- newspapers, 71, 72, 170, 179
- polls, 66, 70–71, 85, 169, 206
- radio, 66, 170, 179
- television, 66, 68, 72–73, 78, 170–72, 176, 179, 181, 205

Campbell, Howard, 23
Campbell, William, 69–70
Capitol Policemen, 34, 39, 149
Carl, J. M., 31
Carnegie Library, 3, 9, 14
Carrillo, Leo, 102
Carver, John, 49–51
Carver, Terry, 98
casino-type gambling, 53–54, 107, 112–14, 116, 119, 121, 126, 169–70, 172, 178, 181–82, 197
Cavallero, Carmen, 43
Cenarrusa, Pete, 199, 202
Charlton, Fred, 67, 88, 93, 106, 120
Charnock, Richard, 111, 155, 173
Chavez, Cesar, 108
Chicago Northwestern Railroad, 3, 6
Church, Frank, 94–95, 97, 100, 106, 121, 168, 170, 182
Clark, Barzilla W., 24–25
Clark, Chase, 77, 88
Clark, D. Worth, 32, 34, 35, 39, 45, 104, 151, 172
Clark, Virgil, 45, 47
Clark, William, 101
Clyde, George, 207
Coast Guard. *See* United States Coast Guard
Coe, Richard, 33, 37
Cole, Eugene, 14
Cole, F. M., 2, 13–14, 23, 32, 45, 47, 49
Cole, Leila, 2, 10, 13, 14–15, 17, 20, 45, 47, 49, 74, 79
College of Idaho, 10–11, 13–14, 15–17, 23, 29–30, 79, 219, 225
- debate team, 26
- football, 15, 17, 18, 19–20, 21–22, 27, 106, 222
- Sterry Hall, 15, 16, 25, 223
- *The Trail*, 26, *28*, 29
- *See also* Albertson College of Idaho

College of Southern Idaho, 93, 200
Collier, Charles, 36
Collins, Leroy, 129
Cook, Charles, 92
Cook, Russel, 23
Corlett, John, 71
Coughlin, James, 23
Council of State Governments, 143
Covington, Burling, Rublee, Acheson, and Shorb, 36, 39–41, 42, 46
Craig, Larry, 221
Crean, John, 45
Crookham, George, Jr., 166–67, 197, 200, 203
"Crown Prince," the, 110–11, 182
Cruzen, Jim and Doris, 171
Cuban Missile Crisis, 197
Cunningham, Laura, 62

Darrow, Clarence, 15
Davis, Ralph, 78

Dean, Nadine, 81
death sentence. *See* Walrath and Powell trial
Democrats, wool-hat. *See* wool-hat Democrats
Department of Economic Development. *See* economic development
Derr, Alfred M., xii, 91, 106–08, 112–14, 116, 121, 165
Dewey, Thomas E., 205
Dolph, William, 46–47
Doolittle, Robert, *96*, 115, 122
Drevlow, William, 110–11, 112, 115, 127–28, 174, 182, 198
Driscoll, Lynn, 70
Durtschi, Ray, 50–51
Dworshak, Georgia, 174
Dworshak, Henry, 56, 100, 126, 153–54, 173–75

Eberle, William, 178
economic development, 64, 67, 71, 84
education funding, 116, 118, 121, 167, 212, 224
  higher education, 64, 119
  public schools, 64, 67, 71, 84–85, 97–98, 119, 124, 126, 160, 185, 191, 201, 204
  "Save Our Schools," 203–4
Edwards, Lydia Justice, 221
Eisenhower, Dwight D., 94, 96–97, 128, 155, 211
  Highway Act of 1956, 118, 160
  visits to Idaho, *55*, 59–61, *159*, 179–81, *181*
Elder, Robert, 70
Elks Club, 53
Ellison, James, 40, 42, 43
Elmore, George, 40
Engelking, Delmer, 109–10
Ernest, Allen, 202
Evans, Blaine, 50–51
Evans, John, 117, 220
Evans, Luther, *129*

Faherty, Murial, 43
Falks, Leo, 61
Farragut State Park, xii, 161–62
Fiesta del Pacifica, 102
Friar, William, 36
Frondizi, Arturo, 138–39, 143, 149

gambling. *See* casino-type gambling
Garber, Jan, 9
Gardener, Larry, 68–69
Garrett, H. Fred, 188
Geneen, Harold, 217–18
George Washington University, xi, 18, 26, 29, 31–36, 37, 104, 133
Gillette, Guy, 8
Gipson, J. H., Sr., 65
Gipson, Jim, Jr., 29
Girl Scouts, 161–62
  Girl Scout tea, *114*
Glasby, John, 107, 121
Goldwater, Barry, xii, *181*, 208, 210–11
Gooding, Frank, 32
Gore, Albert, 100
Gossett, Charles, 69, 101, 116, 117
Governors' Conference of the United States, 127, 144, 205
governor's residence, 80, 86–87, 103, 165, 176, 216
Graeber, Fred, 98
Great Depression, 6, 9, 12, 21, 31, 193
Great Smiley Creek Fiasco, 170–71
Greenfield, George, 18, 24, 26–27, 28, 33, 79, 175
gubernatorial succession amendment, 86, 90–93

Hailey, John, 150
Haines, John M., 1
Hall, Leonard, 94, 127
Hall, William, 219
Halleck, Charles, 117
Hamilton, Clark, xi, 69–71, 73
Hamilton, John Daniel Miller, 24
Hammill, John, 8

Hampton, Elvon, 88–89
Hansen, Orval, *159*
Harding, Lloyd, 7
Harding, Ralph, 172
Harlow, Bryce, 179
Harriman, Averell, 162–66, 187–88
Harriman, Gladys, 187
Harriman, E. Roland, 162–66, 178, 187–88
Harriman State Park, xii 162–66, 187–88
Hatfield, Mark, 206
Hawley, Jack, *159*
Hawley, James, 1, 179
Hayman, Herbert H., 14, 18
haystack near Sutherland, 12, 19
Haywood, William D. "Big Bill," 15
Healey, William, 153
Heath, Thomas, 68, 185
health reform. *See* public health reform
Hechtner, Howard, 89, 91, 117, 125
Highway Act of 1956. *See* highway system
Hinman, George, 208–10
highway system, xii, 64, 85–86, 119, 160, 167, 185, 191, 194, 223
  Highway Act of 1956, 118, 123–24
  Lewis and Clark Highway, 100–101
Hirohito, 143–44, 149
hitchhiking, 12, 19–20, 28–29, 32–33, 74
Hodge, Robert, 50, 80–81, 173
Hodges, Luther, 139
Hogg, Rebecca, *114*
Holden, Robert, 49
Holmes, Sue, *114*
Hoover, Herbert, 149, 163
Hopkins, Harry, 193
House, Henry, 18, 23–24
Howell, Glen, 49
Hyatt, Paul, 49, *50*, 56

Idaho Centennial Commission, 220–21
Idaho Education Association, 85
Idaho Park System, xii, 64, 161–64, 187
Idaho Statesman, The, 60, 71, 83, 88, 109, 172, 219
Idaho State College, 67, 119–20. *See also* Idaho State University
Idaho State Historical Society, 153
  Friends of the Museum, 152
  museum, 150–52
  traveling library, 150–52
  Idaho Yesterdays. See *Idaho Yesterdays*
Idaho State University, 189. *See also* Idaho State College
Idaho Territory, 183–84
Idaho Yesterdays, xv, 152
Idaho's water resources. *See* water resources
Iowa
  Corwith, 4, 8
  Cresco, 6, 9, 19, 29, 33
  Hartley, 1–2
  Hull, 4, 7
  Marcus, xi, 1
  Missouri Valley, 2–4
  Rock Valley, 4–5, 7
Irwin, Carl, 96
Irwin, Lucille. *See* Lucille Smylie

Japan, 143–47, 149
Jeffers, William, 29
Jensen, Dwight, 173
Johnson, Jimmy, 46–47
Johnson, Lyndon B., 95, 155, 206–07, 220
Jonasson, bill, 65, 67, 93
Jones, Alton, *52*
Jones, Arthur Curtis, 23
Jones, Ralph, Jr., *96*
Jordan, Leonard "Len," *55*, 182
  governor, 64–65, 69, 76, 79–80, 93, 194
  senator, *159*, 175, 177–79, 213, 220
  state budget deficit, 77, 87, 89
Julia Davis Park, 151, 152

Kaiser, Henry, 140
Keenan, Frank, 55–56
Kennedy, John F., 110, 124, 139, 155, 206–08
Knight, Goodwin, *102*
Knight, Virginia, *102*
Koelsch, M. Oliver, 56, 154–55
Kramer, Ted, 93
Kremlin, 132, 133
Krushchev, Nikita S., 128, 132–34, 136, 149, 207

Kubitschek. *See* Juscelino Kubitschek de Oliveira
Kunz, Alma, 163

Landon, Alfred M., 24–25, 26–27
Langley, Frank, 59
Langlie, Arthur, 55, 61
Langroise, Bill, 47, 61, 217
Lanting, William, 199, 202
Larsen, J. Berkley, 83
lawyer, 39–42, 46, 217–18
Laylin, John, 41
Leach, Raymond Hotchkiss, 29
League of Curtis Salesmen, 4
Leggat, J. M., 50
Lewis-Clark Normal School. *See* Lewis-Clark State College
Lewis-Clark Normal School Bill. *See* Lewis-Clark State College
Lewis-Clark State College, xi, 89, 91–93
  four-year degree program, 117
Lewis, Meriwether, 101
Lezamiz, John T., 222
Lincoln, Abraham, 183
Lindquist, Elvon, 166–68
Link, Charles, 65, 67
Lombardo, Guy, 9
Lorance, Frank, 78
Love, John, 211
Luce, Claire Boothe, 37
Luther College, 9, 16
Lyon, Caleb, 183

Manning, Darrell, 187
Manley, Art, *214*
Marcus, Claude, 65, 67–68
Markham, Harley, 163, 175, 177–78
Marshall Plan, 41
Matthews, Colin, 21
Mazo, Earl, 210
McCabe, Thomas, 166, 178
McCall, Robert, 208, 210, 215
McClenahan, Don, 50–51
McCormick, Kip, *114*
McDonald, Mrs. James, 61–62
McGill, Frank, 7
McIntosh, Carl, 119–20
McKay, Douglas, 61
McKeldin, Theodore, 205
McNichols, Ray, 110, 115
McQuade, Henry, 102
merchandise trading stamps, 160–61
Mexico, 147–48, 149
Meyner, Robert, *129*
Millar, James, 18, 20
Miller, Bert, 56
Miller, Fred. *See* Butler-Miller Hardware Company
Miller, Fred A., 96
Monroe, James, 89, 91, 117, 125
Moon, Ruth, 117
Morningside College, 2, 7, 8, 15, 16–17
Morrison Knudsen Company, 45, 134, 141, 146
Morton, Thurston, 153, 163
Mossman, Frank, 8
Mountain Bell, 57–59
Mountain House, 165–66, 182, 208–10, 209, 215
Murphy, Cleora, 199
Murphy, Jack, 199, 201–03
Murphy, Paul, 17, 24

Naegle, A. W. "Tony," 178, 185
National Youth Administration, 20–21
Nichols, Red, 9
Nielson, J. P., 52
Nixon, Richard, *98*, 156–57, 166, 220
North Idaho College of Education. *See* Lewis-Clark State College

Oliveira, Juscelino Kubitschek de, 141, 143, 149
Olson, Charles, 40, 42
Orchard, Harry, 15
Ordaz, Gustavo, 147
Orion fraternity, 19, 25
Otter, Butch, 221
Overgaard, Knute, 17

Paddleford, Clementine, 165,
Page, Harland O., 27, 106
Palmer, Mary, 34
Paris, 128, 139
park system. *See* Idaho Park System
Peckham, Hubert, 25
Permanent Building Fund, 124, 126, 160
Perón, Evita, 138
Perón, Juan Domingo, 138
Perry, Hart, 217
Petersen, Philip, 201
Peterson, Clint, 50–51
Pfost, Gracie, 97, 175, 177, 182
Pieper, Don, 117
Pittman, Key, 35
polls. *See* campaign tools
Pope, James R., 32
Popejoy, E. Keith, 6
"potato plan," 108, 112, 114
Powers, Gary, 137
Preston, E. C., 18, 24
Property Relief Act, 53
public health reform, 98–99, 119–20, 126
public school equalization formula. *See* education funding
Pugmire, Smoky, 69, 71

Railroad Ranch, 162–64, 187
Randall, Les, 195
Rankin, Bill, 80
Rankin, Joseph, 18, 24
Rankin, Sarah, 24
Reagan, Ronald, 33, *216*
Republican Governors' Association, 206, 209–10, 212
retirement fund, 188–89, 191, 198
  teacher, xi, 85, 160, 196
right-to-work issue, xii, 107–08, 113–14, 205
Roberts, George H. R., 150
Roberts, Margaret, 150
Robins, C. A., 1, 46, 48, 49, *50, 52*, 55, 59, 101, 117–18, 151
Robbins, Ray, 106
Roblyer, Joseph, 18, 23–24
Rockefeller, Mary, *123*
Rockefeller, Nelson, xii, *123*, 166, 178, 206, 208–10
Rodwell, Beth, *114*
Rohatyn, Felix, 217
Romney, George, 206
Roosevelt, Eleanore, 25, 37
Roosevelt, Franklin Delano, 8, 24, 25, 43, 115, 133, 193, 210
Ross, C. Ben, 151, 193–94, 204
Rubin, Cora, 34
Russia, 127; Leningrad, 128–29, 130, 136; Red Square, 129, 132, 136
  Red Star, 128–29
  Sochi, 131–32

Sabin, Albert B., 54
sales tax. *See* tax reform
Samuelson, Don, xii, 125, 156–57, 213–14, 215–16
Sanborn, John, 68–69, 70, 71
Scatterday, George, 32
Scheideman, Henry, 68
Schrader, Gus and Betsy, 142–43
Scott, Bill, 22–23
Scranton, William, 178, 206, 210
Sellars, Carroll, 78
Seaton, Fred, 60–61, 153–54
Shackelton, Allen, 9
Shadduck, Louise, xv, 49, 101, 161
Shapiro, Henry, 136
Shawver, Ellis, 96
Shepard, Allen, 50–51
Simplot, J. R., 113, 151, 152
Slanksky, Cyril, 18
Sloan, Robert, 18, 33
Smead, J. R., 49, 50, 56
Smirnoff, Ivan Ivanovich, 129–30
Smith, Orma J., 23–24
Smith, Vernon K., xii, 114, 165–66, 169–72, 178, 181–82, 197
Smylie, Dorothy, 2, 3, *5*, 29, 79
Smylie, Lorne Francis "Father," 1–7, 10, 79, 218
Smylie Frances, 2, *5*, 79
Smylie, Lucille, *164*, *186*
  before marriage, 39, 42–44

campaigning, 73, 75, 76, 78, *81, 82,* 171, 173
Fiesta del Pacifica, 102–03, *102*
international travels, 44, 137–48, 218–19
marriage, xv, 45–46, 48, 61–62, 65, 77–78, 79–81, 86–87, *103*, 131, 182, 208, 215–16, *216, 219*
Plum Prune Chutney, 164–65
Smylie, Richard Steven
adulthood, 217, 218, *219*
youth, 62, 79,87, *103*, 130, 131, 165, 179–80, *180*, 215
Smylie, Robert William
adulthood, 217, 218, *219*
youth, 62, 79,87, *103*, 130, 131, 165, 179–80, *180*, 215
Spaudling, Hector Galloway, 36
Spinharney, Phyllis, 81
Springer, Francis C., 18
Stagg, Alonzo, 27
Stalin, Joseph, 10, 135
Statesman, The. See *Idaho Statesman, The*
Steunenberg, Frank, 1, 15
Stommel, Herman, 58
Stovel, George, 19, 20, 21
Stubblefield, Lila, 31
Stubblefield, Mary Alice, 34
Sutton, W. Clay, 108
Swinney, Holman Jerome, 151–52, *153*
Swisher, Perry, 96, 196, 203

tax reform, 67, 71, 88, 99–100, 184
gasoline tax, 124
"head tax," 124, 160, 197
income tax, 120, 124
sales tax, xii, 95–97, 107, 126, 155, 158–60, 166–68, 186, 188, 190–91, 192–204, 224
Taylor, C. J., 79, *80*
Taylor, Glen, 95, 106, 172
Teacher Retirement Fund. *See* retirement fund
Theophilus, Donald, 119–20
The Trail. See College of Idaho
Thomas, John, 116–17
Thompson, Boyd, 6
Thompson, June, *114*
Thurber, James. *See* the "Crown Prince"
Tilford, Charles, *96*
Toole, Jim, 18
Troyanovski, Oleg, 133
Truman, Harry, 35, 41, 115
Trumball, Jonathan, 205
Twin Falls *Times-News*, 92–93, 105

Underwood, Cecil, *129*
Union Pacific Railroad, 14, 29, 221
Union of Soviet Socialist Republics, 127–37, 149, 207
United States Coast Guard, xi, 43–45
University of Idaho, 119–20, 201, 219
Law School, 50, 97
library bill, 89–93, 223
Upton, Ervin, 7

Vanbleck, William Cabell, 36
Volpe, John, 206

Wallace, William Henson, 183
Walrath and Powell trial, 56–57
Walters, T. A., 26
Warren, Earl, 54, *55*, 61
water resources, 67, 189–90
Watkins, Don, 72
Wayland, Charles, 48
Welker, Herman, 94, 96–97, 172
Wells, Merle, *153*
West, Harold, 93
Westcott, Ike, 32, 79
Westcott, Lola, 79
Western Federation of Miners, 15
Western Governors' Conference, 54–55, *55*
Weyerhauser, George, 217
White House, 37, 40, 94–95, 128, 133, 137, 154, 155–56, 197, 207
White, Raymond, 22–23
Wickberg, Ralph, 89, 95–96, *96*, 195–96
Wilbur, Lyman, 134
Wilbur, Roland, 167, 169
Williams, Arnold, 48, 109, 116

Williams, Joe, 109, 117
Wilson, Meredith, 102–03
wool-hat Democrats, 71, 108, 115–16
Woozley, Ed, *52*
World War I, 2, 10, 39–40, 174
World War II, xi, 6, 35–36, 38, 41, 43–45, 131, 150, 162, 188
Worthwine, Oscar, 49
Young, Bill, 18, 26, 33–35, 45, 79, *80*, 83, 92
Young, Cy, *52*
Young, Jim, 81, *96*, *153*
Young Republicans. *See* Ada County Young Republicans
Young, R. H., Jr., 79
youth, xi, 1–11